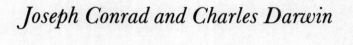

Joseph Conrad and Charles Darwin

Joseph Conrad
and
Charles Darwin

*

*The influence of scientific thought
on Conrad's fiction*

*

REDMOND O'HANLON

1984
The Salamander Press
Edinburgh

The Salamander Press Edinburgh Ltd
34 Shandwick Place, Edinburgh EH2 4RT

*The publisher acknowledges subsidy
from the Scottish Arts Council
towards the publication of this volume*

First published May 1984

British Library Cataloguing in Publication Data
O'Hanlon, Redmond
  Joseph Conrad and Charles Darwin.
  1. Conrad, Joseph—Knowledge—Science
  2. Darwin, Charles—Evolution
  I. Title
  823'.912   PR6005.O4Z/

ISBN 0-907540-42-2

Made and printed in Great Britain.
Set in Linoterm Baskerville
by Hewer Text Composition Services, Edinburgh.
Printed and bound by Robert Hartnoll Ltd, Bodmin, Cornwall.
Designed by Tom Fenton at the Salamander Press.

To my wife, Belinda

Acknowledgments

A great many people have helped me with all manner of kindnesses during the long preparation of this book; but I particularly wish to thank Raymond Carr, Theodore Zeldin, Alistair Horne and the Fellows of St. Antony's College, Oxford, for their continued support of my work and for their electing me to the Alistair Horne Research Fellowship; my tutors, friends and colleagues in Oxford, Jean and John Jones, Katherine Ing, Charles Webster, and, especially Theodore Zeldin, Gill and Tony Cockshut, Dorothy Bednarowska, and Jeremy Treglown: all of whom read the manuscript at various stages.

I am also much indebted to the staffs of the London Library, the Bodleian Library, the Radcliffe Science Library, The Library of Merton College, the Oxford Union Society Library, the English, Zoology and Botany Faculty Libraries in Oxford, and the Library of the Wellcome Unit for the History of Medicine.

More recently, Miss Jane Havell has traversed typhoons of untamed typescript and Linda Hopkins has typed the final drafts and remained calm through cataracts of contradictory corrigenda.

Contents

I

Biology and the politics of progress; physics and the politics of permanence

Joseph Conrad's picture of the world, grimly framed by his knowledge of Victorian physics, is Darwinian in its overall perspective, its experimental intention and its particular details. Even his grotesque humour, even the swarming multitude of exotic and apparently incidental characters which peoples his best work, are at once released and controlled by his Darwinian convictions.

But his guiding biological conceptions are late Darwinian, Lamarckian; he believes, as did most of his scientist-contemporaries when he was arduously forming his own ideas about nature, in the inheritance of acquired characteristics, in the lasting effects of use and disuse, of habit, as well as of natural and sexual selection. And this world, in turn, is modified within and encircled without by the orthodoxies of contemporary physics, particularly by its classical dogma of permanence, by the laws of thermodynamics, and by the very first signs of the new physics to come.

Yet, lest this compressed summary sounds misleadingly complex, we must remember that Victorian science was still almost immediately accessible to all intelligent men, and that Conrad's world is itself more rational, more intelligible, than any of its critics would have us believe—even in those apparently hopeless and obscure reaches where Leavis was led to curse, as he lost his way, that "emotional insistence on the presence of what he can't produce".[1]

To take first the particular idea of permanence which fascinated Conrad: a passage from one of Clerk Maxwell's lectures to the British Association, for instance, will suffice to give us an insight into this aspect of Conrad's thought (as well as warning us that it is not only men of letters who betray their subjective desires in the guise of objective deduction):

No theory of evolution can be formed to account for the similarity of molecules, for evolution necessarily implies continuous change, and the molecule is incapable of growth or decay, of generation or destruction.

None of the processes of Nature, since the time when Nature began, have produced the slightest difference in the properties of any molecule. We are therefore unable to ascribe either the existence of the molecules or the identity of their properties to the operation of any of the causes which we call natural . . .

They continue this day as they were created—perfect in number and measures and weight, and from the ineffaceable characters impressed on them we may learn that those aspirations after accuracy in measurement, truth in statement, and justice in action, which we reckon among our noblest attributes as men, are ours because they are the essential constituents of the image of Him who in the beginning created, not only the heaven and the earth, but the materials of which heaven and earth consist.[2]

Temperamentally, there are strong reasons for Conrad's attraction to this dogma of contemporary physics; as Bernard Meyer puts it, the "seemingly endless pursuit of the quality of solidity in things and people is hardly surprising in a sensitive individual, who in his formative years, had witnessed the merciless march of disaster, disease, and death pass before his frightened eyes".[3] Intellectually, too, it is plain that Conrad's life and training would familiarise him with the basic ideas of contemporary physics rather than biology. Conrad, as his friend Retinger remembers, "could not and did not attach himself to any particular corner or nook of Poland" so that "his patriotism lacked a physical pivot".[4] He was "carried away from his native Berdyczew as an infant"[5] and into a world of vague forces, impassioned ideas, far from the immediate life of nature. His father, Apollo Nałęcz Korzeniowski, poet and patriot, member of the "Red" or extremist wing of the Polish cause,[6] was arrested by the Russians in 1861 for his part in the illegal National Committee, and with his wife and child was deported to Vologda when Conrad was five years old; his mother died two years later, and his father when Conrad was barely eleven. Devotion to the future, to political change, evolutionary or revolutionary progress, had indeed brought disaster and death; and it is this emotional base which helps to explain the particular world view which Conrad selected from contemporary science, as well as the subsequent tension within it, because, as Zdzisław Najder speculates:

On the one hand he could not escape the powerful appeal of Apollo's fascinating personality and of the heroic fidelity with which he had served to the tragic end the ideals of patriotism as he had conceived them. On the other hand he was by no means sure if these ideals had had any reasonable basis. Conrad's father must have seemed to him at once awe-inspiring and absurd; his attitude towards him was a mixture of admiration and contemptuous pity. And he could never forgive his father the death of his mother.[7]

The insecure Conrad looks for permanence, for ineffaceable characters, "perfect in number and measures and weight", for "those aspirations after accuracy in measurement, truth in statement, and justice in action"; all static qualities dear to the nineteenth-century physicist defending his beliefs against evolutionary biology; and he does find a certain comfort in his half-belief in those absolutes, in "the materials of which heaven and earth consist", in the unchange-ability of the elements. The a-human, inscrutable intention of the indifferent, immovable laws of classical physics will preserve the inanimate world intact long after all merely biological activity upon it, all local evolutionary progress or regress, has ceased.

For Hardy, say, death is a bleak fact of nature, but at least it is necessary, a part of the biological process in which variety, change, and a new future are possible. For Conrad, seeking refuge in classical physics from time and death, in Clerk Maxwell's first law of thermo-dynamics, which states, in its generalised form, that the quantity of energy in the universe is constant, imprisoned in this static world, death paradoxically seems more unbearable when it does come; a stepping outside the circle rather than a break in the line linking past and future which someone else may continue; it is a sordid and solitary business, a waiting. No wonder he writes to Cunninghame Graham that

> Marionettes are beautiful . . . Their impassibility in love, in crime, in mirth, in sorrow—is heroic, superhuman, fascinating. Their rigid vio-lence when they fall upon one another to embrace or to fight is simply a joy to behold. I never listen to the text mouthed somewhere out of sight by invisible men who are here today and rotten tomorrow. I love the marionettes that are without life, that come so near to being immortal![8]

It is indeed a rigid immortality, but Conrad knows of no other; he does not follow Clerk Maxwell's extrapolations from eternal molecules to the Eternal Designer, and neither is he in sympathy with his father's late relapse into mysticism. Conrad early abandoned his family's Roman Catholicism: "It's strange how I always, from the age of fourteen, disliked the Christian religion, its doctrines, ceremonials and festivals . . . And the most galling thing is that nobody—not a single Bishop of them—believes in it. The business in the stable isn't convincing."[9] Writers who solve the problems of life with the old Christian formulas are not convincing either:

> *Dislike* as definition of my attitude to Tolstoy is but a rough and approx-imate term. I judge him not—for this reason. That his anti-sensualism is suspect to me . . . Moreover the base from which he starts—Christian-ity—is distasteful to me. I am not blind to its services but the absurd oriental fable from which it starts irritates me. Great, improving, soften-ing, compassionate it may be but it has lent itself with amazing facility to cruel distortion and is the only religion which, with its impossible standards, has brought an infinity of anguish to innumerable souls—on this earth.[10]

He writes to Edward Garnett, after reading *The Brothers Karamazov* in Constance Garnett's translation, that "it sounds to me like some fierce mouthings from prehistoric ages";[11] the same prehistoric and prescientific age in which Saint Teresa lived her devotional life, which Conrad found "absorbing like a dream" as he read Mrs. Cunninghame Graham's biography of her, "and as difficult to keep hold of"; a dream that he found "profoundly saddening" (in the understanding language of his pre-1910 period), for "It is indeed old life re-vived."[12]

Conrad himself knew too much to want to revive the old life, however, and attempts made to claim a residue of Roman Catholicism in his life and work are misplaced—the three pieces of documentary evidence are tenuous in the extreme: Conrad invented a baptism date for Borys in a London church that does not exist, for the benefit of some devout Polish relatives;[13] he urged his Roman Catholic heritage by way of a polite refusal to join an Anglican Club;[14] and in an early letter to his "aunt" Marguerite Poradowska he writes, in the overblown rhetoric with which he admires her from afar: "Charity is eternal and universal Love, the divine virtue, the sole manifestation of the Almighty which may in some manner justify the Act of Creation," but he then qualifies such empyrean exuberance with comment both more caustic and more characteristic: "in my opinion abnegation carried to an extreme . . . becomes not a fault but a crime, and to return good for evil is not only profoundly immoral but dangerous, in that it sharpens the appetite for evil in the malevolent and develops . . . that latent human tendency towards hypocrisy in the . . . let us say, benevolent."[15] This letter follows one of September 15th, 1891, in which Conrad contemplates the idea of "expiation through suffering", and incidentally throws light on his later views on Dostoyevsky, because

> that doctrine, a product of superior but savage minds, is quite simply an infamous abomination when preached by civilized people. It is a doctrine which, on the one hand, leads straight to the Inquisition and, on the other, discloses the possibilities of bargaining with the Eternal . . . moreover, there is no expiation. Each act of life is final and inevitably produces its consequences in spite of all the weeping and gnashing of teeth and the sorrow of weak souls who suffer as fright grips them when confronted with the results of their own actions.[16]

The insistence on the strict operation of cause and effect might be George Eliot's, but the superficial savagery of its action in Conrad's world is really closer to Hardy; and he continues his letter to Cunninghame Graham, stimulated by his recent excursion into the "old life", with an outburst which might have been provoked by a reading of Hardy, where

> old life is like new life after all—an uninterrupted agony of effort. Yes. Egoism is good, and altruism is good, and fidelity to nature would be the best of all, and systems could be built, and rules could be made—if we could only get rid of consciousness. What makes mankind tragic is not that they are the victim of nature, it is that they are conscious of it. To be part of the animal kingdom under the conditions of this earth is very well—but as soon as you know of your slavery, the pain, the anger, the strife—the tragedy begins. We can't return to nature, since we can't change our place in it. Our refuge is in stupidity, in drunkenness of all kinds, in lies, in beliefs, in murder, thieving, reforming—in negation, in contempt—each man according to the promptings of his particular devil. There is no morality, no knowledge and no hope; there is only the consciousness of ourselves which drives us about a world that whether seen in a convex or a concave mirror, is always but a vain and fleeing appearance.[17]

We would expect Conrad to admire Hardy, and indeed Retinger remembers that "among his contemporaries he praised Thomas

Hardy and Henry James for the virility of their conceptions, the economy of their techniques, the precision of their style",[18] whereas "he could not stand *Wuthering Heights*",[19] and had a "strong antipathy to G. B. Shaw",[20] but, as he wrote to Galsworthy: "I suppose there is something in me that is unsympathetic to the general public,— because the novels of Hardy, for instance, are generally tragic enough and gloomily written too,—and yet they have sold in their time and are selling to the present day."[21]

Conrad's own explanation for that "something" is too inclusive and too simple: "foreignness, I suppose";[22] yet it is half true— Hardy's novels are revolutionary within the old tradition, Conrad's are outside it altogether. Hardy's universe is a simple negative mirror image of the providential one it replaces; whereas Conrad's is more advanced, unfamiliar, bearing little trace of the old metaphysical comforts—not even by their outraged denial.

Hardy never doubts the reality of his external nature; evolutionary thinking sustains his interest in the relations of all living things, amongst whom the most advanced is the man of widest sympathies, a Jude. Conrad continually doubts the reality of his nature, "a vain and fleeing appearance";[23] and far from imagining an evolutionary advance towards the widest possible spread of sympathy to the animal kingdom at large, he considers overdeveloped sympathy to be profoundly corrupting; while, personally, rather than feeling for the suffering of the birds on a frosty morning, he actually contemplated going into business on a whaling expedition.[24] Yet Conrad's nature, although unfamiliar to the "general public" and new in the English novel's development, is nevertheless as real and as soundly based in contemporary science as Hardy's; it is merely less visual, less accessible, at moments of its enforced revelation reflecting the ideas of physics rather than biology; and while Hardy's most powerful image of his nature is Egdon Heath, ancient, massively solid, rich in its highly detailed surface supporting life from insect ephemera to the highly evolved man of the unrealised future, Clym, Conrad's most powerful image is the Golfo Placido, without time, an insubstantial arena for elemental forces, undifferentiated—"sky, land, and sea disappear together out of the world when the placido—as the saying is—goes to sleep under its black poncho."[25]

This nature is not derived from old philosophical speculation on the impossibility of knowledge, but from two discoveries of physics. Conrad remonstrates with his friend Cunninghame Graham, who, as a romantic adventurer, commanded Conrad's respect, and, as an aristocratic socialist, stimulated Conrad's intellectual antagonism without arousing his fastidious distaste; whose "admiration for William Morris", as C.T. Watts says, "helped to convert into socialism his freelance radicalism and to divert into practical channels his aristocratic contempt for the bourgeoisie, his chivalrous sympathy with the underdog, and his aesthetic revulsion against the grime and squalor of industrial Victorian Britain".[26] To Cunninghame Graham's evolutionary ideal of the coming fraternity among men, Conrad replies with his picture of a universe which precludes such a possibility: "there is a—let us say—a machine. It evolved itself (I am severely scientific) out of a chaos of scraps of iron and behold!—it knits. I am horrified at the horrible work and stand appalled. I feel it ought to embroider . . . it's only a question of the right kind of oil . . . Alas no. You cannot by any special lubrication make embroidery with a knitting machine."[27]

Nothing can be done with these machine-made marionettes in the name of evolutionary progress, in any of the multiple meanings of those words. No socialist campaign to change the environment, the living conditions, the "right kind of oil", will necessarily result in the right physical difference (Lamarck's belief, which Darwin later adopted, and for which Marx wished to dedicate *Das Kapital* to him);[28] no capitalist laissez-faire economics will guarantee the emergence of Spencer's "fittest", because human nature is governed by a-human biological law (itself subject to the outer, bounding, larger laws of physics) and "the most withering thought is that the infamous thing has made itself; made itself without thought, without conscience, without foresight, without eyes, without heart. It is a tragic accident—and it has happened. You can't interfere with it."[29] As Conrad says to another of his socialist friends: "the difference between us, Wells, is fundamental. You don't care for humanity but think they are to be improved. I love humanity but know they are not!"[30]

And even if they were to be improved, "If you believe in improvement you must weep," because there is no stepping outside the circle on to the line of progress, "for the attained perfection must end in cold, darkness and silence", in obedience to the second law of thermodynamics, when our reason further tells us that: "In a dispassionate view the ardour for reform, improvement for virtue, for knowledge, and even for beauty is only a vain sticking up for appearances as though one were anxious about the cut of one's clothes in a community of blind men."[31]

Inside the circle, in the system of classical physics, where the amount of energy is constant, but where, in human terms, the system itself is hostile to life because heat cannot pass spontaneously from a colder to a hotter body: "reason is hateful . . . Because it demonstrates (to those who have the courage) that we, living, are out of life— utterly out of it. The mysteries of a universe made of drops of fire and clods of mud do not concern us in the least. The fate of a humanity condemned ultimately to perish from cold is not worth troubling about."[32]

So Conrad's world is heated by a sun that is treacherously dying; burning itself out according to the calculations in William Thomson's paper "On the Dynamical Equivalent of Heat",[33] published, ironically enough, in 1851, when the Great Exhibition was so full of those products of the new industrial capitalism and of the promises of its admirers, prophesying the peaceful progress to the golden economic era which the material interests demanded. Imagined as the very same source of power which had produced those material interests, a ball of coal fire, the sun in late Victorian times seemed to have had a very short past (far too short for evolution by natural selection as Darwin had imagined it), and, more important, to be destined for a short future.

Yet this visual, everyday physics is compounded of common sense laws which life reinforces for us in our experienced sense of their rightness: as Conrad says in his essay upon Henry James, only the novelist can render convincing the old truth that for every gain "a sacrifice must be made, . . . something has to be given up . . . Wherever he stands, at the beginning or the end of things, a man has to sacrifice his gods to his passions or his passions to his gods."[34] This is merely a restatement in rough oral wisdom of a law which also seems to be true of heat transference in sophisticated experiments. And we feel it equally fitting, if a little more distressing as less indicative of justice to one's distant progeny, that the sun is also mortal: Singleton, without the power to think (and so to the evolutionary thinkers, hardly a man at all), is, to Conrad: "simple and great like an elemental force". One of the entities of physics, exalted not by his kinship with biologically advanced life, or even, in Hardy's imagery, with animals or with the traditional oak, Singleton is half spared the indignity of personal death because he will share his unthinking end with burning matter: "Nothing can touch him but the curse of decay—the eternal decree that will extinguish the sun, the stars one by one, and in another instant shall spread a frozen darkness over the whole universe."[35]

But a new order of nature, a different reality beneath the hard surface of Newtonian physics, had begun to crack its way up through these commonsense formulae a few years before this letter was written: the Michelson-Morley experiment, which effectively disproved the existence of the rigid ether (but did not, of course, instantaneously kill this attractive idea in the minds of literary men), was performed in 1887.[36] It was later one of the evidential foundations of Einstein's work, as, indeed, were Maxwell's own equations which defined the electromagnetic theory (in itself an elegant product of Newtonian mechanical ideas) and which contained raw materials for both the relativity and the quantum theories.[37] But two more immediate, more visual discoveries were made in the last decade of the century. In a series of experiments with the "cathode ray tube" (itself dating back to its primitive origins in Faraday's experiments with partially evacuated tubes and electric currents) Wilhelm Röntgen found that he could make a fluorescent screen glow outside the tube when he placed a metal target inside it at an angle to the path of the cathode rays—rays which were known to find glass impenetrable—so it was obvious that some new kind of radiation was being produced: radiation of remarkable properties, too, for it passed through wood as well as glass—and through human flesh. In investigating the nature of this fluorescence which occurred under the influence of Röntgen's rays, or "X" rays, Henri Becquerel discovered that uranium salt itself was capable of its own radiation; a discovery which Pierre and Marie Curie pursued, adding polonium and radium to the table of the elements in 1899, and finding radium, which, as Conrad wrote in 1910, "was quite unnecessarily dragged out of its respectable obscurity in pitchblende to upset the venerable (and comparatively naive) chemistry of our young days",[38] to be more than one million times more radioactive than uranium.

But in 1900 the atom and the molecule were still hypotheses which had not been established in physical terms; and the structure of the atom was entirely unknown. So the concept of the universe which forms the background and dictates the foreground of Conrad's best work, could only have been reached and held on the available evidence from nature during the two decades in which he began and completed that work. His sun and his space are based on Victorian science; the second law of thermodynamics is obeyed, in a system using up its conventional energy; the elements are stable, immortal, and do not change into one another (they merely separate and cool); there are still absolute measurements to be made and absolute conclusions to be reached about physical phenomena; there are entities in the cosmos, elements, atoms, which are not subject to time, chance or change. Yet Conrad has also seen just enough of the new reality; he has had one glimpse behind the veil—and no mere philosophical or religious or mystical glimpse—but a demonstration of an entirely new phenomenon, repeatable in experimental conditions, which is as strange in terms of the old schema as anything which the Society for Psychical Research was called to investigate.

The most excited of all Conrad's many letters to Garnett describes his stay in Glasgow, where he had gone to look for a command of a ship, and where he stayed with a friend of Cunninghame Graham, Dr. John McIntyre, a pioneer radiologist: "All day with the ship-owners", wrote Conrad,

> and in the evening dinner, phonograph, X rays, talk about *the* secret of the Universe, and the nonexistence of, so called, matter. The secret of the universe is in the existence of horizontal waves whose varied vibrations are at the bottom of all states of consciousness. If the waves were vertical the universe would be different. This is a truism. But, don't you see, there is nothing in the world to prevent the simultaneous existence of vertical waves, or waves at any angles; in fact there are mathematical reasons for believing that such waves do exist. Therefore it follows that two universes may exist in the same place and in the same time—and not only two universes but an infinity of different universes—if by universe we mean a set of states of consciousness. And, note, *all* (the universes) composed of the same matter, matter, *all matter* being only that thing of inconceivable tenuity through which the various vibrations of waves (electricity, heat, sound, light, etc) are propagated, thus giving birth to our sensations— then emotions—then thought. Is that so?
>
> These things I said to the Dr. while Neil Munro stood in front of a Röntgen machine and on the screen behind we contemplated his back-bone and his ribs . . . It was so—said the Doctor—and there is no space, time, matter, mind as vulgarly understood, there is only the eternal something that waves and an eternal force that causes the waves—it's not much—and by the virtue of these two eternities exists that Corot and that Whistler in the diningroom upstairs (we were in a kind of cellar)

and Munro's here writings and your Nigger and Graham's politics and Paderewski's playing (in the phonograph) and what more do you want?[39]

Apart from echoes of Conrad's interest in the scientific world of H. G. Wells, whose *Time Machine* he had read,[40] and in the source of the future mechanism of *The Inheritors*, which Conrad and Ford Madox Hueffer began to collaborate upon in November of 1898[41] (and which at least assures us that this was not just a passing enthusiasm), Röntgen's discovery seems to have had a deeper effect on Conrad's own work and thought.

In 1891 Thaddeus Bobrowski had written to Conrad reproving him for his pessimism: "My dear lad, whatever you were to say about a good or bad balance of nature, about good or bad social relationships, about right or wrong social systems, about the boundless stupidity of crowds fighting for a crust of bread—and ending up in nothing-ness—none of this will be new!!"[42] So it seems that Conrad's broad preoccupations were much the same at the beginning of his two remarkable decades as they were to be at the end. His mind moved easily from the facts of nature to man's power to resist that nature in his social systems, to the threat posed from within by "boundless stupidity" and by various extremities ("a crust of bread", food, cannibalism), and, perhaps, to the vanishing into "nothingness", the annihilation of death; or to the annihilation of Decoud's "nothing-ness", and suicide, which, as we know, was a course that Conrad himself had taken (albeit in the press of thoroughly unmetaphysical financial worries).[43] Bobrowski generalises from science, in a par-ticularly arbitrary way, to explain Conrad's feelings: "modern physicists suppose that on the earth there recur alternate periods of dryness and humidity every thirty six years. Why, then, should we not suppose that in the world of humans there are organisms subject to periodic rises and falls of spiritual aridity—by aridity I mean pessimism . . ." and offers his resigned advice in terms of evolutionary development:

> You will never control the forces of nature, for whether blind or governed by Providence, in each case they have their own preordained paths; and you will also never change the roads along which humanity goes, for there exists in social development an historical evolutionary compulsion which is slow but sure, and which is governed by the laws of cause and effect derived from the past and affecting the future.[44]

Around these ideas, which we will see at work in *Lord Jim*, Conrad places his own conceptual frames which contain and limit them: "path" and "road" are always metaphors for illusion in Conrad's most powerful fiction, leading only to the circle which bounds them; the laws of cause and effect, the microcosmic and linear laws, are themselves encircled by the macrocosmic laws of thermodynamics, slower and surer; and in this context the modest hopes of Bobrowski become heroically absurd beliefs, a romantic illusion of biological progress:

> If, on this road, the will and work of man mean anything—if in this field all the endeavours of man and their chosen individuals—the geniuses— are effective—everyone may and even ought to contribute to it his hand or head, according to his strength and talents . . . I have developed in myself this calm outlook on the problem of life, whose motto, I venture to say, was, is, and will be "usque ad finem". The devotion to duty . . .[45]

And yet, as Conrad writes to Cunninghame Graham: "Half the words we use have no meaning whatever and of the other half each man understands each word after the fashion of his own folly and conceit. Faith is a myth and beliefs shift like mists on the shore; thoughts vanish; words, once pronounced, die . . ."[46] So that,

> even writing to a friend—to a person one has heard, touched, drunk with, quarrelled with—does not give me a sense of reality. All is illu- sion—the words written, the mind at which they are aimed, the truth they are intended to express, the hands that will hold the paper, the eyes that will glance at the lines. Every image floats vaguely in a sea of doubt—and the doubt itself is lost in an unexplored universe of incerti- tudes.[47]

To the harsh mechanical certainties of Victorian physics, to the commonplace complaint of the vanity of earthly appearances, to the pessimism of the French writers he so admired (and particularly of Maupassant, as Paul Kirschner demonstrates), Conrad adds his own conviction of man's hopeless illusion in life; an inclusive conviction, which is all the more powerful in its dual basis—not only in Schopenhauer and in contemporary psychologists, an illusion generated by man's own mental processes, but also in the recent discoveries and speculations in physics, an illusion inseparable from matter itself: "the inconceivable tenuity" from which the solid world is made, where the appearance of the peaks of the Cordillera, looking as if they "had dissolved . . . into great piles of grey and black vapours",[48] is the reality behind the surface mass. Conrad is indeed "like a man who has lost his gods", as he remarks to Garnett, whose "efforts seem unrelated to anything in heaven and everything under heaven is impalpable to the touch like shapes of mist".[49]

We are beginning to understand why Leavis should find himself in a strange world, occasionally, where Conrad insists on unimaginable realities; or why Forster should have unknowingly discovered significance in Conrad's casket when he opened it: not the old jewel, the immortal speck of matter which man has endowed with his own power, in a reassuring anthropomorphic view of his relations with the elements, but the reality hidden in the crystal, the vapour, "the eternal something that waves", meaningless.[50]

We are also close to realising the obscure semantic difficulties in Conrad, which stem not only from his "Polonisms" but also from his physics. The passion of deeper significance, the imagery of the sea, is easily read as portentous, until we know that "the eternal something that waves" is close to "waves of the eternal something"; that the horizon for Conrad is not the landsman's horizon—the hope in the unrealised future, the outlook over the new valley—but an enclosing circle which is never reached; that the world of physics, invisible forces, waves, vapours, the stars, is also the world of the seaman, who is "immutable in his slight variations like the closed path of this planet of ours on which he must find his exact position once, at the very least, in every twenty-four hours".[51] The circular horizon limits the world of the ship; the closed path, the circling of the planets, limits them too; and, within both circles, it is a universe of static qualities, where biological man-time is irrelevant, where variations are not different or new, but alternations. Where, Conrad remembers,

starting out on a voyage was like being launched into Eternity. I say advisedly Eternity instead of Space, because of the boundless silence which swallowed up one for eighty days—for one hundred days—for even yet more days of an existence without echoes and whispers. Like Eternity itself! For one can't conceive a vocal Eternity. An enormous silence, in which there was nothing to connect one with the Universe but the incessant wheeling about of the sun and other celestial bodies, the alternation of light and shadow, eternally chasing each other over the sky. The time of the earth, though most carefully recorded by the half-hourly bells, did not count in reality.[52]

Inside this encircled world the novelist's imagination can only productively move in a vertical plane; the absorbing question is not how man may progress into the future, but how well he can match the same enemies in a timeless world; the static structure of his society is therefore more important than the lonely wayfarer of genius, because "a ship's safety, apart from the 'Act of God', rests in the hands of the men who are aboard of her, from the highest to the lowest in their different degrees".[53] But the psychology of these men, the various impulses and restraints, the norms of conduct which are expected of their different degrees, is also of vital interest; in a vertical picture of mind, mirrored in a vertical concept of nature, where the sky and the conscious mind reflect each other and are divided by the thin line of the surface, beneath which lie the depths and the unconscious, the individual struggles to find his true position on the "labouring waves for ever rising, sinking and vanishing to rise again—the very image of struggling mankind".[54]

The waves, in this particular image, are seen from the shore: they rise and fall without progress in any direction; despite appearances, they are essentially static, their movement differing radically from the literary commonplace (dear to evolutionists) of man's life as a river flowing to the sea, in which his death is not a "vanishing", but a merging into larger significance, mysterious and comforting, and where oncoming generations do not merely "rise again" to "vanish", but replenish the metaphysical sea with, perhaps, new elements. Likewise, Conrad rejects the equally commonplace symbol of the stars as man's idealised hopes, guiding him to new goals; round Cunninghame Graham's romantic sentimentalising (in the introduction to his *Thirteen Stories*)[55] where a horseman rides out across the plain of life setting course by Soheil, a small star, Conrad draws his cosmic noose:

> let us look at Soheil and reflect that it is a speck in the eternal night even as we are. Only we don't shine. At least some of us don't. But we are as celestial as the other bodies—only we are obscure. At least some of us are. But we all have our illusion of being wayfarers. No more than Soheil, *Amigo!* The appointed course must be run. Round to the left or round to the right what matters if it is a circle? Ask Soheil.[56]

And Cunninghame Graham's indignation, his literary pessimism that the course is probably the wrong one, is equally out of place in the new world—where there is no one with whom to be indignant on the divine scale and where any such cry is merely an emotional relic from the "old life", because "you may fling contempt and bitterness, and wit and hard wisdom, hard unpractical wisdom, at this world and the next—*l'ignoble boule roulera toujours portant des êtres infimes et méchants dans un univers qui ne se comprend pas lui-même.*"[57]

From one point of view, Conrad was unfortunate in the choices he made from the scientific paradigms of nature open to him: physics, in its last a-historical, reactionary phase, aligning itself, with all its prestige, on the side of a static but mysterious universe which still contained a place for the Deity, gave him the hardened certainty of an early end to the world; which, while it reassured the physicists with its familiar Christian and apocalyptic picture, was doubly bleak when its central belief and comfort was removed. And, further, unlike George Eliot, say, with her belief in gradual and rational progress; or Meredith, with his bland faith in nature as man's stern mother; or Butler's and Shaw's irrational attachment to "creative evolution"; or even the ideas and dreams of the early Fabians and Socialists; Conrad refused to indulge himself in semi-religious hopes of half a heaven on earth. From the old physics, and from the first disturbing signs of the new in the "X" rays, Conrad turned for intellectual comfort to contemporary scientific psychology and anthropology; where the mind could at least rest in a sense of the human community, with its common fears and desires, structured and shared and recognisable—a sense of belonging—which the Christian system (and particularly Roman Catholicism) had once formalised so effectively in an adept classification of the subtleties of feeling, distinctions and directions discovered and formulated over centuries of experience; whose categories, it now seemed, could no longer be mentally encapsulated as separate entities, static, timeless elements of emotion, which (just as the elements of physics could be extracted from matter) could be isolated from consciousness. Guilt, for instance, loses its own identity in the new framework, and becomes a confusion of various fears and desires, trailing a long chain of cause and effect which no confessional can break; and, in discussing its true nature, Marlow rides the new misery-go-round of physiological and psychological questions to which there are no absolute answers. As Bertrand Russell writes, the "truth is, of course, that mind and matter are, alike, illusions. Physicists, who study matter, discover this fact about matter; psychologists, who study mind, discover this fact about mind. But each remains convinced that the others' subject

25

of study must have some solidity".[58] A refuge denied to Conrad, who was an amateur of both disciplines.

Conrad's idea of the unconscious, the second self, no doubt owes something to literary tradition, as well as to Schopenhauer. The doppelgänger motif stretches back, in English literature, to James Hogg's *The Private Memoirs and Confessions of a Justified Sinner* (1824), for which André Gide, Conrad's friend and translator, wrote a preface to the Cresset edition. But of course there is no need to be particularly erudite in such a search; Conrad had only to read Schopenhauer, and, later, Dostoyevsky, who (as Borys remembers) was one of the authors Conrad "read most assiduously".[59] In either case, Conrad's unconscious is clearly pre-Freudian—but in the most precise sense, upon the same line of lonely search amongst the new sciences, part intuitive, perhaps, it is certainly, in its successive shadowed shapes, severely scientific—arduously imagined into life by the predictions and prejudices of orthodox biological beliefs.

When Conrad was staying in Corsica, after his breakdown, unwilling to remember any of his own profound explorations of the mind, H. R. Lenormand lent him "*The Interpretation of Dreams* and *Wit and its Relation to the Unconscious*, the fine translations which Brill published of the two works of Freud. Conrad, who spoke of Freud with scornful irony, carried the books off to his room. He returned them to me on the eve of his departure without having opened them."[60] It was a period of sad decline in Conrad's career, when, as Lenormand also remembers: "the only really tragic cry that a writer may utter: 'I can no longer work!' sounded almost daily in his conversation. Spasms of anxiety shook his composure . . ."[61] The psychic depths he had once entered were now too dangerous for him to admit of their existence, and, as he wrote to William Rothenstein, he felt he must keep "a tight hold on myself for fear my nerves go to pieces";[62] so that work produced from those depths, such as Dostoyevsky's, "seemed to exude a bad and unbearable odour".[63] But perhaps one of the most significant remarks which Lenormand remembered was Conrad's advising him "to write a novel, for which he had found me a subject: the decline of men who had arrived at certainty".[64]

This derives from a mirror image of Conrad's pre-1910 picture of nature; a sad, retrospective and half-hidden knowledge of his earlier world from which he had once advised another novelist, John Galsworthy: "The fact is you want more scepticism at the very foundation of your work. Scepticism, the tonic of minds, the tonic of life, the agent of truth,—the way of art and salvation. In a book you should love the idea and be scrupulously faithful to your conception of life." A conception of life which sees the larger conditions which enclose the characters, the writer's idea of the world—and that idea, behind the created life it patterns, is the intellectual truth where "lies the honour of the writer, not in the fidelity to his personages. You must never allow them to decoy you out of yourself."[65] A voracious reader, and, within his own framework, a much greater thinker than his reputation allowed—which was based on all his work, and, more damaging, his later pronouncements upon it—the Conrad who referred to Freud with scorn, had, at some points in his early career closely paralleled Freud's thoughts. Freud had begun the great exploration of his own unconscious in 1897 and, a year later, Conrad began to chart his own search in *Heart of Darkness*. Freud's much later remarks on nature closely recall early Conrad:[66] nature is "sublime, pitiless, inexorable; thus bringing to mind our weakness and help-lessness, of which we thought the work of civilisation had rid us";[67] his general reflections on society's relation to nature might be a summary of Conrad's views: "It is one of the few noble and gratifying spectacles that men can offer, when in the face of an elemental catastrophe they awake from their muddle and confusion, forget all their internal difficulties and animosities, and remember the great common task, the preservation of mankind against the supremacy of nature."[68]

To turn to the novels and short stories themselves, we must follow these ideas to their surprising conclusions and, in the process, we may judge how well Conrad measured up to his own prescription for success in an article he wrote in 1905:

> The pursuit of happiness by means lawful and unlawful, through resig-
> nation or revolt, by the clever manipulation of conventions or by solemn
> hanging on to the skirts of the latest scientific theory, is the only theme
> that can be legitimately developed by the novelist who is the chronicler
> of the adventures of mankind amongst the dangers of the earth. And
> the kingdom of the earth itself, the ground upon which his individu-
> alities stand, stumble, or die, must enter into his scheme of faithful
> record. To encompass all this in one harmonious conception is a great
> feat; and even to attempt it deliberately with serious intention, not
> from the senseless prompting of an ignorant heart, is an honourable
> ambition.[69]

But our own ambition is necessarily curtailed by the book-space available to contain it, and probably the only way to accomplish a sufficiently detailed and convincing exposition of the way in which a great writer may create by preying upon and transforming extra-literary ideas, not just for his overall convictions and general picture of how the world is structured, but also in its intricate pattern, the characters' relations one to another, the precise images in which they are described, is to resign ourselves to a formal limitation in scope.

To chart the changes which contemporary biology and physics wrought in man's idea of time; the vastating awareness of a stellar space emptily indifferent to all natural theological purpose; the altered conception of sex, newly important and newly debased as an evolutionary mechanism; the different understanding of chance, which became a newly central part of the process by which we had evolved; and in the idea of nature itself, which became so very much more complex and uninviting than its pastoral and romantic past had ever suggested, we will need a major work written by an artist who is almost at the height of his powers.

But in a pursuit which seeks to regain the most elusive of all moments of the mind's time, just before the process of artistry begins and the outlines of merely intellectual assumptions become blurred, we would be wise not to select a real masterpiece. And this is especially true with Conrad, whose pre-creative moments, themselves conditioned by the unstated thoughts common to the educated man of the period (but nonetheless peculiar to those particular times) are yet further withdrawn towards obscurity by their creator's own preoccupations with the metamorphosing natures of an unsuspected scientific series of different times: with the time of physics in space; with the vertiginous time of geology; with biological time; with the ancestral time of the primal hordes; with the domestic time of the cave and river-drift man; with the different times in geographical space; with inherited time; with memory time; and with the projected time of the imagination.

Lord Jim exactly fits our purpose. If our exploration is close enough it will re-order our approach to Conrad, enlarge our respect for the great intelligence he was able to employ and the easy mastery he eventually developed in his increasingly daedal fictional experiments with the intricate potential truths of contemporary science (itself superseded, and now lost to us without an arduous exercise in historical reconstruction). If all goes well, it will give us an intimate portrait of the inner nightmares endured by a massively thinking man trying to make sense of the new outer nature and to protect his old emotional life inside it, in the post-Darwin, post-Kelvin but pre-Mendel and pre-Einstein world of the 1890s.

In fact our pursuit of Jim into time lost might just begin to justify the optimism of that historian of ideas whom, as Lovejoy says, "while he oftenest will seek for the initial emergence of a conception or presupposition in some philosophic or religious system or scientific theory, will seek for its most significant manifestations in art, and above all in literature".[70] And for once we might be able to agree with Whitehead when he tells us that: "It is in literature that the concrete outlook of humanity receives its expression. Accordingly, it is to literature that we must look, particularly in its more concrete forms, if we hope to discover the inward thoughts of a generation."[71]

2

Joseph Conrad's cosmology: time, space, sex, chance and nature in Lord Jim

Jim journeys away from the open light of reason under Western eyes towards the mystical East. He "retreated in good order towards the rising sun" and, in following his dream with his eyes "roaming about the line of the horizon", seeming to "gaze hungrily into the unattainable", he journeys towards the heart of darkness, down the long night of past evolutionary time.

It is important to remember that this journey into lost time is not a voyage of self-discovery in any benign Proustian sense; for whilst both Proust and Conrad believe that nature speaks directly to man's unconscious, for Proust the message is to be actively sought by a devoted descent into unconscious memory; a descent which must be made alone, free from the distractions of the senses. For Conrad such a deliberate pursuit of the individual and racial past is unthinkable; salvation is to be found, if at all, in the greatest possible distraction of the senses, in the external demands upon the self of a society under stress, in the exercise of reason before an implacable universe. For Conrad escape must be found in the small, fragile present of the society of one's kind, poised between an empty sky and the black depths of past time. Proust regained his time past in a delighted loneliness of the imagination, placing himself amongst his characters; Conrad protects himself against the lure of the past and of the unconscious, encircling his imagination in the present with an assembled group of rational and well-fed Western European friends, who can be relied upon to remain unperturbed by their comfortably imperceptive indulgence of Marlow. Conrad's narrator and the group of listeners provide a sense of common belief and social convention strong enough to enable Marlow to embark on his own descent into the unconscious without undue risk, to set out upon his time travels knowing that he will be enabled to find his lonely way back to the safe society of his kind, a society deeply based upon a shared idea, a fixed standard of conduct. For as Karl Pearson wrote in *The Chances of Death* in 1897:

> to form a mental picture of the universe and its history as a connected whole has been the aim of man from the earliest dawn of intellect. His problem has ever been: How am I related to the past, to the future, to the wide expanse of surrounding nature? . . . In our own day we find a light, by no means an all-penetrating daylight, yet a steady search-light, in the principle of evolution . . . In the Middle Ages Ptolemaic conceptions were still supreme . . . But for man then, as now, the vital question was conduct; on conduct depended the very survival of social groups, and the gregarious instinct had early emphasised, with the strong religious sanctions embraced in such terms as sin and righteousness, the fundamental features of social and anti-social behaviour.[1]

In *Lord Jim* Conrad continues his search for an answer to the vital question of moral conduct within his own darkly scientific mental picture of the universe and its history, placing Jim in precise biological relation to time and nature. He despatches Marlow to follow the "steady search-light" of contemporary theories of evolution into the dim complexities of a past where Marlow is indeed bewildered and threatened: "I see well enough now that I hoped for the impossible— for the laying of what is the most obstinate ghost of man's creation, of the uneasy doubt uprising like a mist, secret and gnawing like a worm, and more chilling than the certitude of death—the doubt of the sovereign power enthroned in a fixed standard of conduct." But Marlow asks the wrong questions of conduct, presupposing a static nature; and it is the narrator who realises the true direction of Marlow's voyage, which, like the voyage undertaken by the Marlow of *Heart of Darkness*, takes him very much further in time than in geographical space. Whenever Marlow "showed himself willing to remember Jim" his body, we are told, "would become very still, as though his spirit had winged its way back into the lapse of time and were speaking through his lips from the past". And, on his return, Marlow, like H. G. Wells's Time Traveller, "swung his legs out, got up quickly, and staggered a little, as though he had been set down after a rush through space".

We first see Jim "spotlessly neat, apparelled in immaculate white from shoes to hat", but he carries biological corruption within himself as surely as that other Jim, James Wait. Both of them threaten the

31

ship of society; but, as befits Lord Jim's appearance, the danger within him, whilst no less deadly to his fellows, is better hidden, more subtle. Although he shares his touch of Apollo with the Russian Harlequin, and although, with his "deep, loud" voice, his "gleaming clusters of fair hair" which "seemed to catch all the sunshine"; with his imagination—"he was a finished artist in that peculiar way"—and with those dreams he loves for their "gorgeous virility, the charm of vagueness" which "carried his soul away with them and made it drunk with the divine philtre of an unbounded confidence in itself", with all these characteristics of the mystical idealist, he might appear naturally predestined to follow the Russian and Mr. Kurtz to the heart of darkness, yet his journey, though in direction it indeed follows their descent, is both more dangerous and more interesting. Like them, he imagines he is setting out to scale the heights of man's achievements, to kick himself free of the earth, or, as Brown observes, he appears to be "one of those people that should have wings so as to go about without touching the dirty earth". And, in common with Kurtz, his egoistic yearning for the impossible disrupts the rational working of the recently evolved capacity for conscious restraint of the prehistoric instincts. Marlow watches just such a struggle and such a failure at work in him:

> He was very far from me who watched him across three feet of space. With every instant he was penetrating deeper into the impossible world of romantic achievements. He got to the heart of it at last! A strange look of beatitude overspread his features, his eyes sparkled in the light of the candle burning between us; he positively smiled! He had penetrated to the very heart—to the very heart.

The heart of Jim's bright beatific illusion leads him to the heart of darkness; his unconscious depths rise to take possession of him; his secret dreams of triumph over society, nature, time and space allow him to become an outcast, captured by the Lamarckian or late Darwinian biological bond between external nature and his own increasingly primitive unconscious, which forces him to journey "generally farther East", towards the past. But unlike the rootless artist of mixed descent, the degenerating Kurtz, and unlike the already primitive Russian, Jim is "from the right place; he was one of us"; and as such he serves as a glass through which Conrad hopes to peer into the depths of the collective mind of Western European society.

"Originally he came from a parsonage", Marlow tells us, and Jim

himself twice insists upon his priestly parentage: "Jim's father possessed such certain knowledge of the Unknowable as made for the
righteousness of people in cottages without disturbing the ease of mind
of those whom an unerring Providence enables to live in mansions."
He too has his beatific illusion, his socially protected dream of a nature
subservient to his desires, and Conrad is precise about the length of
this particular sleep in man's history: "The little church on a hill had
the mossy greyness of a rock seen through a ragged screen of leaves. It
had stood there for centuries, but the trees around probably remembered the laying of the first stone." The appearance of antiquity is
an illusion beside the new time-scale of Darwinian nature; but there
has nonetheless been an abundance of time for the effects of inherited
habit to accumulate: "The living had belonged to the family for
generations". Jim's conscious dreams are no match for the acquired
characteristics of these priestly generations and their "certain
knowledge of the Unknowable"; beneath the surface appearance of a
man whom Marlow recognises as "one of us" lies hidden another
biological, Lamarckian inheritance, developed unchecked down the
centuries of rural English Protestant thought, grown unobserved in a
warm mental culture, a mild Anglican "ease of mind".

Jim is the unwitting carrier of hereditary disease which he has
no chance of resisting; denied the conditions to which his ancestors
have gradually adapted themselves and in which his father lives in
perfect biological harmony, he is unable to meet the highly evolved
"standards of conduct" which his own racial tradition demands of
him; unknown to himself, or to those of his own apparent position
in the line of moral evolution, he is inwardly deformed, deprived of
a normally hidden but nonetheless essential instinct which only
habitual use can preserve. As Marlow remembers him:

> He stood there for all the parentage of his kind, for men and women by no
> means clever and amusing, but whose very existence is based upon
> honest faith, and upon the instinct of courage. I don't mean military
> courage, or civil courage or any special kind of courage. I mean just that
> inborn ability to look temptations straight in the face—a readiness
> unintellectual enough, goodness knows, but without pose—a power of
> resistance, don't you see, ungracious if you like, but priceless—an
> unthinking and blessed stiffness before the outward and inward terrors,
> before the might of nature, and the seductive corruptions of men—backed
> by a faith invulnerable to the strength of facts, to the contagion of
> example, to the solicitation of ideas.

Jim's own line of descent, however, has diverged from that of the parentage of his kind into a faith that is not honest, which offers false and tortuous theological comfort against the physical and biological conditions of nature in an artificial, intellectual system, which in turn prevents the exercise of instinctive courage in response to surrounding nature by interposing the mystical dream between the emotional Lamarckian adaption and the external facts which produced it. So Jim lacks "that inborn ability", that readiness to meet the "strength of facts"; and the "power of resistance" to "the contagion of example" has become atrophied by "disuse", as Darwin put it.[2] But Conrad is careful to remind us that Jim is not responsible for his decisive acts in any conventional sense; Jim's behaviour simply cannot be judged in terms of the moral standards which serve to measure character in "the great tradition" of the English novel.

As *Lord Jim* draws to its close the narrator receives Marlow's letter describing the final engulfment of Jim's conscious mind, his dream of himself, his mystical illusion, in the dark rising waters of his own unconscious. After the disaster in Patusan, Jim had himself attempted to write to Marlow, but the pen "had spluttered . . . he had seen a broad gulf that neither eye nor voice could span". And, like the Marlow of *Heart of Darkness* who begins to understand a little of the nature of the powers he faces in his psychical wrestling with Kurtz in the primaeval jungle, Marlow in *Lord Jim* recognises the origins of Jim's loss of the powers of rational expression: "I can understand this" Marlow writes. Jim was "overwhelmed by the inexplicable". He is caught by the last and sudden rising of instincts evolved in an unimaginable time past before the mud creature of man's ancestry developed organised brain mechanisms of any kind, let alone the language to name his desires. Jim was "overwhelmed by his own personality—the gift of that destiny which he had done his best to master"; he was overcome by a personality bequeathed to him from his priestly forbears, in Lamarckian or late Darwinian essences or pangenes,[3] bearing the amassed inheritance of acquired habits of a mystical ease of mind, ill-adapted to restrain the dark depths of the unconscious and the evolutionary past. And as if to make the essential point more explicit, Marlow, in recounting Jim's last characteristic act, sends the narrator a letter which he firmly connects with Jim's first unavoidable surrender: "I send you also an old letter . . . It is from his father . . . a few days before he joined the *Patna*." Secure in his egoistic illusion, which so comfortably ignores the real nature of time and space, chance and death, the

> old chap goes on equally trusting providence and the established order of the universe . . . One can almost see him, grey-haired and serene in the invincible shelter of his book-lined, faded, and comfortable study, where for forty years he had conscientiously gone over and over again the round of his little thoughts about faith and virtue . . .

But his "little thoughts" are no longer any safeguard away from such "inviolable shelter"; the trust in providence and the established order of the universe has bred such weakness in the once highly developed conscious minds of a family which has held the living for generations that his own son is now unknowingly regressing back to the mental level of that other James in Conrad's work. Jim is now burdened with the weight of an uncontrollable instinct for self-preservation, which rules in place of that "inborn ability" for self-restraint possessed by others "from the right place"; so that Marlow can imagine Jim, just as the narrator upon the *Narcissus* saw Jimmy, in the "peopled gloom of that cavernous place" in the depths of the *Patna*, at the moment of testing, "overburdened by the knowledge of an imminent death".

James Wait, taking his place in the work of the advanced Western European world, is in process of emerging from the prehistoric past which Conrad (and Spencer, Darwin, Tylor and Lubbock)[4] imagines is also the African present. The "dear James" of the letter is in process of descending back into that past, moving helplessly on the path set for him by his own weakening ancestors, towards the mystical East, towards a people whom Marlow describes as the "old mankind", inhabiting "one of the lost, forgotten, unknown places of the earth", towards another river, which, as surely as the river flowing from the *Heart of Darkness*, comes from a nature almost as primitive as it once was "at the earliest beginnings of the world, when vegetation rioted on the earth and the big trees were kings".[5] It is a nature adapted for Jim, whose most decisive movements are governed by "an implacable force brooding over an inscrutable intention"[6] as surely as the actions of Kurtz; and who, like Kurtz, attempts to hold to his dream in the face of such a force: "of the cause that tore him out of his immobility" on the bridge of the *Patna* "he knew no more than the uprooted tree knows of the wind that laid it low".

The Marlow of *Lord Jim* struggling to define Jim's final relations with the primaeval nature of Patusan (his Lamarckian adaptation to his environment, for which there are no words), a nature which, like Kurtz, Jim now finds it impossible to leave, might well be the Marlow of *Heart of Darkness* speculating upon the hold which the distant Kurtz in the dark interior has begun to exert upon his own uneasy conscious mind:

> I can't with mere words convey to you the impression of his total and utter isolation. I know, of course, he was in every sense alone of his kind there, but the unsuspected qualities of his nature had brought him in such close touch with his surroundings that this isolation seemed only the effect of his power. His loneliness added to his stature.

The "unsuspected qualities" of Jim's nature show their primitive power early in his life. On his training ship, where in his secret dreams he imagines himself to be "as unflinching as a hero in a book", when faced by the "strength of facts" calling for instinctive, inborn ability, Jim momentarily awakes from his dream, and acts in blind obedience to the commands of his unconscious: "when he got through the hatchway he stood still—as if confounded . . . He stood still. It seemed to him he was whirled around." Jim's conscious idea of himself demands his heroic participation in the rescue of a drowning man, in the kind of immediate action which an evolving tribe or society values most highly and rewards with those vague but powerful stimulants of individual egoism which Jim most craves: fame, honour, trust; but Jim is already a half-drowned man himself in Conrad's world. As James Sully writes in *Sensation and Intuition*, "the whole progress of the individual mind is modified by the action of forces whose origin must be looked for outside the boundaries of the individual life, in the inherited results of ancestral experience".[7] The "Evolution Hypothesis" now means that we may "seek for the antecedent of any habit or emotion just as easily in the psychical life of some remote parental race, as in the experience and impressions of the same individual development".[8] And, as Ribot declares in describing the "Evolution of the Affective Life", distinguishing between "the motor manifestations on one side, the pleasures, pains, and their compounds on the other side" and considering which is fundamental: "My reply to this question is clear: it is the motor manifestations which are essential. In other words, what are called agreeable or painful states only constitute the superficial part of the life of feeling of which the deep element consists in tendencies, appetites, needs, desires, translated into movements."[9]

When Jim, having safely missed his chance to join the ship's boat, is again secure in his conscious dream, the "captain of the ship laid a restraining hand on that boy, who seemed on the point of leaping overboard". Jim receives his training in the self-restraint and instinctive mutual aid which Marlow (and Charles Darwin) believes to be so essential for each individual in society, and, through the inherited effects of habit, so necessary for that society's continued survival. He is initiated into "the craft whose whole secret could be expressed in one short sentence", to be rationally understood; but which, as Marlow knows, to form a mental habit: "must be driven afresh every day into young heads till it becomes the component part of every waking thought—till it is present in every dream of their young sleep!" But Jim's training meets with no inherited tradition to graft itself upon; the captain's soothing remark, "Better luck next time" becomes at least one traditional wish for his future which Jim fulfils in his own way as, next time, he leaps overboard in earnest from the *Patna* in obedience to an older pattern of desires, which Ribot summarises: "All these needs have a point of convergence—the preservation of the individual."[10]

So Jim sets out from a settled and advanced Europe, strong in hopes for the future, but already bearing within him the hidden results of that overprotected life in an environment tamed and civilised. In orthodox Lamarckian fashion, he has lost the power to resist the onslaughts of nature; reacting directly to an external threat not by seeking to join his fellows in an organised common defence but with overpowering instinctive emotion expressed physically, below the mental level of developed language. In a storm possessing that "indefinable something which forces it upon the mind and the heart of a man", that "the sunshine, the memories, the future" may be annihilated for him, Jim's social behaviour is not put to the test, because he is confined to his bunk, recovering from an accident on deck, but: "now and again an uncontrollable rush of anguish would grip him bodily, make him gasp and writhe under the blankets".

And, when faced with "the outward and inward terrors" upon the bridge of the *Patna*, Jim's own words tell us the nature of the impulse which "tore him out of his immobility": "I had jumped . . . It seemed", but he himself gives us a very much clearer mimed picture, later, in a moment of remarkable re-enactment.

Amongst the many passages in the work of now forgotten psychologists which suggest parts of the Freudian synthesis still to come, Ribot's summary of ideas of psychological time is perhaps one of the clearest: "The false or abstract memory of feeling is only a sign, a simulacrum, . . . an intellectualised state added to the purely intellectual elements of the impression, and nothing more."[11] And that is how Jim first describes his feelings—in words—but, as Ribot continues:

> The true or concrete memory of impressions consists in the actual reproduction of a former state of feeling, with all its characteristics . . . Here the recollection does not consist merely in the representation of conditions and circumstances, in short, of intellectual states, but in the revival of the state of feeling itself . . . We have thus (not to speak of the present-future) a present-present and a present-past—viz., that of memory.[12]

For Proust, this passage was one of the keys to the gates of an inner paradisical garden walled in against the outer barren wastes of Darwinian time and limitless space, richly stocked with plants of his own gradual creation which, whether hawthorn blossoms or obscene fungi, held meanings solely for him. For Conrad, such a contained garden is impossible; such a present-past recedes ever further from the small and comforting individual memories into the dark and appalling swamps of that evolutionary past stretching endlessly away into unknown regions where memory and consciousness and humanity themselves alter and regress and disappear.

The sudden upwelling of unconscious memory certainly floods Jim's consciousness with lost time; but its effects are a little more sinister than the artistic revelation which leads Marcel to time regained. For Jim, incapable (through no fault of his own) of living in the present-present ("the perfect love of the work . . . eluded him") and allowing his reason to evaporate into euphoric dreams, into "the present-future", time regained is not a state of beatitude for which he must search, but a disabling, brutal force which pulls him out of his chair as he remembers that terrible moment upon the bridge of the *Patna* which his reason refuses to acknowledge. An unconscious "motor manifestation"[13] raises him up, in mimed re-enaction, "slowly—to his full height, and when his knees had locked stiff the hand let him go, and he swayed on his feet". And, just as the postscript upon the philanthropic report of Mr. Kurtz, "exterminate all the brutes", is as "luminous as a flash of lightning"[14] for Marlow's vision of an older set of instinctive feelings in his dangerous subject, so the Marlow of *Lord Jim* is shaken by his glimpse of a face from the distant unconscious past, leering out at him from the Western and civilised Jim: "The muscles round his lips contracted into an unconscious grimace that tore through the mask of his usual expression—something violent, short-lived, and illuminating like a twist of lightning that admits the eye for an instant into the secret convolutions of a cloud."

Jim's wordless, primaeval past signals its presence in other ways. As Henry Maudsley writes in *Body and Will*: "moral action in any of its modes is not an absolute instinct in any person . . . at any rate there is not the instant, direct, blind, unquestioning obedience to an instinct that there is in a man's walking upright. No one in walking seems to entertain the notion of going on all fours . . ."[15]

Kurtz, of course, excessive in these matters, combines both as he indulges in his last and most startling "motor manifestations"; but Jim, too, gives direct bodily signs of his inner regression, which hint at the evolutionary stage reached by his own unconscious in that most emotive series of gradations between the animal kingdom and man; from the snake condemned to crawl on its belly, to the dog on all fours, to man, proud in his upright and masterful posture. As Marlow listens to Jim, "One of his footfalls somehow sounded louder than the other—the fault of his boots probably—and gave a curious impression of an invisible halt in his gait." Such an otherwise overstated mysterious detail (too curious to be a simple result of his accident) is one of a great many pointers to Jim's sinister journey which, if we manage to map it closely enough, will rediscover hidden horrors in those countries of the mind which are imagined with all the particular harshness of a scientifically sanctioned fear.

The invisible halt in Jim's gait is one small mark of a stage on his journey towards the pre-human past; and although he never reaches the distant depths of a Cornelius, whose "slow laborious walk resembled the creeping of a repulsive beetle", their interaction is close enough to be full of unspoken understanding. Jim has lost a little of that "advantage to man to stand firmly on his feet" which Darwin singles out as one essential advance to mankind's "pre-eminent success in the battle of life".[16] The unhalting, upright gait[17] is reached by gradual stages of development from the "quadrupedal type",[18] the anthropomorphous apes occupying an intermediate position in evolution: "the gorilla runs with a sidelong shambling gait . . . and some kind of Hylobates . . . can walk or run upright . . . yet they move awkwardly, and much less securely than man."[19]

But Jim possesses another highly idiosyncratic, physiological mark which Darwin particularly emphasises in *The Expression of the Emotions in Man and Animals*. A characteristic that points to the reason for Conrad's intense interest in him, Jim's apparently over-developed capacity for blushing is not as trivial as it might seem. Unlike other expressions, which all carry the mark of the beast in their origins, blushing is strictly human, social, moral, and "we may conclude that blushing originated at a very late period in the long line of our descent".[20] Yet Jim's remarkably well developed capacity to express emotions with this most recently evolved of unconscious signs is not necessarily ennobling, merely a mark of his unconscious need to be "one of us", of his social instincts. "We cannot cause a blush" Darwin insisted, "by any physical means, — that is by any action on the body. It is the mind which must be affected. Blushing is not only involuntary; but the wish to restrain it, by leading to self-attention actually increases the tendency."[21] As Darwin concluded: "of all expressions, blushing seems to be the most strictly human",[22] originating, he suggested, in self-attention to bodily appearance, which was later "extended by the power of association to self-attention directed to moral conduct".[23]

So this apparently trivial and maidenly expression receives an unexpectedly detailed description and emphasis in Darwin's work, becoming of enormous theoretical importance in his imagination, the one physiological fact supporting his idea of the evolution of the moral sense. Blushing is an expression which only man has advanced far enough to develop ("Monkeys redden from passion, but it would require an overwhelming amount of evidence to make us believe that any animal could blush")[24] but it carries no divine guarantee of an inner altruism:

> It is not the conscious which raises a blush, for a man may sincerely regret some slight fault committed in solitude, or he may suffer the deepest remorse for an undetected crime, but he will not blush . . . It is not the sense of guilt, but the thought that others think or know us to be guilty which crimsons the face.[25]

Marlow confronts Jim outside the courthouse and, in a scene which in common with many other moments in *Lord Jim* appears to be mysteriously overcharged with emotion unless we realise its intellectual purport, he observes with minute Darwinian accuracy as Jim blushes:

> The red of his fair sunburnt complexion deepened suddenly under the down of his cheeks, invaded his forehead, spread to the roots of his curly hair. His ears became intensely crimson, and even the clear blue of his eyes was darkened many shades by the rush of blood to his head. His lips pouted a little, trembling as though he had been on the point of bursting into tears. I perceived he was incapable of pronouncing a word . . .

And even in Patusan Marlow makes a point of telling us that Jim "had still his old trick of stubborn blushing".

Darwin further remarks in *The Expression of the Emotions*: "Breaches of conventional rules of conduct, if they are rigidly insisted on by our equals or superiors, often cause more intense blushes even than a detected crime."[26] For Darwin, as for Marlow (who could not help feeling that Jim "made so much of his disgrace while it is the guilt alone that matters") there is a biological difference between the conduct and the emotion which results in blushing (an acquired, inherited response to public opinion), and the real suffering which follows a conflict between the egoistic instinct of self preservation and the higher social instinct of a man whose intellect and capacity for sympathy are both well advanced. Darwin, like Marlow, sees a fundamental difference between honour and courage; but in terms of the development of the English novel the similarity between the two qualities in Darwin and in Conrad's thought is more important; neither the possession of social honour nor of inborn courage lends itself to traditional moral judgment: the first major source of the apparent ambiguity in *Lord Jim*.

In *The Descent of Man* Darwin begins his discussion of the evolution of the moral sense in his familiar placatory tone:

> I fully subscribe to the judgments of those writers who maintain that of all the differences between man and lower animals, the moral sense or conscience is by far the most important. This sense . . . is the most noble of all the attributes of man, leading him without a moment's hesitation to risk his life for that of a fellow-creature; or after due deliberation, impelled simply by the deep feeling of right or duty, to sacrifice it in some great cause.[27]

But then "any animal whatever, endowed with well-marked social instincts, the parental and filial affections being here included, would

inevitably acquire a moral sense or conscience, as soon as its intellectual powers had become as well, or nearly as well developed, as in
man".[28]

Darwin's remarks, the bland convictions of a naturalist whose
whole attention is amiably absorbed in the intricate delights of the
small facts and large interrelations of the full organic world, become
bleak sentences of execution for many an ancient illusion when read
without the distractions of such knowledge. Conrad documents the
scientific trial of the old concepts of honour and courage in *Lord Jim*,
and it is interesting that he himself, deprived of the comforts of
professional research, emotionally transposes his own direct indignation—his painful awareness of man's lost self-image which so far
outweighs the intellectual gains—out from Darwin's world, into
which he sends Jim, and into another order of nature with which he
himself is better acquainted. Apollo-Jim dreams the old mystical
dream he shares with his father (and carries within himself its
Darwinian results: unseen, sinister seeds of that embrace of inheritance and environment entwined together, both in the roots of his
family tree and in those "trees of the old mankind", seeds labelled
only by the echoing similarity of the names of the moral climates
in which they will flourish—Pater, Parsonage, Patna, Patusan, the
Past).

Jim enjoys the self-projected world of his father and of Paley where
"the stars, together with the serenity of their rays, seemed to shed
upon the earth the assurance of everlasting security". In "a safe
universe", exulting in thoughts of "valorous deeds" he paces the
deck above the *Patna*'s cargo of "the old mankind" who, like his
father, imagine themselves to be on "the path of souls towards the
holy place, the promise of salvation, the reward of eternal life",
whereas their course is a "straight pencil-line drawn as far as Perim",
a quiet Conradian joke, on a line of mystical wishes firmly bounded
by the real perimeter of the enclosing circle of the new nature.

After the romantic setting of the "thin gold shaving of the moon",
when the ship, full of man's spiritual desires, moves so very smoothly,
the narrator intervenes with his own vision of her: "as though she had
been a crowded planet speeding through the dark spaces of ether
behind the swarm of suns, in the appalling and calm solitudes
awaiting the breath of future creations". Yet it is only really safe to
contemplate the a-human nature of physics and astronomy if your
attention is entirely concentrated upon the description and theory

of such a swarm of suns, when the captive emotions cannot wander unguided into the dark spaces of ether; if, in Marlow's words, you belong to that privileged body of "the astronomers who are paid to talk learnedly" about an obscure star, "its composition, weight, path—the irregularities of its conduct, the aberrations of its light—a sort of scientific scandal-mongering".

It is the same with the irregularities of mankind's conduct, except that Darwin's scientific scandal-mongering fascinates as well as appalls Conrad; but:

> We have not . . . as yet considered the main point, on which, . . . the whole question of the moral sense turns. Why should a man feel that he ought to obey one instinctive desire rather than another? Why is he bitterly regretful, if he has yielded to a strong sense of self-preservation, and has not yielded his life to save that of a fellow-creature?[29]

Unlike Jim's father, who, as Marlow tells us, believes that "Virtue is one all over the world, and there is only one faith", Darwin would first of all have us remember "that with mankind the instinctive impulses have different degrees of strength; a savage will risk his own life to save that of a member of the same community, but will be wholly indifferent about a stranger . . ."[30] Yet Darwin believes that social evolution has indeed altered the balance between egoism and altruism in the advanced Western European nations: "Nevertheless many a civilised man, or even boy, who never before risked his life for another, but full of courage and sympathy, has disregarded the instinct of self-preservation, and plunged at once into a torrent to save a drowning man, though a stranger."[31]

This is the very test which Jim first faces, in the opening pages of *Lord Jim*, when "in the brutal tumult of earth and sky, that seemed directed at him . . . He stood still. It seemed to him he was whirled around." Whereas the "boy with a face like a girl's", who "disregarded" Darwin's instinct of self-preservation, and saved a drowning man, is the "hero of the lower deck". Yet that "powerful stimulus to the development of the social virtues . . . the praise and blame of our fellow men" is not, as Darwin admits, the motive of such heroic actions, and never can be, "for they are performed too instantaneously for reflection, or for pleasure or pain to be felt at the time; though, if prevented by any cause, distress or even misery might be felt".[32] And this is why Conrad is so careful to emphasise Jim's lack of distress or misery after the heroic event; because he was biologically unable to take such heroic action, action which Darwin believes to be "the simple result of the greater strength of the social or maternal instincts than that of any other instinct or motive",[33] Jim is also incapable of genuine distress after his failure: "He could detect no trace of emotion in himself". And he merely returns to his a-rational, mystical dreams: he "exulted with fresh certitude in his avidity for adventure, and in a sense of many-sided courage". But Jim does not possess this inherited quality, courage; whereas Stein, for instance, "possessed an intrepidity of spirit and a physical courage that could have been called reckless had it not been like a natural function of the body—say good digestion . . . completely unconscious of itself"; although it is not courage that Jim desires, but honour.

Honour is a quality bestowed upon an individual by public opinion of a special kind, as Darwin points out:

> The wishes and opinions of the members of the same community . . . either form the sole guides of our conduct, or greatly reinforce the social instincts; such opinions, however, have sometimes a tendency directly opposed to these instincts. This latter fact is well exemplified by the *Law of Honour*, that is, the law of the opinion of our equals . . .[34]

Brierly possesses honour, and so does the French naval officer ("The honour . . . that is real—that is!"). This biological difference between courage (internal, acquired and inherited in a Lamarckian way) and honour (external, the reward of favourable public opinion) is only one source of ambiguity in *Lord Jim*, however: a pointer to a darker and deeper misunderstanding.

Courage, involving no exercise of willpower in the modern sense, no determination, and so carrying no conventional moral value, becomes a biological characteristic, embodied in successive individuals, but also an entity of its own within the species, carrying the past experience and environments of former generations in itself: courage is no longer a simple quality. And the process of losing it leads us, and helped to lead nineteenth-century thought, towards the most widespread early twentieth-century concept of the unconscious.

For if the moral sense had been acquired by man in his evolution from remote mindless ancestors, in a late Darwinian, Lamarckian process, then it could also be lost again; changed surroundings, different habits, social customs that allow Darwin's "effects of disuse"[35] to wither slowly an unexercised characteristic of the civilised moral sense, may all entice man down the "broad and easy way leading to degeneration, decay and death", as Henry Maudsley imagined the new scientific primrose path in 1883, "which is the opposite of the steep and narrow path that leads to evolution and fuller life".[36] Marlow, too, imagines Jim about to take such an easy way: "It struck me that it is from such as he that the great army of waifs and strays is recruited, the army that marches down, down into all the gutters of the earth. As soon as he left my room . . . he would take his place in the ranks, and begin the journey to the bottomless pit."

But for the individual man the bottomless pit lies within himself, the black base of the mind, marking that moment when man as a species first evolved the rudiments of a brain. He is free to plunge into such an abyss here and now, without the help of the future and Mephistopheles. And this intellectual result of an ignorance of the "laws of variation",[37] of genetics, amongst many other very such more serious consequences, is a second major source of ambiguity in *Lord Jim*.

The interior journey (continuously matched by the changing external environment) leads downwards and backwards, a perpetually present threat of another descent of man, which Darwin's idea of heredity lets into the very words of his largely innocent and optimistic work. Conrad would not agree with Darwin's (albeit unenthusiastic) prediction of the strength of the moral sense in "future generations", for whom there is "no cause to fear that the social instincts will grow weaker, and we may expect that virtuous habits will grow stronger, becoming perhaps fixed by inheritance. In this case the struggle between our higher and lower impulses will be less severe, and virtue will be triumphant."[38]

In retracing the evolution of the conscious in a descent to the bottomless pit, the civilised but degenerating individual enters the lost stretches of time towards the heart of darkness, towards the unrestrained desires of pre-rational man as he was imagined by Darwin "on first seeing a party of Feugians on a wild and broken shore" when "the reflection at once rushed into my mind—such were our ancestors".[39] And such were to become the shadowy figures of the new unconscious, evolution at once deprived of its far more vastating, dehumanising dimensions in time and in space, and compressed, preserved outside change and chance; a chamber of horrors where man was at least the central figure, around whom all the other threatening exhibits were arranged, nature in man rather than man lost in nature, and with all the pleasurable fascination of the morally forbidden rather than the unresponsive wastes of the new nature, external to man, Conrad's "appalling and calm solitudes".

Darwin's savages ("absolutely naked and bedaubed with paint, their long hair was tangled, their mouths frothed with excitement"),[40] joined his idea of civilised man "with all his noble qualities, with sympathy which feels for the most debased, with benevolence which extends not only to other men but to the humblest living creature, with his god-like intellect which has penetrated into the movements and constitution of the solar system".[41] The old and new mankind are later placed in a vertical hierarchy of values, more familiar to Christendom, in the new model of mind; where Darwin's savage who "delights to torture his enemies, offers up bloody sacrifices, practises infanticide without remorse, treats his wives like slaves, knows no decency, and is haunted by the grossest superstitions"[42] continues to flourish in the unconscious.

So the unconscious contains the evolutionary past, desires of which Kurtz is an embodiment; but the journey back is not to be a simple restoration to savagery. Spinning the future from the "common law of life",[43] the ages of man and of nations, Maudsley invokes contemporary physics: "If the force at the back of all becoming on earth is that which the sun has steadily supplied to it through countless ages . . . it is plain that when it fails, as fail it one day must, there will be a steadily declining development and a rapidly increasing degeneration" because the environment directly affects the Lamarckian organism, and the "nations that have risen high in complexity of development will degenerate and be broken up, to have their places taken by less complex associations of inferior individuals" until "the last wave of the receding tide of human existence before its final extinction".[44] But, in an interesting afterthought, we are admonished not to imagine it will be a dignified leave-taking, as painless (relatively) as the development of a child from its evolutionary progress in the embryo—as Von Baer described it[45]—to a moral manhood:

> Not that humanity will retrograde quickly through the exact stages of its former slow and tedious progress, as every child now goes quickly forward through them: it will not in fact reproduce savages with the simple mental qualities of children, but new and degenerate

varieties with special repulsive characters—savages of a decomposing civilisation . . . who will be ten times more vicious and obnoxious, and infinitely less capable of improvement, than the savages of a primitive barbarism; social disintegrants of the worst kind, because bred of the corruption of the best organic developments, with natures and properties virulently anti-social.[46]

The new hell is almost as exciting to the scientific imagination as was its predecessor to the mediaeval mind: indeed, perhaps only the weather has changed. Appropriately enough, these Kurtzian savages will perversely mimic savage ancestors in the birthplace of the species at the heart of darkness (as Darwin believed, "it is somewhat more probable that our early progenitors lived on the African continent than elsewhere")[47] but, as the sun dies, they will be "living perhaps in snowhuts near the equator, very much as Esquimaux live now near the pole".[48]

The savage past in the unconscious makes itself felt in other ways, however; for Maudsley there are waking thoughts, the horror of which forbids their utterance, but which in the secret recesses of the mind excite no more revulsion than "similar thoughts do in dreams, when we break all the ten commandments with serene equanimity. Why not, if the inspiration of the moral sense be at bottom social and external?"[49] For Ribot, there are two separate layers of unconsciousness, the "hereditary or ancestral unconsciousness", which is "inherited and fixed in a race";[50] and a "personal unconsciousness",[51] where "affective amnesia"[52] has sealed away disturbing events and their "residuum of affective states"[53]—impressions which may "well remain indelible, though latent, becoming active under given circumstances".[54]

The tantalising half-suggestions of Freud in Conrad's work, the partly distorted echoes, especially powerful from *Heart of Darkness* and *Lord Jim*, are not the result of a conscious, semi-miraculous anticipation of Freud's models of mind and neither are they necessarily the unconscious evidence of a deep disturbance on Conrad's part which can be retrospectively diagnosed (and exorcised for the mental relief of the Freudian analyst); the two men simply thought about the problem of man's behaviour within his society in terms of the same contemporary scientific ideas. The theory of the evolution of a moral sense leads at once to the theory of a conflict of instincts with different histories, fitted for different conditions; a conflict of time past with the present, the desires and needs of the pre-human

47

creature and of savagery with those of civilised society; the desires of
childhood with those of maturity. Conrad and Freud imagined (or
discovered or created) an unconscious past—with their own distinctive personal and monstrous desires at play in it of course—but the
murky landscape of that far country is much the same for both men.
Freud was a Lamarckian all his life, although it was not until 1911
that he declared the unconscious to hold not only infantile material
but also relics from primitive men;[55] and it was only his very late
conclusion that the fundamental aim of all instincts is to revert to an
earlier state, a regression into the past, which eventually reduces the
living organism to inert matter, the so-called "Death Instinct".[56] But
it is easy to see that Freud's thought followed Darwin's in much the
same way, close to Conrad's own preoccupations in *Heart of Darkness*
and *Lord Jim*. Freud's late picture of the mind fits neatly into Darwin's
description of the moral sense at its most developed when it "becomes
a highly complex sentiment—originating in the social instincts"
(beneath which lies the a-social region of the Id in Freud's termin-
ology) "largely guided by the approbation of our fellow men, ruled
by reason, self-interest" (the domain of the ego) "and in later times
by deep religious feelings, and confirmed by instruction and habit"[57]
(the higher realm of the super-ego).

In this Lamarckian explanation of the mechanism of the development of a stable and civilised society the reverse process is an obvious
possibility; with the disappearance of "deep religious feelings", with
the revealed fragility of the only recently evolved "reason", those
"fellow-men" begin to look unpleasantly like a mob (if not a primal
horde)[58] ruled by a different and anarchic "self-interest". Hence
even Huxley's occasional fearful look over his shoulder, just in case
the enemy, religion, might really be dying in earnest,[59] and hence the
great campaign for better instruction, education at all levels;[60] un-
reliable habit is the only remaining dyke before the now rising flood
of unrestrained instinct.

Both Freud and Conrad would have agreed with the stern measures
that Max Nordau proclaims to be the only hope for mankind in the
concluding pages of his exploration of "the *fin-de-siècle* disposition"[61]
in *Degeneration* (translated into English in 1895):

> Progress is possible only by the growth of knowledge; but this is the task
> of consciousness and judgment, not of instinct. The march of progress
> is characterised by the expansion of consciousness and the contraction
> of the unconscious; the strengthening of will and the weakening of

impulsions, the increase of self-responsibility and the repression of reckless egoism . . . And he who places pleasure above discipline, and impulse above self-restraint, wishes not for progress, but for retrogression to the most primitive animality.[62]

Yet, for Conrad as he plays out and encircles these ideas in his work, too much knowledge makes the line of progress appear a mere scratch upon the indifferent surface of things; and if the will is already weakened and the impulsions are growing stronger then there is no point in discussing responsibility. It is easier to attack a social or intellectual class of people or beliefs, of the kind, for instance, which Kurtz and the Russian Harlequin represent; as Nordau continues:

Retrogression, relapse—this is in general the ideal of this band who dare to speak of liberty and progress. They wish to be the future. That is one of their chief pretensions. That is one of the means by which they catch the largest number of simpletons. We have, however, seen in all individual cases, that it is not the future but the most forgotten, far-away past.[63]

Nordau's work, based upon Haeckel's[64] more extreme interpretations of Darwin, upon Morel[65] and Lombroso,[66] seems absurd enough now; but Nordau certainly fulfilled the ambition he declares in his perfervid dedication to Lombroso to enter the "vast and important domain into which neither you nor your disciples have hitherto borne the torch of your method—the domain of art and literature",[67] where, burning with medical righteousness, his torch helped to stoke up the new hellfire. And we must remember that in the absence of any scientific recognition of Mendel's precise demonstration that life upon earth could not have arisen as Lamarck and Darwin in his later work believed, and so was not about to degenerate down an equally fallacious genetic slide to the bottomless fiery pit—when humane institutions had not yet hygienically cleared Europe of village idiots, the sight of monstrous births, or untreated deformities, when all the major disfiguring diseases of the West were still rife, and, in the new industrial cities, becoming apparently far more virulent—then there was simply nothing but vague chimaeras like decent feeling and common sense to set against Nordau's own hybrid nightmares. We must remember, too, that by the 1890s the time scale in which evolution was thought to have taken place had been drastically foreshortened and so, equally, the time in which the easier process of degeneration might complete itself in the future seemed barely long enough for its momentum to be checked and halted; vigorous counteraction was necessary, and the apparent need to be quick about it gives Nordau's work its almost hysterical sense of urgency. We can recognise the emotional insistence of this passage, for instance, in both *Heart of Darkness* and *Lord Jim*:

> whoever preaches absence of discipline is an enemy of progress; whoever worships his "I" is an enemy to society. Society has for its first premise, neighbourly love and capacity for self-sacrifice; and progress is the effect of an ever more vigorous subjugation of the beast in man, of an ever tenser self-restraint, an ever keener sense of duty and responsibility.[68]

The power of the idea of regression upon the contemporary imagination may be crudely measured by balancing the seriousness with which Nordau's work was taken against the stature of the men he chose to attack, almost all of whom force us to size Nordau with that louse which Huxley assured Darwin was always to be found clinging to the back of the intellectual whale. Nordau begins his passage into the dangerously degenerate minds of his age by observing the apocalyptic glow from the Krakatoa dust clouds, and the floating mists, both of which hang so heavily in Conrad's work, too, that they have perplexed later generations of readers (as E. M. Forster writes uncomprehendingly of Conrad in *Abinger Harvest*: "the secret casket of his genius contains a vapour rather than a jewel")[69]:

> Massed in the sky the clouds are aflame in the weirdly beautiful glow which was observed for the space of years after the ruption of Krakatoa. Over the earth the shadows creep with deepening gloom, wrapping all objects in a mysterious dimness, in which all certainty is destroyed and any guess seems plausible. Forms lose their outlines, and are dissolved in floating mist. The day is over, the night draws on. The old anxiously watch its approach. . . . A few amongst the young and strong are conscious of the vigour of life in all their veins and nerves, and rejoice in the coming sunrise. Dreams, which fill up the hours of darkness till the breaking of the new day, bring to the former comfortless memories, to the latter high-souled hopes. And in the artistic products of the age we see the form in which these dreams become sensible.[70]

But it is not merely "artistic products of the age" such as the "course of light holiday literature" which so affect Jim's dreams, his "high-souled hopes" that Nordau castigates; but also Tolstoy,

Ibsen, Nietzsche, Zola, Huysmans, Baudelaire, Gautier, the Pre-Raphaelites, Wagner, and the Impressionists (whose style "becomes at once intelligible to us if we keep in view the researches of the Charcot school into the visual derangements in degeneration and hysteria . . . The degenerate artist who suffers from *nystagmus*, or trembling of the eyeball . . .").[71] Yet Nordau's judgments upon art and literature have a misdirected intensity born of real fear; he clearly did indeed believe that we "stand now in the midst of a severe mental epidemic; of a sort of black death of degeneration and hysteria, and it is natural that we should ask anxiously on all sides: 'What is to come next?'"[72] And therefore it is "the sacred duty of all healthy and moral men to take part in the work of protecting and saving those who are not already too deeply diseased. Only by each individual doing his duty will it be possible to dam up the invading mental malady."[73] Art and literature are powerful forces either for development or for degeneration in this new Manichaean battle; an "invading mental malady" let into a healthy mind by degenerate art will be acquired by habit and then inherited via those Darwinian pangenes collecting in the sex cells for the next generation. Art indeed has a mission in life.

So it is not surprising that the young Freud, for instance, should have "called on Max Nordau with a letter of introduction" as Ernest Jones tells us, nor that "he found him vain and stupid and did not cultivate his acquaintance".[74] It is equally interesting that Nordau should have admired Conrad's work,[75] and that another vigorous exception to his general damnation of contemporary men of letters is Turgenev, who possesses a "splendid sense of artistic proportion" and who, "as a grand and genuine creator of men, stands Prometheus-like over the figures he has inspired with life".[76] Conrad, too, admires Turgenev for much the same reasons: "All his creations, fortunate and unfortunate, oppressed and oppressors are human beings, not strange beasts in a menagerie or damned souls knocking themselves to pieces in the stuffy darkness of mystical contradiction."[77]

Now, for Nordau, the darkness of mystical contradictions is "a cardinal mark of degeneration" and "of all the delirious manifestations peculiar to the hereditarily-afflicted, none indicates the condition more clearly, we think, than mystical delirium".[78] We see "in mysticism a principal characteristic of degeneration. It follows so generally in the train of the latter, that there is scarcely a case of degeneration in which it does not appear."[79] To Nordau as to Conrad "mysticism" means a "state of mind . . . always connected with strong emotional excitement"[80] when the "judgment grows drifting and nebulous like floating fog in the morning wind" and when the "degenerate and debilitated" becomes a victim of his own dreams: "emergent thought-phantoms" which, in a healthy mind, "can acquire no influence over the thought-procedure because attention either lightens up their faces, or banishes them back to their underworld of the unconscious".[81] In the consciousness of the mystical dreamer, however, where will and attention and reason are weakening, the "faint, scarcely recognisable, liminal presentations are perceived at the same time as those that are well lit and centrally focussed".[82]

As Jim lies in hospital in an Eastern port breathing "the bewitching breath of the Eastern waters" with its "suggestions of infinite repose, the gift of endless dreams" outside time, he looks out every day at his new environment, which Conrad describes in deliberate clichés of light and peace to hint at a different reality beneath the surface glitter of that "thoroughfare to the East . . . dotted by garlanded islets, lighted by festal sunshine, its ships like toys, its brilliant activity resembling a holiday pageant, with the eternal serenity of the Eastern sky overhead and the smiling peace of the Eastern seas possessing the space as far as the horizon." The sirens of a falsely reassuring nature, time and space, invitingly free of struggle and decked out with childish and illusory charms, toys and pageants, sing their song of the "far-away past" to Jim's unconscious. And upon his recovery, when he consciously imagines himself to be looking "for some opportunity to get home" to his kind in the advanced West, his unconscious is already looking towards the East. The long instincts of his racial past continue to uncoil, and are at once silently drawn, in direct Lamarckian need, towards a mental environment of similar but more extreme conditions in the surrounding minds, entwining Jim's consciousness to prevent his going home to those "harder conditions" in which the past reawakened within him could not survive. The men Jim "associated naturally with" in the port that stands upon the roadstead to the East are of precisely the same biological make-up as those who cluster naturally in the station that stands upon the river leading to the heart of darkness.

The inhabitants of the Eastern port, like Marlow's pilgrims in Africa, "were of two kinds", Conrad tells us; one kind, "very few

and seen there but seldom, led mysterious lives" like the Russian
Harlequin and Mr. Kurtz, and they possess "the temper of buccaneers
and the eyes of dreamers". These men are the most interesting and
the most dangerous of the two kinds of degenerate—"Borderland
dwellers"[83] indeed, as Maudsley and Ball named them, "dwellers
on the borderland between reason and pronounced madness"[84] as
Nordau adds—and it is from these "higher degenerates"[85] that
writers and artists emerge, those men whose cultural (and so eventually biological) influence Nordau so feared. Kurtz, as mongrel in
the arts as in his hereditary origins, nevertheless is formidable because
of his voice, his eloquence, and, as Nordau writes,

> under the influence of an obsession, a degenerate mind promulgates
> some doctrine or other . . . He does this with vehement penetrating
> eloquence, with eagerness and fiery heedlessness. Other degenerate,
> hysterical, neurasthenical minds flock around him, receive from his lips
> the new doctrine, and live thenceforth only to propagate it.[86]

And the "possessor of an obsession" (the Russian Harlequin,
Conrad's father, and several fascinating members of the biological
chorus which encircles Jim's own journey) "is an incomparable
apostle",[87] Nordau warns his readers. The few men of this kind
whom Jim meets in the Eastern port "appeared to live in a crazy
maze of plans, hopes, dangers, enterprises, ahead of civilisation",
although in a deeper and darker sense they really live far behind
civilised society, "in the dark places of the sea" rather than the dark
land, where, again, "their death was the only event of their fantastic
existence that seemed to have a reasonable certitude of achievement".

As Marlow discovers in *Heart of Darkness*, however, Kurtz's
eloquence bears no open relation to actions, unconscious bodily
expressions, forgotten wordless instincts; so that "speech, that great
auxiliary in the interchange of human thought" is no unmixed
benefit. "It brings to the consciousness of most men incomparably
more obscurity than brightness."[88] Nordau's Englishman, for
instance, "accepts a fit of delirium if it appears with footnotes, and is
conquered by an absurdity if it is accompanied by diagrams",[89] and
"Bunyan depicts the *Pilgrim's Progress* to the mystical kingdom of
redemption in the method of the most graphic writer of travels—a
Captain Cook or a Burton";[90] perhaps Conrad remembered the
national weakness when he came to write his own pilgrim's progress,
using the new biological compass to the full, on his own graphic travels.

The majority of the men Jim meets in the Eastern port resemble the rest of those debilitated "pilgrims" whom Marlow disdained upon his way to the darkness of the primaeval past; waiting upon Providence and Chance (they "talked everlastingly of turns of luck") they have become biologically adapted to their easy environment and are held in Lamarckian bondage at an evolutionary level well below that of their own European societies, whose advanced moral sense has been forcibly produced in adaptation to the fierce Northern nature, harsher lands and more exacting seas. These unconscious exiles "had now a horror of the home service, with its harder conditions, severer view of duty, and the hazard of stormy oceans".

To Jim, their "gossiping crowd, viewed as seamen, seemed at first more unsubstantial than so many shadows"; and this is exactly how his conscious mind, stricken by "the organic weakness of will"[91] of encroaching degeneracy, would notice such unknown familiars sliding out of the unconscious in Lamarckian response to the open presence of so many gossiping shadows. The crowd of seamen, each one wholly ruled by instincts of self-preservation and unrestrained egotistical needs and desires, is itself a group of Nordau's "emergent thought-phantoms" as Jim first sees them. But Jim's own father, after all, believes in constant luck, or rather in "unerring Providence", as befits his higher sanctioned station in life, which is still more conducive to ease of mind and "inviolable shelter" of body, than the "precariously easy lives" of the lower degenerates who unconsciously tempt Jim.

And, much like that secret sharer who is prone to emerge into the consciousness of the scholar in his "book-lined, faded, and comfortable" study (as Conrad describes the habitat of Jim's father "for forty years") in the more unpleasant stories of M. R. James, the beast in man, whose "ever more rigorous subjugation"[92] is Nordau's measure of evolutionary progress, must have been uncomfortably close to rearing itself out of the parsonage shadows—when Jim's father would indeed have been defenceless, because Nordau's only real prescription for safety is to "keep the processes of thought under the discipline of an extraordinarily powerful attention . . . This true depth of strong select minds is wholly luminous. It scares shadows out of hidden corners, and fills abysses with radiant light."[93] More to Conrad's (and M. R. James's) *prédilection d'artiste*, however, is he "who sees the world through the eyes of a mystic" who "gazes into a black heaving mass . . ."[94] So it is not surprising that Jim's unsubstantial shadows, the "spectrally transparent shapes", of Nordau, far from being banished back to the underworld of Jim's unconscious, are allowed to materialise: "beside the original disdain there grew up slowly another sentiment" and "at length he found a fascination in the sight of those men"; men who were "attuned to the eternal peace of Eastern sky and sea".

Jim, "giving up the idea of going home", joins the *Patna*; and we can gain a rough measure of the significance of such a berth, the distance Jim has already travelled in time, in the moral difference between the captain of the ship which brought Jim to the Eastern port and the captain of the ship with whom he elects to journey away; very many biological fathoms, measuring out the laborious development of the moral sense, separate the two men. And, quite apart from the murky fascination of such imagined depths in themselves, it is interesting that Conrad's tortuous exploration of contemporary scientific ideas leads him to the details as well as to the master chart of his novel; its apparently anarchic profuseness of small events and the multitudinous press of all the individual energies of character, the broken, grotesque, constantly changing vitalities of a rich nature (which he only manages to rival once more in his writing life, in *Nostromo*) are all controlled and produced by a germinating cluster of very powerful ideas which enable him to write with such fullness without losing his way.

The captain of Jim's last ship from home, before he becomes attuned to the East, is from "the same place" as Allistoun and MacWhirr, with that "inborn ability" adapted to such an environment. After the ghastly storm which Jim weathers disabled in his bunk, but filled with "uncontrollable" anguish and "a despairing desire to escape at any cost", his "Scottish captain used to say afterwards" in a MacWhirr-like reflection remarkable for the light it throws on to his "instinct of courage" rather than upon his philosophical profoundity: " 'Man! it's a pairfect meeracle to me how she lived through it!' "

Late Darwinian evolutionary thought tended to place the promised land north of the Tweed (Jim himself, Marlow tells us, "came from a long way South of the Tweed") where nature was just hostile enough to promote stern self-restraint and a society tightly bonded together in mutual struggle against the environment, without producing a consequent ease of mind which threatened the south, or the unequal conditions of the far north, which prevented progress altogether (the

Lapps, the Esquimaux). The new industry and technology was no longer an outward reward for an inward moral success dispensed by a severely Protestant Deity to the virtuous congregations in the north of the country, but an inevitable result of the "right way of development"[95] which Maudsley imagined to be the real "categorical moral imperative",[96] the correct interraction of climate and disciplined habits of social duty. These the Scots possessed (but the Irish, despite the propitious weather conditions, did not), and their Victorian virtues were used upon both sides of the debate on racial evolution. Darwin in *The Descent of Man* quotes Greg, for instance, who had observed that the "careless, squalid, unaspiring Irishman multiplies like rabbits: the frugal, foreseeing, self-respecting, ambitious Scot, stern in his morality, spiritual in his faith, sagacious and disciplined in his intelligence, passes his best years in struggle and in celibacy, marries late and leaves few behind him."[97] Darwin counters this apocalyptic vision of the Irishman inheriting the earth, not by admitting that natural selection is an amoral process, but by detailing the various forces of degeneration working to control such prodigious reproductive power: the death rate is higher in towns; "profligate women bear few children";[98] they suffer more severely from the ravages of disease: "Intemperance is so highly destructive".[99] And, although we must not be too complacent because it is "surprising how soon a want of care, or care wrongly directed, leads to the degeneration of a domestic race",[100] yet the civilised who remain at home may congratulate themselves cautiously, because:

> In regard to the moral qualities, some elimination of the worst dispositions is always in progress even in the most civilised nations. Malefactors are executed, or imprisoned for long periods, so that they cannot freely transmit their bad qualities. Melancholic and insane persons are confined, or commit suicide. Violent and quarrelsome men often come to a bloody end. The restless who will not follow any steady occupation—and this relic of barbarism is a great check to civilisation—emigrate to newly-settled countries, where they prove useful pioneers.[101]

And so, in Conrad's world, the Scottish captain, a man from an advanced society, full of instinctive moral courage, returns to the waters of the home service, to the environment which produced him and his kind, leaving Jim behind with Darwin's "useful pioneers", pilgrims of progress, such as Jim's next captain, the "renegade New South Wales German", an inhabitant of a "newly settled country" which, imagined in the time scale of Darwinian development, is an even older environment than the African heart of darkness.

Advanced European man, in orthodox Darwinian theory, evolved out of the African continent, leaving behind him "the old mankind" of savagery, the ancestors whom Marlow visits in *Heart of Darkness* and uneasily acknowledges as such, mesmerised by the Darwinian truth of his remote kinship, "truth stripped of its cloak of time"[102] as Marlow insists. He meets that truth with "his own inborn strength", a strength needed to withstand the powerful direct unconscious attraction of the mind and environment of prehistoric times preserved around him, as Darwin explained, because in the minds of

> our earliest ancestors . . . at this early period, the intellectual and social faculties of man could hardly have been inferior in any extreme degree to those possessed at present by the lowest savages; otherwise primaeval man could not have been so eminently successful in the struggle for life, as proved by his early and wide diffusion.[103]

But European man also left behind him ancestors even more ancient, the Old World apes and monkeys: "as man from a genealogical point of view belongs to the Catarhine or Old World stock, we must conclude, however much the conclusion may revolt our pride, that our early progenitors would have been properly thus designated."[104]

The African "old mankind" and his remote ancestors, the Old World Simiadae, in their turn evolved from still earlier progenitors, the Lemuridae, the Lemurs, whom they left behind, not in Africa, but in remote and protected environments where no superior intruder would bother to venture. Their "remnants" are to be found not upon Darwin's "well-stocked continents"[105] but "on islands, such as Madagascar and the Malayan archipelago",[106] where they might hold safely to their own lower and weaker levels of life in the easiest possible surroundings; in environments, for instance, like Patusan, in the Malayan archipelago which, as Marlow reiterates, is "indeed, one of the lost, forgotten, unknown places of the earth". There nature has been preserved in lost time, the "stream of civilisation, as if divided on a headland a hundred miles north of Patusan, branches east and south-east, leaving its plains and valleys, its old trees and its old mankind, neglected and isolated". The stream of development has left the Lemuridae to degenerate in peace. As Darwin observes: "This group is diversified and broken to an extraordinary degree, and includes many aberrant forms."[107] It is biologically fitting that such aberrant forms of life should inhabit an environment like Patusan, which, as Marlow tells us, "was referred to knowingly in the inner government circles in Batavia, especially as to its irregularities and aberrations". In orthodox late Darwinian logic the acquired characteristics of all the inhabitants of such a place match their surroundings. And Patusan, in "the irregularities of its conduct, the aberrations of its light", matches Darwin's "aberrant forms"; "diversified and broken", its people allow Conrad's imagination to range "insensibly from the crown and summit of the animal creation" (as Huxley follows the range of the gradations of development in the Lemuridae in *Man's Place in Nature*) "down to creatures from which there is but a step, as it seems, to the lowest, smallest, and least intelligent of the placental mammalia".[108]

The diverse group of the Lemuridae hidden away upon islands in "the original dusk of their being" (as Marlow puts it) in turn evolved from ancestral forms related to the marsupials, who "appeared at an earlier geological period" than the placental mammals, whose "range was formerly much more extensive than at present", and whose own ancestral forms were akin to the Monotremata (the duckbilled platypus and the spiny anteater), "forming a third and still lower division in the great mammalian series". And as Darwin continues, they are "represented at the present day solely by the Ornithorhynchus and Echidna; and these two forms may be safely considered as relics of a much larger group, representatives of which have been preserved in Australia through some favourable concurrence of circumstances."[109]

The duckbilled platypus and the spiny anteater give Conrad's imagination, understandably, even greater licence than the Lemuridae; he at last feels free to unleash his ferocious humour with perfect personal and artistic safety in the compound of strong Darwinian theory; and the degenerates of *Lord Jim* are contained by such ideas and attacked with a grotesque laughter not to be found in *Heart of Darkness*. The captain of the *Patna*, attuned to Australia (and specifically, as Marlow twice details, to New South Wales, where the duckbilled platypus, to the perplexity of the natural theologians and the later delight of Darwinian theorists, was first discovered in 1797), is a degenerate who, like Kurtz, on his distorted descent into the past, has become one of Maudsley's "new and degenerate varieties with special repulsive characters".[110] Like Kurtz in Africa, the "New South Wales German . . . brutalised all those he was not afraid of" and his "aspect", like that of Kurtz, is certainly "voracious" with an insatiable instinctive appetite which has overwhelmed all conscious restraint, an inner surrender expressed not in the wraith-like figure of a Kurtz consumed with desires, but in their triumphant gratification, in "the fattest man in the whole blessed tropical belt clear round that good old earth of ours". As befits someone who has become adapted, in degenerate form, to the primaeval home habitat of the duckbilled platypus, itself a relic of the ancestral species from which the mammals evolved, the captain is the victim of Conrad's intellectual humour, although his potential effect upon Jim is not in the least comic. Conrad, with that particular anarchic visual enjoyment which is the privilege of those who read a naturalist's description of his subject without the ordered intrusion of any of their own independent knowledge, privately laughs at Darwin as he evolves his monstrous characters: "There was something obscene in the sight of his naked flesh. His bared breast glistened soft and greasy as though he had sweated out his fat in his sleep . . . the fold of his double chin hung like a bag triced up close under the hinge of his jaw . . . a clumsy effigy of a man cut out of a block of fat."

The captain of the *Patna* oozes and secretes; and he would certainly earn a place in Darwin's oily and intimate discussion of the emergence of male and female from an androgynous ancestor, because the "possession by male mammals of functionally imperfect mammary organs is, in some respects, especially curious",[111] and, given his environment, fascinating in this case; because the Monotremata, as Darwin eagerly points out, "have the proper milk-secreting glands with orifices, but no nipples; and as these animals stand at the very base of the mammalian series, it is probable that the progenitors of the class also had milk-secreting glands, but no nipples".[112] A land of milk indeed, if not of honey, a nature of ease, the nature of Jim's dreams, "the great certitude of unbounded safety and peace that could be read on the silent aspect of nature like the certitude of fostering love upon the placid tenderness of a mother's face". A nature in which Jim "sighed with content . . . and felt a pleasurable languor running through every limb as though all the blood in his body had turned to warm milk. His skipper had come up noiselessly . . ."

The captain's power of unconscious Lamarckian suggestion is strong. And Archie Ruthvel, naturally susceptible, an amiable degenerate ("The race—the two races rather—and the climate" as Marlow remarks darkly upon the effect of his mixed descent) is astonished, when the captain stands in his office, by a vision full of the promise of honey (well, sugar) when: "he saw, in his own words, something round and enormous, resembling a sixteen-hundred-weight sugar-hogshead up-ended in the middle of the large floor space . . . he did not realise the thing was alive . . ." The captain appears to have degenerated a little further since the *Patna* desertion perhaps, losing all trace of his parsimonious allowance of backbone, or retaining only a remnant like the transitional amphioxus which is related to the "Ascidians . . . invertebrate, hermaphrodite, marine creatures . . . They hardly appear like animals, and consist of a simple, tough, leathery sack, with two small projecting orifices".[113] Yet his final disappearance is vigorous enough to earn him a higher place in our esteem, the assurance of an inborn ability rediscovered from a past not quite so distant; both the surviving members of the Monotremata in Australia burrow, but the spiny anteater is particularly skilled: "it can move with great rapidity. In a few moments, particularly if frightened, it can burrow well out of reach." Such unconscious skill saves the frightened captain, who forces his way into a waiting gharry, when "the immense heaving . . . the whole burrowing effort of that . . . sordid mass troubled one's sense of probability . . . like one of those grotesque and distinct visions that scare and fascinate one in a fever". But his head, morphologically suspicious, "hung out, distended and tossing like a captive balloon", a degenerate transposition, no doubt, "for morphology plainly tells us" Darwin says "that our lungs consist of a modified swim-bladder, which once served as a float".[114]

But Conrad also explores such ideas in *Lord Jim* with high seriousness. The "old mankind" flows aboard the *Patna*, people of a kind Jim later seeks in Patusan, who have come from "huts in the wilderness, from populous campongs, from villages by the sea". And the captain's remark "Look at dese cattle" reminds us of Kurtz's "Exterminate all the brutes".[115] The long evolutionary line of Marlow's journey to the heart of darkness is swung up upon its axis on board the *Patna*, the Darwinian world transformed into the emerging world of Freud. Below the officers upon the bridge (ostensibly, at least, the seat of reason, discipline, and command) the old mankind, in search of the impossible fulfilment of wishes for immortality, "upheld by one desire", in a mystical dream of eternal self-preservation, "flowed forward and aft, overflowed down the yawning hatchways, filled the inner recesses of the ship—like water filling a cistern, like water flowing into crevices and crannies, like water rising silently even within the rim". And whence comes the power and insistence of this image for Conrad?

Silently rising water, the unconscious depths, the speechless desires of the instinctive evolutionary past; we are reminded of that earlier and artistically much cruder image in "The Return", where Conrad's intellectual excitement is much too strong to be absorbed by the events he describes. Alvan Hervey and his wife, we may remember: "skimmed over the surface of life . . . like two skilful skaters cutting figures on thick ice for the admiration of the beholders";[116] but with the shock of eruptive instinctive emotion the ice of social and conscious restraint breaks and he is overwhelmed by darkness: "as if ascending from a well . . . rising like a silent flood . . . it leaped up the walls like an angry wave . . . It flowed from outside—it rose higher, in a destructive silence".[117]

And likewise the past "like water rising silently even within the rim" threatens Jim's consciousness. Yet a more exact, immediate and sinister meaning is contained in such an idea, which we can now only reach and emotionally recreate with a large effort of historical imagination. Quite apart from the often dramatic loss of faith, the complex conflicts of Victorian belief and Victorian science, the intellectual acceptance of Darwinian evolution brought a multitude of emotionally disturbing reorientations in its accompanying details, and one such was man's past emergence from water, his slimy development out of the estuary mud. If the time travelling of *The Origin of Species* and *The Descent of Man* took the Victorian reader back to his early ape-like progenitor, if he suspiciously felt for the vestigial points upon his ears, and surreptitiously found he could still waggle them, as Darwin invited him in one of those horribly telling asides ("The early progenitors of man must have been once covered with hair . . . their ears were probably pointed, and capable of movement")[118] then, just as Marlow is swept on into the far distance as he tells his story of Jim, "as though his spirit had winged its way back into the lapse of time", so the reader of Darwin would be borne remorselessly back to "a still earlier period" when "the progenitors of man must have been aquatic in their habits",[119] and held there with an equally telling comment: "In the lunar or weekly recurrent periods of some of our functions we apparently still retain traces of our primordial birthplace, a shore washed by the tides."[120] The uncomfortably obvious evidence of embryology allowed for no escape: "The clefts on the neck in the embryo of man show where the branchiae once existed."[121] And further, in a time-scale drastically shortened since Lyell and Darwin's original estimate, in which development has been so fast, degeneration may be equally rapid; as Darwin himself writes in *The Descent of Man*: "with mankind some of the worst dispositions . . . may perhaps be reversions to a savage state, from which we are not removed by very many generations."[122] Nordau, less inhibited, makes the point clearly, in a burst of unwarranted enthusiasm with his own embryological erudition:

> The relapse of the degenerate may reach to the most stupendous depth. As, in reverting to the cleavage of the superior maxillary peculiar to insects with sextuple lips, he sinks somatically to the level of fishes, nay to that of the arthropoda, or, even further, to that of rhizopods not yet sexually differentiated; . . . or by excess in the number of fingers (polydactylia) to the multiple-rayed fins of fishes, perhaps even to the bristles of worms; . . . so in the most favourable case, as a higher degenerate, he renews intellectually the type of the primitive man of the most remote Stone Age; or, in the worst case, as an idiot, that of an animal far anterior to man.[123]

And so the captain of the *Patna* makes his degenerate escape with a display of burrowing virtuosity, and we may safely place his aberrant form with those Monotremata which are themselves, as Darwin writes, "eminently interesting, as leading in several important points of structure towards the class of reptiles"[124] with whom man shares a common ancestor in some amphibian-like creature, and this again "from some fish-like animal".[125]

But the captain's companion, the chief engineer (they had been "cronies for a good few years") does not manage to maintain his degenerate position. "Outwardly they were badly matched", Marlow tells us, "one dull-eyed . . . and of soft fleshy curves" (a degenerate resemblance to the ancestor man shares with the platypus) and "the other lean, all hollows, with a head long and bony . . . with an indifferent glazed glance of sunken eyes . . . smoking, without relish, doctored tobacco" in an extraordinary long pipe—"a cherrywood stem four feet long"—and "with the imbecile gravity of a thinker evolving a system of philosophy from the hazy glimpse of a truth". Here is Nordau's degenerate mystic[126] in a befuddled haze, another dreamer, poisoning himself according to Morel's prescription for "degeneracy and hysteria" with "alcoholic drinks, tobacco, opium, hashish";[127] but, perhaps, Conrad also pairs him with the captain in his appropriate biological niche: thin, spiky, bony, with sunken eyes and long snouted pipe—a degenerate resemblance to the ancestor of the spiny anteater himself. Inwardly, the two men perhaps are very well matched indeed. But, in line with the psychological and bio- logical theory of the diverse and aberrant forms of degeneration, their further travels in time take different directions.

The captain disappears into his burrow underground (or under- water); the chief engineer degenerates still further beyond the stage of such decisive mental retreat. Conrad is as scientifically precise in describing his descent, and as accurate in terms of contemporary theories, as he was in observing Jim's blushing; the chief engineer follows Morel's atavistic signpost to Mariani's "grog-shop" and on to three days' hard drinking in a room by himself, until he is driven further "in flight from a legion of centipedes" (a nicely judged horror for an anteater) and on to a "garbage heap" whence he is carried to the hospital. When Marlow visits him he sees a "spectral alarm" in the "blank glitter of his glance", the false light which is not the light of reason, "resembling a nondescript form of a terror crouching silently behind a pane of glass." And this nondescript form eventually emerges.

The consciousness of the chief engineer is threatened by a deeper descent towards the past of the species. He begins to see Nordau's "spectrally transparent shapes"[128] from a lower level, "towards the class of reptiles" as Darwin said, almost deep enough to meet that rising water, towards "some amphibian-like creature".[129] He reminds Marlow, and us, that he is well qualified for such torment: "I am an old stager out here." The sinking *Patna* he now remembers as "full of reptiles"; full of Darwin's "lowest Vertebrates which breathe air . . . Amphibians"[130] in suitably diverse and aberrant form: "Millions of pink toads . . . All pink—as big as mastiffs, with an eye on top of the head and claws all round their ugly mouths." Here is a vision from past evolutionary time which Nordau would consider appropriate enlightenment for such a philosopher, who is "straining to see, thinks he sees, but does not see—in which a man is forced to construct thoughts out of presentations which befool and mock conscious- ness".[131] Conrad emphasises the clear-sighted mystical confidence of this visionary, who informs Marlow with proper pride: "Only my eyes were good enough to see, I am famous for my eyesight . . . I tell you there are no such eyes as mine this side of the Persian Gulf . . . there's no eyes like mine . . ." His perceptive power has indeed become remarkable, as the doctor whom Marlow meets emphasises for us:

> the curious part is there's some sort of method in his raving . . . Most unusual—that thread of logic in such a delirium. Traditionally he ought to see snakes, but he doesn't. Good old tradition's at a discount nowadays. Eh! His—er—visions are batrachian . . . I never remember being so interested in a case of jim-jams before . . . most extraordinary man I ever met—medically, of course.

Traditional snakes, biblical serpents, the old symbols of man's fall have been displaced; Darwinian snakes are advanced modifications of lizards, a specialised branch away from the line of man's ascent, and so a direct fall from Huxley's garden of civilisation within wild nature would eventually produce evolutionary memories of Darwin's amphibia, "the lowest vertebrates which breathe air" and (most suitable for mystical revelation) of these only "frogs and toads possess vocal organs".[132]

But Marlow himself certainly does not find these visions humorous, and he is not protected by a mere scientific interest. "The perspiration dripped . . . off my head, my drill coat clung to my wet back", even though "the afternoon breeze swept impetuously over the row of bedsteads". Jim's "weakness" has become "a thing of mystery and terror" for Marlow; and, just as Jim's "unconscious grimace that tore through the mask of his usual expression" reveals this "something violent, short-lived", so the "spectral horror" in the chief engineer "broke through his glassy gaze", and "Instantly his face of an old soldier, with its noble and calm outlines, became decomposed before my eyes by the corruption of stealthy cunning, of an abominable caution, and of desperate fear." And this constant, apparently over-emotional, feverish intensity of narration in *Lord Jim* itself arises from Marlow's constant and urgent need to struggle against his own unconscious, a wrestling with the "inconceivable", a continual powerful unconscious attraction towards the instinctive desires of the past, which Conrad must express in terms of wordless emotion, overstressed and aberrant feelings, pitted against all the strength of Marlow's conscious and rational aversions.

The chief engineer's eyes do not play him entirely false, but equally his eyesight is not as remarkable as he imagines: his consciousness has itself descended down through the blurred lenses of his own interior telescope and stands perilously near its object. Marlow, too, sees remarkable visions; and Jim's consciousness half recognises Marlow's powers of perception.

Marlow's eyes reflect a consciousness disciplined by reason, an advanced curiosity which strives to remain intellectually detached; unlike the rest of those in court whose glance reflects their mesmerised trance, their surrender to the unconscious, Marlow's "quiet eyes ... glanced straight, interested and clear" and Jim realises that the "glance directed at him was not the fascinated stare of the others. It was an act of intelligent volition." But Marlow's strong will, his "powerful attention" as Nordau put it, is fastened upon those "thought phantoms" in an attempt to "banish them back to their underworld of the unconscious".[133] Marlow's clear gaze illuminates shadowy forms, the instinctive desires from their common racial past, which Jim's own consciousness is now unable to acknowledge at all. Jim "met the eyes of the white man" and this "fellow — ran the thought — looks at me as though he could see somebody or something past my shoulders".

With this "somebody or something" Conrad is as careful as always in his choice of words; for who is to say whether it is a man or an animal, this composite organism preserved in deep memory, this compressed time compacted of unconscious presents gathered in places stretching from the primordial mud to the civilised parsonage? Here is the real character which holds Conrad's interest at the centre of *Lord Jim*.

3

A biological familiar

Jim's conscious mind is bemused by his hopeless attempt to meet the inquiry of advanced and recently evolved reason into his conduct with the only explanation which such a new and still fragile faculty can easily acknowledge: a description of the external events in terms of social time and the mere surface of geographical place. "The facts those men were so eager to know had been visible, tangible, open to the senses, occupying their place in space and time, requiring for their existence a fourteen-hundred-ton steamer and twenty seven minutes by the watch;" but it is not upon this scale in time and space, within the present of civilised social morality where, as the Marlow of *Heart of Darkness* says, man lives "in the holy terror of scandal and gallows and lunatic asylums",[1] that the biological truth is to be discovered. Behind the face of such actions, an "aspect that could be remembered by the eye", there waits the really central character of *Lord Jim*, the "somebody or something" Jim sees Marlow looking upon past his shoulder, a "something else besides, something invisible, a directing spirit of perdition that dwelt within, like a malevolent soul in a detestable body". This "something else" cannot be fully realised in the recent faculty of speech; at the inquiry Jim "doubted whether he would ever again speak out as long as he lived. The sound of his own truthful statements confirmed his deliberate opinion that speech was of no use to him any longer." And only Marlow "seemed to be aware of his hopeless difficulty". But Jim has begun to feel the power of that "directing spirit of perdition" in his own consciousness, and will never be able to meet Marlow's strong "intelligent volition"; Jim "looked at him, then turned away resolutely, as after a final parting".

This "something invisible", the directing spirit of perdition, the biological force of regression, cannot be measured by the comforting time of reason, by the chronometer which Brierly himself later ties so neatly to the rail as he jumps into the waiting depths of another order of time, like those days which mark the passage of the *Patna*, "disappearing one by one into the past, as if falling into an abyss for ever open in the wake of the ship".

And so Jim's conscious mind sinks gently into the past as befits his "fate"—his mild anglican inheritance (and, as Marlow sadly remarks "as if the initial word of each our destiny were not graven in imperishable characters upon the face of a rock"). The directing spirit, the "somebody or something", attunes Jim to the company which had at first disgusted him upon the *Patna*. When he had first seen the captain "in a revealing moment", through a gap in the mist of that dream of unreason as "the incarceration of everything vile and base that lurks in the world we love", he had "started" in momentary shock because, as Marlow explains, in our emotional life, "in our own hearts we trust for our salvation in the men that surround us, in the sights that fill our eyes, in the sounds that fill our ears, and in the air that fills our lungs". The environment, the nature which keeps its own time and space utterly unrelated to the time of a Brierly's chronometer or the position on his chart, permeates the mind through the unguarded sense, produces its own equilibrium. And soon Jim is well adapted; while his Western reason is ensnared in secret dreams, the "quality of these men did not matter; he rubbed shoulders with them, but they could not touch him; he shared the air they breathed, but he was different . . ." He is entwined in Lamarckian attachments to his surroundings without his rational knowledge: "The line dividing his meditation from a surreptitious doze on his feet was thinner than a thread in a spider's web." The trap is web-like, because it radiates invisibly from enclosing nature upon the intruding victim, but in the vertical picture of mind of Conrad's imagining, the web attaches itself to different positions upon the prey, positions of enfastening and of webs which change in time and in space.

The Lamarckian-Darwinian web upon the *Patna* holds Jim against all his reason's attempts to escape into self-knowledge; into the open nature to the West; and he is held at a precise level, sunk to deep strata of mind which match the recently plumbed geological strata of Darwinian nature, trapped in time and its particular space. In the courtroom of his own racial reason and evolved tradition, confronted with the questions of his kind, which pass over his head and seem irrelevant to his new resting place in the past, his own remnant of corresponding reason seeks to rejoin the Darwinian environment of advanced man, but "his mind positively flew round and round the serried circle of facts that had surged up all about him to cut him off from the rest of his kin: it was like a creature that, finding itself imprisoned within an enclosure of high stakes, dashes round and round, distracted in the night, trying to find a weak spot, a crevice, a place to scale." But the Lamarckian, late Darwinian web of interrelations between an organism and its habits and habitat, invisible though the multitude of criss-crossing threads may be, was imagined as the very strongest of all possible traps. And so the half-bemused, ineffectual struggles of Jim's reason are not likely to modify the conditions of his biological captivity; re-experiencing the actions of his unconscious, which first forced his reason to acknowledge the web-like entanglement around him, after re-living, in the present-present of true memory, the terrible compulsion of his jump to Marlow, he pathetically, in transient but genuine revulsion, "raised his hand deliberately to his face, and made picking motions with his fingers as though he had been bothered with cobwebs".

And lest this seems too far-fetched, general enough to lead us to imagine his meaning to be mere impassioned commonplace about the evils of keeping bad company, we must consider Marlow's own confusion; a confusion which marks Conrad's intellectual intention pushing his narrative momentarily out from the duskier shelter of his artistic approval, pointing the aesthetic limits upon Marlow's knowledge (which are also intellectual limits—for if Marlow's reason knew all about Jim's directing spirit, his Darwinian unconscious, then Jim would cease to mesmerise Marlow). After Marlow's assurance and encouragement: "I make myself unreservedly responsible for you. That's what I am doing. And really if you will only reflect a little what that means . . ." Jim's reason finds false escapes in Marlow's keeping, "a weak spot" in that enclosure of high stakes.

Jim's weakened reason responds to Marlow's encouragement according to the epigram of Novalis with which Conrad begins *Lord Jim*: "It is certain any conviction gains infinitely the moment another soul will believe in it." And so, with his advanced reason left in trust with Marlow, indulging in dreams of an impossible future ("I always thought that if a fellow could begin with a clean slate . . ."), Jim's unconscious once more overwhelms him. And Marlow is deeply

A biological familiar

confused by Jim's sudden surrender to the speechless expression of unconscious emotion as:

All at once [Jim] sprang into jerky agitation, like one of those flat wooden figures that are worked by a string . . . I had pulled the string accidentally, as it were; I did not fully understand the working of the toy . . . He darted—positively darted—here and there . . . I had no idea it was in him to be so airily brisk. I thought of a dry leaf imprisoned in an eddy of wind, while a mysterious apprehension, a load of indefinite doubt, weighed me down in my chair.

Jim is once again caught by the powerful forces which "tore him out of his immobility" upon the bridge of the *Patna*. These unconscious movements are "so airily brisk" because "the old mankind" were imagined as full of mindless energy, a character which may still be observed in the "arrested development" of "microcephalous idiots" who, as Darwin explains in *The Descent of Man* "somewhat resemble the lower types of mankind . . . They are strong and remarkably active, continually gamboling and jumping about . . ."[2] The civilised Marlow remains in his chair, unable to trace the cause of his apprehension or the nature of his doubt; while Jim's unconscious reveals its prehistoric pleasure, bound to the East rather than to the West, towards the prehistoric rather than the advanced homeland. And it is perhaps worth remarking that contemporary scientific ideas of the probable place of man's origins had themselves changed in the years since the publication of *The Descent of Man*: Africa might well have provided the environment which nursed the early evolution of the apes and the pre-human ancestors but "the missing link" itself seemed to have been found in the East.

Ernst Haeckel, the best known, most aggressive, and least scrupulous of Darwin's popularisers and champions upon the continent, lacking Darwin and Huxley's scientific inhibitions, had already named the missing pre-Ice Age creature he needed to complete his evolutionary tree of man's descent, *Pithecanthropus alalus*, the "speechless ape-man". And when Eugène Dubois, a young Dutchman fired by Haeckel's convictions who had obtained a post as a military surgeon in the Dutch East Indies expressly to look for remains of this speechless ape-man, in 1894, did indeed announce his discoveries of an ape-like skull-cap and a much fossilised human thigh-bone in his excavations on the bank of the Solo River in Java, Haeckel sent his congratulations by telegraph: "From the inventor of *Pithecanthropus* to his happy discoverer!" Dubois displayed his finds in Berlin in 1895, in Leiden, Paris and London; and Java man became firmly established, within the short time-scale of a Lamarckian, late-Darwinian mechanism of evolution by the inheritance of acquired characteristics, as a simple and direct link between modern man and the apes.

So perhaps Jim's unconscious, momentarily released, responds violently to the Lamarckian pull of an older nature to the Eastwards, towards a probable home of "the old mankind", towards Patusan, towards the Java of Haeckel's speechless ape-man, the Borneo of "the wild man of the woods", the orang-utan (whose candidature as an ancestor of man had survived Monboddo).[3] Jim becomes "another man altogether" as Marlow watches his rationally uncontrolled movements, his "jerky agitation" as he darts "here and there" in the room; a more primitive, speechless creature has perhaps briefly re-emerged, as it had surfaced before upon the training ship in the face of an advanced social challenge, and upon the *Patna* when "there was a hot dance of thoughts in his head, a dance of lame, blind, mute thoughts—a whirl of awful cripples." Such thoughts are perhaps not just a Bosch- or Brueghel-like image upon Conrad's design, but lame because they cannot walk erect, blind because darkly instinctive without the light of reason, and mute because they are speechless, pre-human. They arise from a past preserved deep in the mind, whence comes, as Nordau writes:

> the really impelling force in thought and deed . . . the emotions, those disturbances elaborated in the depths of the internal organs, and the sources of which elude consciousness, but which suddenly burst into it like a horde of savages . . . submitting to no police regulations of a civilised mind, and imperiously demanding lodgment. All that wide region of organic needs and hereditary impulses . . .[4]

And, just as the Marlow of *Heart of Darkness* is uneasily aware of the Lamarckian pull of "the night of first ages" where just such a hot dance is being enacted in the jungle, so the Marlow of *Lord Jim* is uneasily aware of the Lamarckian pull of the primitive man emerging from within Jim. Marlow "can't explain" the "mixed nature" of his feelings because his response is itself arising from the unconscious level which Jim has already reached, and to which Jim unconsciously appeals. As Marlow exclaims: "It seemed to me I was being made to comprehend the Inconceivable—and I know of nothing to compare with the discomfort of such a sensation. I was made to look at the convention which lurks in all truth and on the essential sincerity of falsehood."

The speechless past, the invisible "someone or something" momentarily rising to take possession of Jim's consciousness, brings the Marlow of *Lord Jim* into dangerous Lamarckian exposure to an encapsulated, mind-embodied tract of primitive nature. This is the nature to which the "prehistoric man" once adapted himself; a small part of "prehistoric earth", which so powerfully affected the Marlow of *Heart of Darkness* as he made his journey back into a lost nature and so inevitably back into lost regions of the mind; and when he, too, was "cut off from comprehension" of his surroundings, "wondering and secretly appalled" before the equally mysterious and frenzied movements of the men he uneasily glimpses amongst the "old trees", men adapted to "this strange world of plants" and emerging before him with "a burst of yells, a whirl of black limbs, a mass of hands clapping . . . a black and incomprehensible frenzy".

The Marlow in *Heart of Darkness* knows that he is confronted with an emotional truth about himself and about civilised man and society, "truth stripped of its cloak of time", a truth about the nature of unrestrained instincts. To resist the onslaught of such instincts "He must meet that truth with his own true stuff—with his own inborn strength."[5] The Marlow of *Lord Jim* is confronted with just such a truth—"the convention which lurks in all truth . . . the essential sincerity of falsehood"—the truth from the prehistoric past, the nature of those instinctive desires which social conventions in civilised Europe pretend do not exist, disregarding "the essential sincerity" of a biological, pre-social need behind all anti-social conduct and its explanatory falsehoods. But Marlow has inherited and nurtured "his own true stuff", a biological "inborn courage" socially developed in his race, whereas Jim's ancestors have left him only principles—and as the Marlow in *Heart of Darkness* remarks, "Principles won't do. Acquisitions, clothes, pretty rags—rags that would fly off at the first good shake."[6] Such principles are of no use amongst the minds and nature of the lost, instinctive heart of darkness when, Marlow remembers, the "smell of mud, of primaeval mud, by Jove! was in my nostrils, the high stillness of primaeval forest was before my eyes".[7] And they are equally useless in that nature of Patusan which the Marlow of *Lord Jim* is later so glad to leave on his journey downriver to the sea, when "the way at times seemed to lead through the very heart of untouched wilderness" and "the smell of mud, of marsh, the primaeval smell of fecund earth, seemed to sting our faces".

Both Marlows are more than simply rationally relieved to escape the oppressive enclosures of the old nature and the old mankind. After all, the greatest single advance in the recent evolutionary progress of man was thought to be his escape from just such a nature; his descent from the trees and the easy life of the forest into the open arena of the plains where struggle for survival forced upon him his upright posture and his enlarged brain, social cohesion in hunting groups, the development of speech. Even more open and more hostile are the seas, a nature where only the fittest among men are at home. And so it is with a sense of biological reunion, a deep feeling of a returning balance between inner and outer worlds, a snapping back into place of each Lamarckian, late Darwinian link between his racial self and his proper environment that Marlow leaves behind the evolutionary past of Patusan: "I revelled in the vastness of the opened horizon, in the different atmosphere that seemed to vibrate with a toil of life, with the energy of an impeccable world. This sky and this sea were open to me . . . there was a sign, a call in them—something to which I responded with every fibre of my being." For Conrad, the sea is the particular possession of the British, the real nature which forced the advanced social development and individual "inborn courage" of a race which lives upon an island moored like a ship in the sea, as the narrator of *The Nigger of the Narcissus* greets it upon his homecoming;[8] an island in which the narrator of *Youth* quite unjustifiably believes that the "men and sea interpenetrate, so to speak—the sea entering into the life of most men, and the men knowing something or everything about the sea".[9]

Yet all is no longer so simple, for a man who comes "from the right place" and looks "so sound" may still not be fit to withstand the sea, to captain a ship, because "by Jove! it wouldn't have been safe" as Marlow reflects, and no wonder that "There are depths of horror in that thought." The depths of that horror fathom down below the rational fear of a creeping social degeneration amongst the civilised races, of generalised despair as to the possibility of sustained human progress because luxury brings decay. Jim, like Kurtz, arouses a very particular horror by stirring the past alive in those who come under his Lamarckian powers of enchantment: "He appealed to all sides at once—to the side turned perpetually to the light of day, and to that side of us which, like the other hemisphere of the moon, exists stealthily in perpetual darkness, with only a fearful ashy light falling at times on the edge." And, half-aware that he is himself approaching the heart of darkness, Marlow juxtaposes Jim's superficial heroic dreams against the rituals of a jungle past: "It's extraordinary how he could cast upon you the spirit of his illusion. I listened as if to a tale of black magic at work upon a corpse."

These thoughts of magic and darkness oppress Marlow while Jim is recounting those moments upon the *Patna* when time past was indeed regained; when Jim responded to a degenerate echo of the prehistoric cry Marlow heard upon the "prehistoric earth"[10] of Africa. Jim jumps in answer to such a call: the "three voices together raised a yell. They came to me separately: one bleated, another screamed, one howled. Ough!" The animal cries of the officers of the *Patna* provoke a violent obedience in Jim's unconscious, and, once such a cry has been obeyed, once one has stepped backwards in time and gone ashore for "a howl and a dance"[11] then, measured against the hard won progress of the civilised mankind, it is indeed, as Jim tells Marlow, as if he "had jumped into a well—into an everlasting deep hole". Marlow, too, hears such a cry in *Lord Jim*, when his "familiar devil" exposes him to the reptilian visions of the *Patna*'s chief engineer whose "wolfish howl", the authentic expression of emotions lost in the half-animal past, "searched the very recesses of my soul" and, as he escapes, the "howl pursued me like a vengeance". But Jim's impulse was not to run from such a cry; having joined his fellow officers in the boat, he tells Marlow: "There are no words for the sort of things I wanted to say. If I had opened my lips just then I would have simply howled like an animal."

Jim is bereft of any other means of expression of his emotions because those emotions are themselves too primitive and unfamiliar to be acknowledged by the recent labels of articulate speech; he has fallen down the "everlasting deep hole" to levels of social behaviour close to that of his degenerate companions whom he later describes to Marlow as "yapping before me like a couple of mean mongrels at a treed thief. Yap! yap! . . . Bow-ow-ow-ow-ow!" This imagery of mongrels, curs, dogs, is plentiful and precisely placed in *Lord Jim*. Marlow's "familiar devil", he tells us, "lets me in for that kind of thing . . . the inquiry thing, the yellow-dog thing", and "to run up against men with soft spots, with hard spots, with hidden plague spots, by Jove!" (And how very different are these particular plague spots, we might remember, from the outwardly similar marks of "egoism" in Conrad's immediate predecessor in such impassioned moral studies: George Eliot's conception of those ordered "spots of commonness"[12] with which she stamps her patronising and self-congratulatory revenge upon a Lydgate.)

Jim's "plague spots", virulently infectious, eventually necessitate the formal declaration of his own kind that after diagnosis under their Western eyes he is to be considered unclean and cast out; Jim's plague is certified at the "inquiry thing", and the course of the disease is predicted in "the yellow-dog thing". Jim, leaving the court, deprived of his seaman's certificate, mistakenly imagines Marlow and his friend to have jeered at his back "Look at that wretched cur". He turns and confronts Marlow, who is at first at a loss to know why he is so earnestly threatened, "very much like a meeting in a wood", but eventually realises the nature of Jim's misunderstanding, which he considers with extraordinary solemnity: "It was, indeed, a hideous mistake; he had given himself away utterly. I can't give you an idea how shocked I was . . . There had never been a man so mercilessly shown up by his own natural impulse." And, when "his eyes followed downwards the direction of my pointing finger" Jim himself reacts with equally over-emphasised emotion to the discovery of the real yellow dog, which "suddenly snapped at a fly like a piece of mechanism". Jim contemplates "the wretched animal", and, fresh as he is from the hopeless attempt to define and so to find a cure for his plague by the once potent help of the reason evolved by his race (itself exercised by the court to make him an outcast) unwittingly allows Marlow to watch that reason, the advanced faculty he still retains, as it is forced to acknowledge that kinship with the brute which his unconscious has already proclaimed by assuming the ownership of an insult which fits the primitive animal nature of his actions: "He appeared at first uncomprehending, then confounded, and at last amazed and scared as though a dog had been a monster and he had never seen a dog before."

Here Marlow too is uncomprehending, because the particular cur that scares Jim's reason is indeed monstrous. And Marlow, like his predecessor, comes a little too close to that distant abyss into which time and space themselves appear to be pulled, the abyss of the evolutionary past from which the tracks of the many races of man lead in different directions and for varying distances across the Conradian plain, towards that other distant abyss of the evolutionary future and the common annihilation predicted by Kelvin's physics.

In *Heart of Darkness* biological, tropical nature, and the old mankind, bear the full weight of Conrad's intense efforts to capture and contain time and space on such a vast scale. In *Lord Jim* time and space are enclosed in Jim's own heart of darkness, with much less artistic striving and more confidence of method upon Conrad's part, but with an added obscurity, because the amplitude of *Lord Jim* is not created by a more leisurely exposition but by an intense and much more various exploration of as much of that undiscovered country of the past as is compatible with the return of the traveller and with the especially limited power of words in such changed landscapes.

The Marlow of *Lord Jim*, like the Marlow of *Heart of Darkness*, is chastened and often psychically exhausted by his journey in evolutionary time, that real measure of the powerful instincts behind Jim's words (which, like those of Kurtz, were "common everyday words . . . But what of that? They had behind them . . . the terrific suggestiveness of words heard in dreams, of phrases spoken in nightmares").[13] After Jim's everyday words to Marlow about his desertion from the *Patna*, words of broken froth upon the surface of those depths of darkness whose great undercurrents dictate Jim's bodily movements: "A pause ensued" Marlow remembers, "and suddenly I felt myself overcome by a profound and hopeless fatigue, as though his voice had startled me out of a dream of wandering through empty spaces whose immensity had harassed my soul and exhausted my body."

And, in those immense empty spaces upon the Conradian plain, Jim "had advanced his argument as though life had been a network of paths separated by chasms", Marlow reflects, with the same rueful wisdom with which he contemplates the dreamer's equally self-flattering idea that "a fellow could begin with a clean slate". Jim has inherited such easeful images from his father—but the new knowledge decrees otherwise; there is more than Jim's "thickness of a sheet of paper" or the "breadth of a hair" between path and chasm, between the "right and wrong of this affair". The great thickness of the thought and habitual actions of many generations and every moment of his own childhood and youth determine the path itself and its direction; and the comfort of clean slates has no place in an unclean world of complex late-Darwinian interrelations of man and nature. As Conrad wrote to Marguerite Poradowska in 1891: "Each act of life is final and inevitably produces its consequences in spite of all the weeping and gnashing of teeth and the sorrow of weak souls who suffer as fright grips them when confronted with the results of their own actions."[14] Like George Eliot's characters caught in those often earnestly machine-spun webs, Jim is the deed's creature; but for Conrad the real interest lies in the creature which itself springs the deed; his intellectual idea of egoism has genuinely sinister depths not to be measured or contained or corrected in the rationally horizontal, well-lit social webs of a *Middlemarch* or an *Adam Bede*, in the extended family of her ordered clarity, her intellectual domesticity, where virtue is still "one all over the world".

To Jim's desperate reason it all seems "a beastly unfair thing"; as Marlow ironically says, "nothing less than the unconceivable itself could get over his perfect state of preparation. He had been taken unawares." Or as Jim tells Marlow after their talk: "I am afraid I don't feel as grateful as I would if the whole thing hadn't been so brutally sprung on me." The beastly something is of course unfamiliar with the refinements of civilised justice and the niceties of the English gentleman's code of honour ("It was not like a fight, for instance" says Jim). It has a life of its own lost in the night of first ages and the darkness of unconscious emotion, a "somebody or something", powerful in a time and space of immense evolutionary processes measureless to man, but also in the small unguarded present of personal consciousness and the needlepoint spaces of personal events and decisions. The "unconceivable itself", impossible to conceptualise within the limits of social language, part of the unconscious, must always take consciousness "unawares" when "allowed" to overwhelm the developed defences of the race evolved in each member mind. So Jim's everyday words with their social clichés and struggling ordinariness of the "good, stupid kind" yet ride, like consciousness, upon another order of time, space and nature, which gives a deeper meaning to so-called chance, a "something else besides" to the face of events, as Marlow says. Jim's reason decides that the "whole thing" has been "brutally sprung" upon him—and so it has, but not as a random accident, indifferent chance in the interconnecting causes of the inanimate world, but literally, beneath the common words, in the brutal spring, the spring of the brute, instinctively leaping to preserve itself. Caged in by no stockade of developed social restraint, the jump to safety is easily and powerfully accomplished; and it is the antagonistic remnants of the irksome social discipline and altruistic behaviour of reasonable heroism which finds itself "imprisoned within an enclosure of high stakes".

Conrad emphasises the victory of Jim's unconscious as strongly as he can; as Darwin writes in *The Descent of Man*, the "instinct of self-preservation is not felt except in the presence of danger; and many a coward has thought himself brave until he has met his enemy face to face."[15] Jim is not afraid of a gentleman's disagreement with Marlow outside the courthouse, an honourable man to man and socially ritualised fight; but that is not "inborn courage" in Conrad's world, there is no terror in such a duel. Yet, once Jim has seen the "yellow-dog" itself, and realises he has unintentionally pitted himself against his own inner beast, he appeared terrified. Jim brags to Marlow about the prowess of his outwardly strong muscles should he have been forced to pit them against other animal-like opponents; opponents who are assuredly not bound by the rules of gentlemanly conduct, but who are, like the frightening yellow dog, two "mean mongrels . . . trying to outbark each other . . . Yap! yap! . . . as if trying to drive one overboard with the noise". The captain advances upon him suddenly in the small boat with "wheezy grunting", and the "beast was coming at me . . . big, big—as you see a man in a mist, in a dream". The degenerate captain sensibly runs out of breath and lumbers back to his oar. "I would have tumbled him over like a bale of shakings" Jim assures Marlow. But not so. Conrad once again places the unspeakable, inconceivable, the "inscrutable intention" (because in the unconscious untamed jungle of pre-historic mind) with its "implacable force", unrestrained, beneath the confident commonplace. The suggestion of "the beast . . . big, big . . . in a dream" in Jim's "present-present"[16] of that genuine unconscious memory, rises to overwhelm Jim's outward protestations of heroic intent as implacably as upon the *Patna* itself. And the characteristic-ally violent bodily movements expressing its instinctive emotion are signs of an inner possession, a time regained; signs as unmistakable as that wild, broken mechanism of attempted escape which accom-panies the chief engineer's visions of his mastiff-sized toads when "Quick jerks as of galvanic shocks disclosed under the flat coverlet the outlines of meagre and agitated legs."

On this occasion Jim, with the very present image of the beast, the captain of the *Patna*, filling his consciousness while he nominally talks to Marlow, "with a convulsive jerk of his elbow", knocks over the cognac bottle. Marlow "started forward, scraping my chair"; and Jim, with a prehistoric and instinctive, instantaneous agility, jumps. He jumps from the unconsciously suspected danger, himself springing like a brute just as he imagines his disastrous *Patna* misfortune was "brutally sprung" upon him; and, like the brute which he has momentarily become, "He bounced off the table as if a mine had been exploded behind his back, and half turned before he alighted, crouching on his feet to show me a startled pair of eyes and a face white about the nostril." Jim crouches like that other unrestrained degenerate brute, a man-beast or beast-man, a "somebody or something", which Marlow sees behind the blank glitter of those eyes of the demented chief engineer, "a nondescript form of a terror crouching silently behind a pane of glass".

When placed beside Marlow and, more obviously, beside a Captain Elliot whose weaknesses extend solely to the dismal matrimonial prospects of those daughters who appear to have inherited his acquired facial characteristics, and do not encompass anything as pathologically abnormal as an intellectual doubt; beside two such men of his kind, Jim's "scared" acknowledgment of a kinship with the "native tyke", that "yellow-dog", seems a fitting enough placing of the levels to which he has unconsciously regressed.

In an advanced society, Jim's increasingly pre-civilised, animal-like alertness of the senses, his agility and strength, seem disturbingly primitive. But when he eventually reaches a tribal society of the old mankind in the old nature then these very characteristics are an obvious and advantageous adaptation; particularly as he still bears traces of his own lost ancestors, whose evolutionary development, in late-Darwinian logic, must have fitted them more vigorously for mastery and escape from their successive environments at every stage, towards that present dominance amongst the races of mankind. So Jim's primitive characteristics fit him for survival and success in Patusan; and Conrad is again biologically precise in the images he uses to suggest the nature of Jim's success. "There was his readiness", as Marlow says. "Amazing. And all this had come to him in a manner like keen scent to a well-bred hound."

Jim, no longer regarded as a native tyke by his peers, shows the signs of his selective breeding; but in wider terms the yellow dog outside the courthouse and the well-bred hound of Patusan are also interesting; without a knowledge of particulate genetics it was easy to imagine the dog as an animal in the direct line of man's evolutionary descent, as a near and familiar reminder of man's immediate animal instincts.

Darwin frequently refers to the dog to point his argument in *The Descent of Man*: the first illustration is a comparison of the embryo of a man and of a dog to show how alike they appear, copied from Bischoff;[17] and while man himself is not altogether dog-like in Darwin's estimation, neither are dogs. Dogs have a sense of smell "highly developed", but man "inherits the power" too, albeit "in an enfeebled and so far rudimentary condition, from some early progenitor";[18] and Cornelius in *Lord Jim*, with his degenerate "dark and secret slinking" after various carrion, has recovered his sense of smell metaphorically well enough for the native Tamb'Itam to characterise his behaviour with "singularly felicitous" allusions, Marlow tells us, "to dogs and the smell of roast meat". Dogs are endowed with ferocious teeth, but he "who rejects with scorn the belief that the shape of his own canines, and their occasional great development in other men, are due to our early forefathers having been provided with these formidable weapons, will probably reveal, by sneering, the line of his descent", writes Darwin. He "will unconsciously retract his 'snarling muscles' (thus named by Sir C. Bell), so as to expose them ready for action, like a dog prepared to fight".[19] And this is exactly how Conrad describes Jim's "grimace" as he re-lives that moment of finding himself in the *Patna*'s boat; Jim reveals the line of his own descent, his kinship with the animal-men, "the mean mongrels" in the same boat as himself, by retracting his snarling muscles like a dog prepared to fight: "the muscles round his lips contracted into an unconscious grimace . . . something violent, short-lived, and illuminating."

Jim in Patusan appears to Marlow to have discovered hidden abilities within himself, senses which have come to him as naturally as that "keen scent to a well-bred hound", but such breeding is only visible against such a natural background. Jim proves his "grasp of the unfamiliar situation, his intellectual alertness in that field of thought" because that situation is familiar to the brain mechanisms from his own lost racial time. His success, after all, is a result of his grasp of tribal warfare, Darwin's "never-ceasing wars of savages"[20] or, as Marlow puts it, his "word decided everything", which is simply the "moral effect of his victory in war". Jim's animal alertness, his hound-like instincts, are indeed "well-bred", restrained, beside the native dog-like instincts of his opponents amongst the old mankind. "Several times" Marlow tells us, Tunku Allang's "council was broken up, and the advisers made a break helter-skelter for the door and out on to the veranda. One — it is said — even jumped down to the ground — fifteen feet, I should judge — and broke his leg."

Yet we can judge just how small a vestige of well-bred or inborn courage separates Jim from the natives of Tunku Allang's court by in turn measuring him with another "well-bred" control essential to the development of truly advanced society in Conrad's world. The Marlow of *Heart of Darkness*, we might remember, could not "bear a lie . . . It makes me sick, like biting something rotten would do. Temperament, I suppose."[21] But no such highly evolved, innate morality now afflicts Jim; on the contrary: "some conviction of innate blamelessness had checked the truth writhing within him at every turn", and it is not until he has fallen deep into that "primaeval mud" itself that he feels the same inborn revulsion: "I remember how sick I felt wriggling in that slime. I mean really sick—as if I had bitten something rotten."

Jim's dreams of a gentlemanly heroism, the conflicts between his own biological inheritance and the larger cultural inheritance of his racial tradition, his relations with Marlow, and the unseen effects he has upon those he meets as he journeys, all obscure his linear movement and unconscious search beneath a multitudinous if superficial complexity; and so it is essential to bear in mind that biological goal he eventually finds in Patusan, if we are to clearly follow the hidden, animal "desires" of his unconscious, driving him onwards upon his interior travelling in time and his outward quest in time and space.

For the moment, our meagre glimpse of Patusan will have to suffice to give us the compass bearing in Conrad's idea of the uncharted regions of such a soul. To summarise: Jim's unconscious expresses its unsatisfied need to interlock with an environment upon the correspondingly primitive Lamarckian layer of development by driving him to demonic activity until, in Patusan, he at last arrives in a nature which matches his own depth of reversion with its primitive peoples and jungles; his "wild vitality"[22] on predictable occasions, his Darwinian characteristic of continual "gamboling and jumping about" in often disastrously inappropriate moments in civilised society, are still valued and preserved in the nature of Patusan.

But within organised and Western influenced communities and their surrounding nature such pre-civilised agility and strength is at best a disturbing curiosity. The young mankind has progressed beyond the old virtues and now values other characteristics very much more highly than the primitive, reckless bodily activity of one of its water-clerks; even though Jim's effortless adaptation to the wildest nature makes him the nonpareil of his profession. His virtuosity is itself disturbing to those of his own kind, whose ancestors have long since discarded such hunting and nomadic abilities; and they are as bemused as is Marlow by Jim's "airily brisk" rapid movements, his grotesque and quick facial expressions, when he becomes "another man altogether", already resembling those "lower types of mankind": sure signs, we remember, of "arrested development" in civilised idiots, who are social vestiges of Western man's savage progenitors, towards whom Jim is unconsciously regressing.[23] That "jumping about" of Darwin's seems a little unkind, if wholly accurate, when applied to Jim's agonies; with his inheritance of "some conviction of innate blamelessness" which Marlow thinks "had checked the truth writhing within him at every turn", Jim's misty, mystical dreams, his clear patches of shocked and frightened reason, make his remarkable activity difficult to see as the clear stages of his implacable, inscrutable journey into the past. But the startled sea captains, more or less responsible men from their European societies, endorse Darwin's opinion in their comments upon Jim, comments which also have that "suggestiveness . . . of phrases spoken in nightmares".[24] As Egström boasts of his departed water-clerk to Marlow:

> the first thing they would say would be, "That's a reckless sort of lunatic you've got . . . Egström. I was feeling my way in at daylight under short canvas when there comes flying out of the mist . . . a boat half under water . . . a yelling fiend at the tiller . . . shoots ahead whooping and yelling . . . more like a demon than a man. Never saw a boat handled like that in all my life . . . Such a quiet, soft-spoken chap, too—blushed like a girl when he came on board."

Jim is indeed degenerating internally and unconsciously, his personal past and racial tradition beginning to subside into the abyss of the lost past within him down towards the primitive mankind, or towards Darwin's savagely active lunatics. The captains who voice their amazement to Egström would have to set sail in time past as well as in space to see a boat handled like that again; Marlow in *Heart of Darkness*, for instance, following the coastline "of a colossal jungle", the monotony relieved only by an occasional boat coming out from the surf-line "paddled by black fellows" who "shouted, sang; their bodies streamed with perspiration; they had faces like grotesque masks . . . but they had bone, muscle, a wild vitality, an intense energy of movement, that was as natural and true as the surf along their coast. They wanted no excuse for being there."[25] These primitive men are perfectly adapted in a late-Darwinian interrelation of their needs and habits with surrounding nature; but Jim's equally intense energy of movement as a water-clerk is far from wanting "no excuse for being there"; his efforts are so full of that primitive "wild vitality" that he himself appears as a "familiar devil", or else crudely displaced from his proper, intelligently reasonable relation with an advanced society's semi-tamed nature: "Couldn't have been drunk—was he?" asks a captain. It is in any case time for Jim to move on in search of more primitive surroundings to satisfy the needs of his unconscious, long before Captain O'Brien of the *Sarah W. Granger* pronounces his memorable biological judgment upon the officers of the *Patna*: "Skunks!"

4

The degenerate chorus

To comment upon and extend the possible ramifying evolutionary branches and roots of Jim's pilgrimage, Conrad surrounds Jim's path of pilgrim's regress with a chorus of Jim's diverse and degenerate kind. The chorus of late-Darwinian souls is itself moving in time and in nature, and open to Jim's own late-Darwinian unseen influences. The first victim of such biological enchantment is Big Montague Brierly.

Lacking Marlow's inborn courage, exposed to the continual presence of the prehistoric nature within Jim, Brierly is himself trapped in the web, encircled by the rising past of his own reawakened unconscious. And Conrad is careful to emphasise the orthodox late-Darwinian causes of Brierly's otherwise inexplicable behaviour. Brierly shares many inherited and acquired characteristics with Jim and comes from the same social environment and place in nature. "Fact is," Brierly says to Marlow of Jim, "I rather think some of my people know his. The old man's a parson, and I remember now I met him once when staying with my cousin in Essex last year." Like Jim, Brierly's biological inheritance has bequeathed him nothing more reliable than the mystical dream. In place of the inborn courage once possessed by all his race, he has only a conscious desire for the outward show, honour, the name. Brierly, Marlow tells us, "was acutely aware of his merits and of his rewards"; his reason is ensnared in impossible subjective projections of his own desires ("you don't think enough of what you are supposed to be" he reprimands Marlow); in place of real instinctive social behaviour there is only the empty symbol which is all that Brierly feels Jim has betrayed: "We aren't an organised body of men, and the only thing that holds us together is just the name for that kind of decency."

Brierly, too, attracts Marlow's uneasy friendship; despite Brierly's

Jim- and Kurtz-like "exalted egoism", the dream which lifts his consciousness free of the earth, Marlow is drawn to him, once again: "for the sake of something indefinite and attractive in the man. I have never defined to myself this attraction . . ." But Brierly has another familiar. On his way (like Jim's but very much foreshortened) to another order of time: "the dog, that was always at his heels whenever he moved, night or day, followed, sliding nose first after him." At the last moment, Brierly sends the dog back: "He was afraid the poor brute would jump after him," as Jones the mate observes; but Brierly himself jumps, in obedience to the precise and superficial dictates of his threatened reason, in fear of the brute within. He jumps to escape from those "wakened ideas", as Marlow puts it in one of those explanations with which he warily circles the "unconceivable" truth and so, eventually, outlines for us a composite shadow of the rough beast itself.

Brierly's ideas, Marlow reasons, are of a kind which "start into life some thought with which a man unused to such companionship finds it impossible to live". Brierly prepares for his jump with meticulous care; Jim jumps in response to unconscious impulse. Brierly surrenders to the implacable force of the inscrutable nature and instincts awakened within him, with a knowledge of his defeat; Jim's more priestly "innate conviction of blamelessness" enables him to make his various brutish jumps without such knowledge. And in the last act of both Brierly and Jim, the difference and similarity is again precise. As Ribot blandly writes in *The Psychology of the Emotions*: "The act of suicide results from two very different mental states, that of reflection and that of impulsion."[1] Jim's "exalted egoism" is a part of the empty honour, the name, nothing to do with the inbred courage that is not even aware of itself. In Conrad's intense Western eyes, Brierly's "contemptuous pity" for the "twelve hundred millions of other more or less human beings" upon the earth is all of a biological piece with his suicide, and Jim's dream, the disdainful sense of superiority within his heroic achievements, is the same dream which entices him to his death. For as Ribot observes: "if self-love, in its positive form, reaches its culminating point in megalomania, it seems to me quite legitimate to maintain that self-feeling, under its negative form, attains its supreme negation in suicide."[2]

Jim is overwhelmed by the "yellow-dog" instincts, primitive impulses which in advanced society are dangerous and identified, without understanding, by their outward signs in conduct: yellow cowardice, the actions of a "wretched cur". The same past rises in Brierly, awakened by Jim's direct influence. Jim's reason circles the primitive enclosure of "high stakes" like "a creature distracted in the night"; Brierly, with more civilised desperation, "dropped into his seat looking done up, as though he had spent the night in sprinting on a cinder-track". And Conrad distinguishes, with equal care, between the relative positions of the two men in time and nature by his precise placing of animal imagery around them. Jim's sign of the inner familiar, the "yellow-dog", is a "native tyke"; whilst Brierly's constant companion is a civilised and domesticated, well-bred "black retriever", a dog which has itself advanced a great distance in late-Darwinian time and which remains instinctively faithful, the object of Brierly's degenerate betrayal. For Brierly's dog is unlike the primitive animal of man's ancestry, resembling instead that paragon of virtues resulting from generations of European domestication, the dogs which Darwin tends to compare favourably with his "savages".[3] Brierly knows he possesses "the love of worship" of his black retriever "the most wonderful of its kind—for never was such a man loved thus by such a dog" or, as Darwin puts it, the "love of a dog for his master is notorious; as an older writer quaintly says 'A dog is the only thing on this earth that luvs you more than he luvs himself.' "[4]

Brierly's ideal conception of his own profession is one of those illusions which allows the Englishman to gain a firm hold on the substance, as Conrad remarks through his own dark intellectual doppelgänger who emerges in *Nostromo*, Decoud, about an Englishman for whom Brierly might be a brief study, Charles Gould. But Brierly has artistic ancestors as well as descendants in Conrad's work. Kurtz, too, formed an ideal conception of "what he was supposed to be" and, in kicking himself free of the earth in the mystical degeneration of his dream of godhead fell into "the everlasting black hole" in "the horror!" of his awakening; Brierly's ideal conception of himself is merely another expression of biological relapse, a decay into the past which self-enchanted reason allows to pass unobserved, a monstrous dream preoccupying his weakened capacity to face the inward terrors, whilst, as in the presence of Kurtz, "had you been Emperor of East and West, you could not have ignored your inferiority in his presence". And Marlow's sympathetic attempt to catch the inner conscious nature of such a dream also helps us to see the late-Darwinian webs of evolutionary time and biological nature spidering out to draw together the Russian

85

Harlequin with the arch-priestly father, Kurtz the mongrel philan-thropist, and Brierly the god-like captain, whose origins are almost as rotten with degenerate complacency as are the priestly mystical beginnings of Jim's mental world. The Marlow of *Lord Jim* might here be reflecting upon the Russian Harlequin: "By Jove! he was amazing. There he sat telling me that just as I saw him before my eyes he wouldn't be afraid to face anything . . . I tell you it was fabulously innocent and it was enormous, enormous!" The Russian Harlequin was also "enthusiastic, fabulous" and ruled by the "unpractical spirit of adventure"[5] (and certainly "remarkably active, continually gamboling about and making grimaces"):[6] and such a description would also fit the young Kurtz and the young Brierly. As Marlow continues, speaking of Jim: "Can you fancy it? A succession of adventures, so much glory, such a victorious progress! and the deep sense of his sagacity crowning every day of his inner life. He forgot himself; his eyes shone; and with every word my heart, searched by the light of his absurdity, was growing heavier in my breast."

Such heaviness and darkness comes upon the Marlow of *Heart of Darkness* and the Marlow of *Lord Jim* at exactly the same inappropriate moments within the same old nature as they listen to the optimistic assertions of the Harlequin and of Jim. And this darkness makes very clear one crime which mystical dreamers, remarkable men in the mere power of their illusion, all commit in Conrad's world: betraying the real possibility of a happiness to be found in immediate nature for the distant illusory promise of a glory which nature cannot provide, because it exists in Conrad's "surface glitter" upon the real dark depths, in the deceptive sign of the word only.

The Marlow of *Heart of Darkness* is at first relieved and amused to hear that Kurtz had spoken to the Russian Harlequin of love, but: "'It isn't what you think,' he cried, almost passionately. 'It was in general. He made me see things—things.'"[7] And for Marlow, we remember, as he looks upon the prehistoric nature enclosing him, it seems as if the heart of darkness has reached the blackest pitch of its desolation, emotional pigments compounded of a past and a future equally hopeless: "I assure you that never, never before, did this land, this river, this jungle, . . . appear to me so hopeless and so dark, so impenetrable to human thought, so pitiless to human weakness."[8] Conrad adds the incongruous meeting with the "intended" to the end of *Heart of Darkness* partly to underline Kurtz's betrayal of a "love of worship" genuine enough, if more limited, than the impossible love of worship of his primitive subjects. Likewise, if in miniature, Brierly dreams the impossible ideal of god-like reputation, and so in reality limits himself to the worship of his primitive pre-human subject, the black retriever, who, like the savages deprived of their god in *Heart of Darkness* whose desolate cry so haunts Marlow, when asked to remember his god's inexplicable desertion ("Where's the Captain, Rover?" enquires Mr. Jones) "looked up at us with mournful yellow eyes, gave one desolate bark, and crept under the table". The Marlow of *Lord Jim* listens to Jim enthusing about his love in Patusan: "You take a different view of your actions when you come to under- stand . . . every day that your existence is necessary—you see, absolutely necessary—to another person . . . it is a trust, too . . . I believe I am equal to it . . ." Or, as Brierly said to Marlow equally unnecessarily: "We are trusted. Do you understand?—trusted! . . . A man may go pretty near through his whole sea-life without any call to show a stiff upper lip. But when the call comes . . . Aha! . . . If I . . ."

Similarly, Marlow in *Lord Jim* listens to the fair haired, white- clothed, exalted and Apollo-like Jim who in Patusan is apparently dauntless with Harlequin-like courage, and emptily named, like Kurtz, the Lord of surrounding nature, the god of his own secret ideal dream. Jim still imagines himself to be living in the fictional time of "light holiday literature"; he has forgotten his own social clock-time, and no longer possesses sure hold upon the time of his own racial consciousness: an order of time whose instinctive measurement would dictate his planning to leave for "home" and a nature which in late-Darwinian fullness still holds the external half of that internal needing and willing of the habitual thought and action of the Englishman. And so, as Jim boasts of his future ability to live up to the trust which Jewel's "love of worship" confers upon him, it seems to Marlow as he looks upon the nature enclosing him, precisely as it seemed to his predecessor listening to the Russian Harlequin, that the darkness has grown darker still: "I don't know why, listening to him, I should have noted so distinctly the gradual darkening of the river . . . the irresistible slow work of the night settling silently on all the visible forms, effacing the outlines, burying the shapes deeper and deeper, like a steady fall of impalpable black dust." This is the order of time in which such words of Jim's belong, with the formless darkness of the monstrous "somebody or something" of instinctive emotion; not linear time at all any more, but time of the unconscious, "deeper and deeper" in man, and implacable and inscrutable in the old nature.

"Love in general" means self-love disguised in the dream; the dream, subjective desires foisted upon nature, is itself a distinctive part of the thought of primitive man, as Darwin, Lubbock, Tylor and Frazer all insist. When the dream is threatened, or simply in its service, the unrestrained instinct to preserve the extended self will not only betray all other selves who no longer feed its god-like expansion, but even preserve its primitive idea of dominion in suicide. Brierly betrays a half-primitive dog; Jim will later betray a half-primitive woman. And this kind of juxtaposition of Jim and his unconsciously commenting chorus—action is particularly important in this area of Conrad's work partly because it is only in bodily movement that the speechless somebody or something can express its desires—this violent and bizarre dumb-show of a multitude of characters, controlled by powerful strings from external nature and their own unconscious, is one reason why Conrad disregards narrative continuity so radically and with such intellectual labour. Traditional fictional time, stretched ever more superficially linear by the pull of suspense, is even more rarefied, more a part of the wishful waking dreams of impossible paths to eternal futures, than the socially agreed, reason-made clock-time. And clock-time is itself more super-ficial than the time measured in consciousness, which, in its turn, is mere surface glitter upon the Conradian depths of the time of un-consciousness which cannot be measured at all and which language cannot directly comprehend, but in which those forces that obses-sively interest Conrad in all his best work are to be found.

Lest this short and summary placing of Brierly in such a relation to Jim's pilgrim's regress seems a little mystically degenerate itself, there are other, more traditional, pointers to Brierly's real crime in the small details of Conrad's tortuous thought. In his characteristic way, Conrad evokes the group of classical myths with which he associates Brierly. Like Jim, Brierly, in his "exalted egoism" sus-taining his "exalted existence", and attempting to become of god-like reputation amongst men, becomes half-beast; and, appropriately enough, he commands a ship named the *Ossa*, in a line which also boasts the *Pelion*. Big Montague Brierly (Giants, Mountains, Woods) like the giant sons of Aloeus, who attacked the gods in their own "exalted egoism" and attempted to build mountain steps to heaven by placing *Ossa* upon *Olympus*, and *Pelion* (a wooded mountain near the coast of Thessaly and the home of the Centaurs) upon *Ossa*, is destroyed by his impossible dream.

Brierly's dream is particularly English; his exalted egoism, whereby he creates a mystically ideal role from the commercial function he performs and a magic formula for self-respect from his real responsibility serves Brierly as well and as tyrannically as it will later serve Charles Gould. It is a dream which hangs like a mirage in social time and social space and seems to others to have quenched the dreamer's wildest thirst for honour and success: Brierly "had one of the best commands going in the Eastern trade" and he had "saved lives at sea, had rescued ships in distress". He is the proud possessor of two fitting rewards for his moral conduct within such a time and space: "a gold chronometer" commemorates his awareness of social, practical time measured by Greenwich rather than the amphioxus in the estuarine mud, and "a pair of binoculars with a suitable inscription" puts the trinket of society's approval upon his ability to see in social, external space, in a nature measured by comforting instruments in distances that bear no relation to Decoud's empty universe, and which are no improvement upon the remarkable eyes of the chief engineer of the *Patna*, for instance, as he looks into another order of time.

Brierly's idealistic dream, inseparable from incidental material success, is one of Conrad's answers to the kind of question put by Darwin in *The Descent of Man*: "The remarkable success of the English as colonists, compared to other European nations, has been ascribed to their 'daring and persistent energy' . . . but who can say how the English gained their energy?"[9] Another equally interesting answer, which we must explore later, lies in the energy of Gentleman Brown. Gentleman Brown, too, has the final barbaric word in Conrad's debate upon the nature, the biological nature, of the English gentleman in *Lord Jim*, that vague racial idea of pure blood preserved through the generations and linked with impeccable social conduct. Marlow makes a point of telling us that Jim considers himself entitled to claim such a label of social approval, and to claim it almost in the same breath as he remembers the outward event which has made him a social outcast. Jim remembers his jump with a "convulsive effort, whose stress" Marlow felt, "as if propagated by the waves of the air, made my body stir a little in the chair". The true Conradian English gentleman, instinctively courageous and acting with firm altruism towards his fellows, resists such primitive and direct

Darwinian calls to his own restrained unconscious; and is even able to resist Darwin's "instinct of self-preservation".[10] But Jim's conscious mind naturally clings to the surface meaning of a social distinction to be found in the trivia of social time and space: "of course I wouldn't have talked to you about all this if you had not been a gentleman . . . I am—I am—a gentleman, too . . ."

However, when Jim is "overburdened by the knowledge of an imminent death" in the cavernous hold of the *Patna* and has "started unsteadily to run" towards the bridge, he is entreated for water by a man on deck who holds on to his coat and repeats "the word water . . . in a tone of insistence, of prayer, almost of despair"; and Jim, the bearer of light, remembers that he "hauled off" with his free arm "and slung the lamp in his face". Jim's brutal response is particularly sinister when measured against the conduct of that most famous exemplar of the true code of the English gentleman who, when likewise burdened with knowledge of his imminent death, on the battlefield of Zütphen, yet passed the only cup of water to another wounded man with those famous words (which echo throughout *Lord Jim*): "Thy necessity is yet greater than mine."

The deep, biological inability to think or act socially in terms of Sir Philip Sidney's words marks out the distance which Jim's ancestral line has already traced for itself into the racial past, a line winding gently down from the heroic heights of moral and social evolution reached in the south of England in the golden age of the sixteenth century. Conrad further marks the line of this regression in the milestone figures he places unobstrusively along Jim's course.

The Protestant English myth of the self-sufficient man of practical reason, saving himself bodily and spiritually is, for Conrad, a dangerous egotistical dream; but Conrad attacks such pretentions to individual salvation with a more precise aside in *Lord Jim*. After Bunyan's seventeeth-century *Pilgrim's Progress*, the best-known work in the racial literature which celebrates the comforting conviction to be won from the self-projected dreams of impossible righteousness and godly rewards, is the eighteenth-century *Robinson Crusoe*. This particular English myth, in Conrad's world, is quite different from his own belief in those Englishmen whom Marlow praises as he contemplates Jim and "the parentage of his kind". This "parentage" (from whom Jim's biological inheritance differs by "the least drop of something rare and accursed"), the racial ancestors of all those who, like Jim, come from "the right place" (and Marlow speaks with Lamarckian literalness) possessed "that inborn ability to look temptation straight in the face", we remember, "a readiness unintellectual enough . . . but without pose—a power of resistance" to the disease of decay-in-time; an "unthinking and blessed stiffness" against the unseen miasma of easy environments, "before the might of nature" in all the varieties of its "implacable force" and before the equally testing environment of the "seductive corruption of men". They possessed an unconscious biological characteristic, naturally selected and progressively evolved (by Darwin's "effects of habit")[11] and this racial characteristic was not only "unthinking" but rooted deep enough in the buried life of the emotions to be "a faith invulnerable to the strength of facts" (external nature) and to the "contagion of example" (dangerous individuals within society) or to "the solicitation of ideas" (artifical systems of wishful thought, impossible dreams), ideas which prey upon the healthy individual with slow stealth, each idea itself a social outcast, "tramps, vagabonds, knocking at the back door of your mind, each taking a little of your substance".

Just such an idea is the "exalted egoism" of the dream of self-perfection and the especial favour of Providence, an idea taking a little of that hard-won "substance" of character because it lulls away the exercise of discipline and the sense of struggle with nature in the mystical assurance of impossible ease to come, that all will be well no matter how terrible the onslaught, as Brierly boasts, "when the call comes". But neither Robinson Crusoe nor his god are a match for the Darwinian unconscious or Darwinian nature in Conrad's evaluation of the hidden strength of the English character, posied on the edge of the twentieth century.

As Darwin writes of instinctive self-preservation in *The Descent of Man*, "Nor is it easy, perhaps hardly possible, to call up with complete vividness the feeling, for instance, of hunger" because the "instinct of self-preservation is not felt except in the presence of danger",[12] whether it be the danger of the "tumbling tide" beside Jim's training ship where a man is drowning, or the danger of death by starvation; in other words the instinct is unacknowledged, unconscious, but at the "moment of action, man will no doubt be apt to follow the stronger impulses; and though this may occasionally prompt him to the noblest deeds, it will more commonly lead him to gratify his own desires at the expense of other men."[13] Conrad's Robinson gratifies his own desires at the rather excessive expense of other men—by eating them. The chanting of his psalm tunes and all the noble "impulses" in man they celebrate is hardly enough to disguise that classical Darwinian competition for food within the limited environment of an ocean island, producing "favoured races in the struggle for life",[14] or Spencer's "survival of the fittest";[15] the "fittest" whom Darwin and Huxley later both insisted had no necessary relation to "the best".[16] And what of these new saved souls, the individuals within the species whose "instinct of self-preservation" is the strongest, the Darwinian "fittest"? Conrad has no difficulty in calling up with "complete vividness" the feeling of hunger, and neither has he any illusions about instincts of self-preservation when there is a shortage of meat. His Darwinian "fittest" in this sense survive their pacts with the devil without fear of damnation, and their outrages against the law of the natural creation are now only at the dictates of the new nature, but their survival is itself no cause for reassurance. Ghost-like himself, "Holy-Terror" indeed, his once unrestrained biological instincts withered by approaching biological death, Conrad's own Darwinian victor in the struggle for life is "an emaciated patriarch in a suit of white drill" whom Marlow watches "crossing the street in a trotting shuffle . . . 'How do you do? how do you do?' he piped amiably, and tottered."

And his real Terror lies not in his past exploits but crouches behind the Conradian pane of glass of his appearance now: "a nondescript form of a terror". The open terror of the beast which so triumphantly sated its voracious appetite and survived—certainly; but two nondescript forms of an intellectual terror are now more potent. Survival upon Darwinian terms is hardly worth the energy needed to eat one's fellows, after all, when Darwinian death (itself a process evolved and naturally selected for the developing biological complexity it allows) works so much more implacably than any other kind. Robinson's death will be without that limited Darwinian hope in the continuity and development of the species by means of sexual selection, which is, for Conrad, simply another Darwinian instinct responding to a need like hunger (and with which he expressly links it later in *Falk*). And it will be without that Lamarckian joy in the continuing life of the species of a Schopenhauer (the thought of individual death gives Schopenhauer great vicarious pleasure, as he contemplates the altruistic self-sacrifice of the ant and the bee in the greater continuing life of their species). Death totters out, in dotage, without the quietly optimistic faith of Robinson Crusoe's own century's secular illusion in the Age of Reason (Robinson's intellectual power is less important than that vested in his jaws); and, equally, it will be without the mystical self-flattery of the nineteenth-century romantic faith in the interrelated importance of man with a mystical order of nature, a nature where the fall of a sparrow continues to be marked, and where the fall of an albatross is proportionately more serious (but the Ancient Mariner Robinson breaks rather stronger taboos with impunity, and, as Conrad says of him: "'He! he! he!' laughed the Ancient"). And so, as Marlow remarks with an image which might have emerged unchanged from Tylor or Frazer's work on savage animism, the only comfort to be derived from death is its power to end the natural tyranny of "fate", the "directing spirit" of the power of the Darwinian environment and unconscious adaptation, of the biologically predestined distress of travelling the wrong way in time: at least it is "End! Finis! The potent word that exorcises from the house of life the haunting shadow of fate."[17]

"Old Robinson . . . Holy-Terror Robinson" Chester tells Marlow, was a man of voracious Darwinian appetite, gratifying the instinctive desires which ensured his survival. He survives from a time long before a Sidney could have re-uttered those words of highly evolved social man—"Thy necessity is yet greater than mine"—an expression of a genuine code of moral conduct, developed by the struggle and slow success of societies which, as Darwin writes, "included a great number of courageous, sympathetic and faithful members".[18] The society capable of producing a Sidney certainly possessed Darwin's measure of evolutionary success in the "advantage which disciplined soldiers have over undisciplined hordes", and which "follows chiefly from the confidence which each man feels in his comrades".[19] Robinson, however, like Jim, bears the mark of the brute, the Conradian outcast, a criminal in Marlow's sense where the "real significance of crime is in its being a breach of faith with the community of mankind". And he himself marks a reversion to the past in English society and the ideals of its "public opinion" in the eighteenth century as compared with the sixteenth. Robinson's actions in his holy terror adventures express the unconscious desires of the somebody or something of the brutish Darwinian past most clearly and contemptuously; his instinctive assertion of his very own necessity, in itself, carries a derisive comment from the speech-less past upon a Robinson Crusoe's trust in Providence, upon that dangerous egoistic dream of individual salvation and god-like self-sufficiency triumphing alone against nature. A mystical delusion whose great material success hides the impossibility of its real attainment and the actual submission to the primitive instincts and unrestrained "exalted egoism" it entails; a Brierly- and Gould-like English Protestant dream still powerful and dangerous in the nineteenth century. And so Old Robinson lives happily far from "home" attuned to a time and nature which is also old, but fit to receive the man who "used to board the sailing-schooners up Alaska way" in Robinson Crusoe-like partnership with his egoistic God "when the fog was so thick that the Lord God, He alone, could tell one man from another".

The most famous story in "Holy-Terror" Robinson's career is even more appropriate: "A shipwreck . . . that's right" Chester confides to Marlow, "seven of them got ashore" and, when found by "Her Majesty's ship *Wolverine*" (suitably bearing the name of the most voracious mammal upon earth), Robinson, alone, was "found kneeling . . . chanting some psalm tune or other" and chased "for an hour up and down the boulders" until, in Defoe-like connection of reason and Providence, "a marine flung a stone that took him behind the ear providentially and knocked him senseless".

Still nearer the present in Conradian time, and still further into the past, is the decline towards nineteenth-century romanticism. To the East of his meeting with Old Robinson, Marlow comes across a more desperate dream of unreason. He hears "Blake's strained voice . . . as the voice of one scolding in a wilderness". As if in marginal illustration of the psychological dangers and the safeguards of the intricate mechanism of social evolution at work, poised between progress and reversion, the a-social, degenerate Blake "every day from the moment the doors were opened to the last minute before closing . . . could be heard rowing his partner with a sort of scathing and plaintive fury" in one long fiery delusion which appears to be as much a biological part of him as his "unhappy, beady eyes". And the "sound of that everlasting scolding was part of the place like the other fixtures" amongst which Blake's partner Egström, one of those imperturbable Northmen whom Conrad (and Darwin) thought to be bred with Marlow's "blessed stiffness" in the lands of perpetual struggle near the Ice Cap, "a raw-boned, heavy Scandinavian", unaffected by such sustained mystical outrage that nature should be ordered as it is, "comported himself in that clatter exactly as though he had been stone-deaf".

Jim and Marlow will later meet other still more powerful characters conjured out of the sustaining illusions or past realities of the English racial consciousness; but we must first break our pursuit into lost time to consider the two sages who are invariably treated with the greatest deference by the readers of *Lord Jim*, and whose oracular judgments are often accepted as moral guidelines to Jim's conduct and to Conrad's thought.

Marlow tells us that "this affair" of the *Patna* has in itself "an extraordinary power of defying the shortness of memories and the length of time" as it lives "with a sort of uncanny vitality, in the minds of men". With a persistence worthy of the intrusions of Galton's unconscious in his word-association experiments or of Freud's unfortunate jokes and slips of the tongue[20] it plagues men "on the tips of their tongues", and hints at the hypnotically fascinating depths its acted symbols stir by "emerging from the remotest possible talk, coming to the surface of the most distant allusions".

The brute, the mark of the beast, itself possessed of an "uncanny vitality, in the minds of men", mesmerises others besides Marlow; and one such is the French lieutenant whom Marlow meets in a Sydney café and whom he discovers to have been the officer put aboard the abandoned *Patna* by the French gunboat which towed it to port.

Marlow is at first impressed by the apparent bravery of the Frenchman; but Conrad encircles Marlow's admiration of those thirty hours upon the stricken *Patna* (perturbed only by the barbarous lack of wine) with a noose of details which eventually knots tight to leave nothing but another lifeless illusion upon Marlow's haunted search to find a sovereign power in a fixed standard of conduct. The French lieutenant has much in common with Jim's father, but he comes from further south, from a less hardy cultural and social environment, set in an easier nature. Marlow twice tells us how priest-like he is: "he reminded you of one of those snuffy, quiet village priests, into whose ears are poured the sins, the sufferings, the remorse of peasant generations"; and we must remind ourselves of Conrad's attitude to such Roman Catholic dignitaries in the story of "The Idiots", for instance, where "the placid and simple expression" of priestly concern is also only "like a veil thrown over the mystery of pain and distress". This distress is akin to just such a story as Jim's, in crude miniature: the more extreme and terrible reversion to a Darwinian past in the degenerate aping of the apes, in idiocy; a biological horror which the priest veils in a cloud of unknowing, delivering himself "with joyful unction of solemn platitudes about the inscrutable ways of Providence".[21]

Just as Jim and Brierly are outwardly possessed by the secular version of their ancestors' Protestant dream of personal salvation guaranteed by their sustained progress, their continuous right action judged in worldly achievement as a gauge of godly pleasure, so the priest-like French lieutenant, in his comfortable and static world ("Time had passed indeed: it had overtaken him and gone ahead"), dwells in an illusory—and weakening—world of reassuring incantations from the Roman Catholic past. Only the words have changed; the beliefs still leave him reassured, but "hopelessly behind with a few poor gifts"; as unfitted as his ancestors for the real struggle in Darwinian nature, time, and a space emptied of all deities.

Conrad writes of Marlow's perception of the French lieutenant's relation to time—recent, historical time—with an insistence, an excited emphasis upon an intellectual discovery, which, if its significance is not immediately apparent, might lead us to decide that Conrad is writing portentously to fool us into ignoring his lack of a portent; insisting "on the presence of what he can't produce"[22] as Dr. Leavis has it; but, in Conrad's world, Marlow's insight does indeed portend terrible events.

The French lieutenant's exclamation "*Mon Dieu!* how the time passes!" brings Marlow "one of those rare moments of awakening when we see, hear, understand ever so much—everything—in a flash . . . I saw him as though I had never seen him before. I saw his chin sunk on his breast . . . his clasped hands, his motionless pose, so curiously suggestive of his having been simply left there."

Time has indeed "overtaken him and gone ahead"; and he and his kind are also hopelessly displaced in Darwinian nature. Inside the café, which Marlow uncomfortably feels to be "intolerably stuffy, and very hot" (whilst outside he remembers it "was a brilliant day; a southerly buster was raging"), the French lieutenant listens to Marlow's account of Jim's pain and distress "looking more priest-like than ever". And priest-like he is, mentally adapted to the artificial hothouse ease of centuries of received dogma. "His imperturbable and mature calmness was that of an expert in possession of the facts, and to whom one's perplexities are mere child's-play" Marlow tells us, and he "delivered himself" of his pronouncements "as immovably as though he had been the mouthpiece of abstract wisdom". But his calmness and his immobility are merely the reverse images of Jim's boastful and restless activity; the very different outward behaviour results from a different image of self, reflected back by the different angle from which he contemplates their common illusion. The Protestant dream lures the dreamer towards impossible futures of achievement and self-perfection. The Roman Catholic dream calms the dreamer into an impossible sense of security by relieving him of the burden of the need for individual struggle in his static, vertical world. He nurtures the illusion of Authority and accepts a revealed religion (which has nothing to do with external nature). "It was judged proper" that the uniformed French lieutenant should remain upon the *Patna*; and the dreamer is not alone with his god and his conscience but part of a corporate whole: "Brave—you conceive—in the service—one has got to be—the trade demands it". The confessional will return him to the immovable centre of the static dream, banishing time and chance: "Take me for instance—I have made my proofs. *Eh bien!* I, who am speaking to you, once . . ." he admits to Marlow, but then: "'No, no; one does not die of it,' he pronounced, finally . . ." because, after all, the dreamer enclosed in the elaborate and enchanted castle of Roman Catholicism does not believe with Jim's father in his book-lined study that "virtue is one all over the world", but that vice is one all over the world. Or, more accurately, that without the divine assistance of Grace the individual cannot be expected to reach or even vaingloriously strive towards moral excellence, but that the lowest estimate of the moral worth of human nature is most likely to be both individually correct and universal, because, as the French lieutenant easily pronounces: "there is somewhere a point when you let go everything". The dream of original sin is one of those most potent illusions which at once pardons moral failures and adds glory to moral successes achieved in the face of such good reason for defeat; as the French lieutenant dreams, "Man is born a coward . . . It is a difficulty—*parbleu!* It would be too easy otherwise".

Lest these still powerfully attractive ideas seduce his readers with the promise of calm (even if a calm of "stagnant water") and rest from struggle (even if it resembles airless torpor) Conrad follows them, at once, with the life and death of an insurance canvasser, "Little Bob Stanton"; his conduct makes the priestly wisdom of the French lieutenant, so solemnly pronounced in the drowsily degenerate café, in every way fit to add to its old and stale air. Bob Stanton, "undersized and bearded to the waist like a gnome", possesses that true instinctive courage which Marlow admires. And he possesses, too, that touch of the grotesque, which often marks Conrad's artistic approval of actions and emotions. He scrambles back on board a sinking ship to save an outsize, hysterical lady's maid who is still clinging to the rail "like grim death"; a comically masked death, in the dance of death. But unlike Jim upon the *Patna* running from such a spectre, Bob Stanton grapples unhesitatingly with death, "pull devil, pull baker", a bravery not openly demanded by the men of the merchant service who do not wear uniforms and brass buttons like the French lieutenant, but whose society includes individuals who are indeed not born cowards and whom habit and the eye of others cannot always influence; whose courage is more than proof against the debilitating opinion that "there is somewhere a point when you let go everything". Bob Stanton wrestles with death for the life of the girl until, exhausted, he "just stood by looking at her, watchful like", as a sailor tells Marlow, instinctively refusing to jump, and shouting at his boat below to keep clear: "he must've been reckoning that, maybe, the rush of water would tear her away from the rail by and by and give him a show to save her. We daren't come alongside for our life . . ."

Bob Stanton drowns; his deep biological courage and social sense ensured that there was nowhere a point when he "let go everything". The French lieutenant spoke cryptically of his own "proofs": some incident in which his instinct of self-preservation overwhelmed all civilised social restraints in a mechanism similar to the biological springs of Jim's jump. He sloughs off his feelings of guilt and potential remorse (one of Darwin's rather naively imagined factors in the evolution of a moral sense) in a comfortable conviction that mankind having universally fallen to much the same original sinful depth, then to acknowledge that given "a certain combination of circumstances, fear is sure to come" is to return once more with a heavily immobile consciousness to the warm righteous centre of a static world in which all may be forgiven. "No, no; one does not die of it" the French lieutenant pronounces upon his own past cowardice; indeed not, and neither does Jim, but one often dies of courage, and often, like Bob Stanton, without consoling dignity.

Within the old order of Roman Catholicism perhaps the refusal, over the centuries, to brace the mind against a nature in which "each act of life is final and inevitably produces its consequences"[23] as Conrad wrote in a letter to Marguerite Poradowska, has also weakened the social instincts of the faithful, because Darwin's "nature and strength of the feelings which we call regret, shame, repentance or remorse"[24] are severely limited within the dreams of the priestly confessional and the doctrine of "expiation through suffering", which is, as Conrad believes, "a product of superior but savage minds" and "quite simply an infamous abomination when preached by civilised people".[25] The biological reality has disappeared and only the public name is left. As the French lieutenant pronounces, "one may get on knowing very well that one's courage does not come of itself . . . There's nothing much in that to get upset about . . . But the honour—the honour, monsieur! . . . The honour . . . that is real—that is! And what life may be worth when . . ." Bob Stanton thought life was worth a great deal; his advanced biological courage did come of itself; and, anyway, he had lost his mere social honour long ago as an insurance canvasser, when his mistreated "immortal soul was shrivelled down to the size of a parched pea after a week of that work".

But at the thought of losing his honour (already lost in secret fact, but not in public word) the French lieutenant, in giving way to anticipatory fear, gives us a hint of the extent of unnoticed encroachment which the emerging past of the brute has already made into that comfortably drowning and placidly static consciousness; anaesthetised gently against the pain and distress of external nature, linear time, empty space, all the implacable forces and inscrutable intentions of an uncaring universe.

In a moment of fear before Marlow's words, like the captain of the *Patna* in sudden fear of confronting Captain Elliot when "some sort of animal instinct made him hang back and snort like a frightened bullock", the French lieutenant "got on his feet with a ponderous impetuosity, as a startled ox might scramble up from the grass". Just before this animal-like movement Marlow has his second revelation of the real nature of this priestly confessor when, Marlow tells us, for the first time, he "drew up his heavy eyelids . . . and at last was disclosed completely to me. I was confronted by two narrow grey circlets, like two tiny steel rings around the profound blackness of the pupils." Marlow looks down into the bottomless pits of the past, to the profound blackness of the heart of darkness, where his predecessor, likewise, looking into the eyes of the Manager of the Central

Station, felt that "he certainly could make his glance fall on one as trenchant and heavy as an axe";[26] a characteristic shared by the French lieutenant whose "sharp glance, coming from that massive body, gave a notion of extreme efficiency, like a razor-edge on a battle-axe". Efficient he may well be—efficient in executing the mechanical trivia, the practical details of superficial social action in the time and space of charts and compasses and reassuring rules made by Authority, exactly as Kayerts and Carlier or Brierly himself could function efficiently within a society which, as Conrad writes in *An Outpost of Progress* "not from any tenderness, but because of its strange needs, had taken care of those . . . men, forbidding them all independent thought, all initiative, all departure from routine; and forbidding it under pain of death. They could only live on condition of being machines."[27] Beneath the machine-like social action, the biological courage needed to meet that "departure from routine", when, as Brierly says "the call comes", has withered away; the only really reliable strong social instincts, the genuine feelings of uncalculating sympathy which Bob Stanton possesses, have decayed. In the pre-social, unfeeling glance of the French lieutenant Marlow sees a form of that beast-like something or somebody from the past which Conrad described earlier in the glance of the peasant father of the atavistic idiots who, looking into the cot where the next generation bearing his primitive inheritance lies:

> glanced in . . . with that indifference which is like a deformity of peasant humanity. Like the earth they master and serve, those men, slow of eye and speech, do not show the inner fire; so that, at last, it becomes a question with them as with the earth, what there is in the core; heat, violence, a force mysterious and terrible—or nothing but a clod, a mass fertile and inert, cold and unfeeling, ready to bear a crop of plants that sustain life or give death.[28]

Over this reversion to man's origins, to that almost inanimate past reached by the Manager at the heart of darkness whose "unconscious" smile made "the meaning of the commonest phrase appear absolutely inscrutable"[29] and which fits him to survive in a nature of "implacable force" and "inscrutable intention";[30] over this biological nature within, the French lieutenant now has only the thin veil of "infinite politeness" and a conversation of "empty sounds" as meaningless as those inscrutable common phrases. And even his excessive virtuosity in the Alvan Hervey-like artificial gestures of mechanical manners is itself characterised in a mockingly sinister image of the brute within, as he and Marlow "faced each other mutely, like two china dogs on a mantelpiece".

To bloodhound our way back upon Jim's escape towards lost time, we might notice other characters who mark his path, all men of Nordau's "degenerate mind" which "promulgates some doctrine or other—realism, pornography, mysticism, symbolism, diabolism".[31] Marlow's chief mate Selvin (self-in) for instance, otherwise "an excellent man" is the "victim of such black imaginings" that he all but drives the crew "to the verge of mutiny" and makes "a little hell on earth for himself" whenever a letter from his wife is late, paying her the excessive compliment of imagining himself defeated in the great biological struggle of sexual selection, and forgetting that even the males of the species exercise an aesthetic sense of some kind in these matters, as Darwin might have reassured him. And then there is Chester, with his primitive "immense girth of chest" from primitive West Australia, "pearler, wrecker, trader, whaler, too, I believe . . ." an angry advocate of realism—"You must see things exactly as they are"—an impossible realism, which relies upon eyes almost as remarkable as those of the chief engineer to really see a primitive vision of nature, where reason does not intervene between the internal wish and the external fact, a nature where the wealth and power of a dream lies buried in a pile of bird droppings upon a reef-ringed island where no rain falls for years on end and where the lack of an anchorage is an oversight of perceptive reason on Chester's part made optically more interesting by sheer cliffs, currents and hurricanes. But Chester's view of Jim upon his island does give us two extreme visions of Jim's alternative biological destiny which Conrad contemplates a moment, and leaves to explore more accurately elsewhere.

At the most advanced level of civilised intellect, later most hauntingly reached by Decoud, we for a brief (and unconvincing) moment are invited to place Jim in that particular Conradian nature where Maudsley's remarks, for instance, on the end of life upon earth are realised:

> If a disillusioned and degenerative end of mankind on earth has been forefixed from the beginning . . . May it not be that we are in daily presence of such foretokens without thinking enough of their meaning?

Metaphysical disquisitions concerning the reality of an external world; scepticism as to the very foundations of knowledge, and doubts whether all that we see and seem is not pure illusion—a dream within a dream . . . the increase of sorrow that increase of knowledge is . . . the multiplication of suicides from life-weariness or from impotence to face life's struggles: all these and the like maladies of self-consciousness, notably absent in the animal and uncivilised man . . . what are they but proofs that the highest achievements of thought sever the unity of man and nature and bring doubt and disillusion?[32]

Conrad would agree with Maudsley's conclusions and the apparent truth of the scientific theories upon which they are based, but not with his confused moral judgments; there is in any case no comfort to be won from the mystical "unity of man and nature"; Darwinian "animal and uncivilised man" is not a part of biological nature that the man of courage and of reason would ever want to seek in spiritual union, and reason and courage will sooner or later enable him to discover that biological nature is itself only an incidental development, a chance nonsense lost in the measureless time and space of empty physical nature. But Jim's path is not winding upwards towards such advanced disintegration, although Conrad's interest in such a path is already clear in Chester's plan for Jim which gives Marlow "a rapid vision of Jim perched on a shadowless rock, up to his knees in guano, with the screams of sea-birds in his ears, the incandescent ball of the sun above his head; the empty sky and the empty ocean all a-quiver, simmering together in the heat as far as the eye could reach."

For Decoud's final revelation it is instructive that Conrad deliberately removes the last vestige of biological nature, the sea-birds, to leave Decoud alone in the raw nature of physics. Decoud's sceptical intelligence is itself developed enough (Maudsley would say degenerate enough—and Conrad makes a show of trying to feel likewise) to be sensitive to such a bleak withdrawal of all the biological points of external reference, which soothe the self, point to its own place in a real world, and so enables the sceptic, the self-assured practitioner of scientific method and scientific trust in the senses, to doubt the dreams of all other men. The multitudinous presence of his Lamarckian relatives, a seethe of life classified and documented, and rooted, too, in the evolution of his language and culture, normally allows the nineteenth-century sceptic to ignore the new meaning of the comforting conviction, as Maudsley puts it, "of the utter vanities of all things under the sun, which has been the experience of the greatest sages and is the central truth at the heart of all religions".[33]

Yet Jim is already too "animal and uncivilised" for the intellectual dignity of such a fate; the other vision of him upon Chester's island is perhaps more convincing, abandoned like Holy-Terror Robinson, as Chester exclaims: "simply nothing to do; two six-shooters in his belt . . . Surely he wouldn't be afraid of anything forty coolies could do—with two six-shooters and he the only armed man, too!" Suicide or cannibalism—for the moment Conrad abandons both; and Jim serves further Darwinian time as he unconsciously prepares for the next stage upon his continuing descent.

As Darwin looks back upon such a route leading up to European civilisation, he writes that progress "seems to depend on many concurrent favourable conditions, far too complex to be followed out" but amongst which he is most insistent upon the advantages of "a cool climate" which "from leading to industry and the various arts, has been highly favourable".[34] He is equally insistent upon the disadvantages of "Nomadic habits, whether over wide plains, or through the dense forests of the tropics, or along the shores of the sea" which "have in every case been highly detrimental".[35] The Russian Harlequin wanders through the dense forests of the tropics, Jim wanders "along the shores of the sea". Jim the water-clerk "wanders", driven by primitive unconscious instincts which, unacknowledged in his conscious dream, give his wandering a desperate brokenness of unconscious fits and starts, his instinct of self-preservation lending a memory of the earlier jumps to his later movements; his dream-preservation, the egoism of his fear of a loss of honour, the empty name, making him scramble away, animal-like, as does the French lieutenant. He is kept company within by the real presence of the external embodiment which at one of his brief halts drives him on again: "I couldn't stand the familiarity of the little beast" Jim writes to Marlow of the second engineer of the *Patna*, who is also "wandering", and who arrives in Jim's workplace where Jim feels he is "infernally fawning and familiar—and that sort of thing". The little dog-like beast, infernally familiar, is nonetheless Jim's master within; Egström, the imperturbably stable man from Darwin's "cold climate", delivers an unconscious bolt of a kind which only those almost upon Olympus are safe and sure enough to throw so accurately. "What scared you? You haven't as much sense as a rat; they don't clear out from a good ship . . . This business ain't going to sink," says Egström; to which Jim's unconscious answers with the direct bodily expression of the beast. "He gave a big jump", like the native tyke, or the rat, and his instinctive action is glossed over by the ideal action from his quickly reasserted dream in words which gather the force of Conrad's title and whisper their way through the rest of the novel: " 'Goodbye', he says, nodding at me like a lord."

5

Wallace lines and shadow lines

Jim's Darwinian nomadic wandering along the shores of the sea where to "the common mind he became known as a rolling stone . . . within the circle of his wanderings (which had a diameter of, say, three thousand miles)" has evidently taken its "highly detrimental" effect when the beast within openly emerges once more; and then dramatically enough to shock even those "perfect strangers" who "took to him as one takes to a nice child", unconsciously recognising something undeveloped within him, but still attracted by "his personal appearance, his hair, his eyes, his smile" which "made friends for him wherever he went".

Conrad once again apparently overemphasises Jim's involvement in a common enough incident, which "belonged to the lamentable species of bar-room scuffles", but after which Jim "was universally condemned for the brutal violence". Jim is insulted by a degenerate "cross-eyed Dane of sorts . . . in the Royal Siamese Navy", but his reaction, the violent bodily expression of the brute, is so extreme that even the hardened onlookers in Schomberg's billiard room had "all precise recollection scared out of them by the appalling nature of the consequences that immediately ensued". The "appalling nature" hidden within Jim reveals itself by the reverse of Darwin's model action of his idea of moral perfection. Instead of the advanced conduct of Darwin's "many a civilised man . . . full of courage and sympathy", who "has disregarded the instinct of self-preservation, and plunged at once into a torrent to save a drowning man, though a stranger",[1] instead of mere instinctive self-preservation holding him inactive, as upon his training ship, Jim's instinct sweeps away all civilised restraint to compel him to throw a fellow man into that very torrent: the river below Schomberg's veranda flowed "very wide and black" and it was "very lucky for the Dane that he could swim".

Jim's brutal violence erupts, as Darwin says, "too instantaneously for reflection".[2]

The setting for this "worst incident of all in his—his retreat" is also a fitting place for Jim to end the "wandering" in geographical space which leads him further upon his time travelling descent into the past; and beyond a Schomberg, for instance, who is roughly placed upon the Darwinian journey by Marlow's description of him as "a hirsute Alsation of manly bearing", because, as Darwin remarks, there "can be little doubt that the hairs thus scattered over the body are the rudiments of the uniform hairy coat of the lower animals".[3] Although the "different races differ much in hairiness; and in the individuals of the same race the hairs are highly variable" we should not assume that "the more hairy races . . . such as the European, have retained their primordial condition more completely than the naked races", but rather that hairiness indicates "partial reversion; for characters which have been at some former period long inherited, are always apt to return. We have seen that idiots are often very hairy, and they are apt to revert in other characters to a lower animal type."[4]

Marlow himself takes Jim upon the next stage of his journey, towards Stein; after the "truly regrettable incident" of his pitching a man into the Menam river, Marlow tells us, "Jim turned up at about midnight on board my ship without a hat", without that symbol of a civilised social identity. On the "longish passage" Jim is clearly no longer a "seaman" who, "in every sense of the expression" as Marlow says, is " 'on deck' ". Indeed, Marlow now carries a dangerous cargo, a burden from the past, a nigger of the Narcissus, the weight of his African origins, which can still pull him into the deadly depths of his unconscious as he gazes unknowingly into the self-reflected glitter of his egoism upon its deceptive surface; a Jim Wait, a "my Jim", as Marlow now calls him, and, after all, as Marlow earlier admits, if "he had not enlisted my sympathies he had done better for himself—he had gone to the fount and origin of that sentiment, he had reached the secret sensibility of my egoism". And so, as Marlow half apologises to his audience, "I suppose you will understand that by that time I could not think of washing my hands of him." The bond between the two men is now of a different, more sinister nature; for Marlow it is debilitating, pulling him towards an unacknowledged past: "He infected me so that I avoided speaking on professional matters . . . For whole days we did not exchange a word; I felt extremely unwilling to give orders to my officers in his presence. Often, when alone with him . . . we didn't know what to do with our eyes." And "my Jim, for the most part, skulked down below as though he had been a stowaway".

Marlow, later, bound for home, knows he must shed his own secret sharer, leave Jim behind him in the forgotten nature of Patusan: "it may be I desired, more than I was aware of myself, to dispose of him . . . before I left. I was going home, and he had come to me from there, with his miserable trouble and his shadowy claim, like a man panting under a burden in a mist." In relation to civilised man Jim is already a part of the past, half absorbed into the "inconceivable" unconscious of instinctive action, which is why Marlow finds Jim's adaptation to the nature and peoples of Patusan "inconceivable. That was the distinctive quality of the part into which Stein and I had tumbled him unwittingly." And that is why Marlow so oddly remarks: "I cannot say I had ever seen him distinctly—not even to this day, after I had my last view of him", and, because there is a fine gradation from speechless darkness up into the full light of Western civilised reason, why Marlow feels obscurely bound at a level of mind inaccessible to his developed intellect—vaguely conscious of something uncomfortably demanding awakened in himself yet whose "shadowy claim" is hidden by mists which the empirical "why and the wherefore" of reason will not disperse. As Marlow attempts to explain: "It seemed to me that the less I understood the more I was bound to him in the name of that doubt which is the inseparable part of our knowledge. I did not know so much more about myself."

The nature in which the habitually empirical turn of mind of Western man with his scientific reason and his habitual respect for law and disciplined justice have evolved is itself, in Darwinian logic, inimical to such vague awareness of instinctive sympathy and the upwelling mist and darkness of a secret sharing of mind with the brutish past. As Marlow insists, in a passage which is the intellectual centre of *Lord Jim* (balanced by an emotionally central *cri de coeur* later): "And then, I repeat, I was going home—to that home distant enough for all its hearthstones to be like one hearthstone"—a racial home with racially evolved beliefs about fixed standards of conduct—and "for each of us going home must be like going to render an account". The apparently absurdly inadequate concept of "home" has taken the place of Divine Judgment. But it is an advanced Darwinian "home" and, imagined pictorially, no less exalted than the old heaven in relation to the lowest savage kingdom of the degenerate past (peopled, appropriately, by the truly damned souls, who have fallen from at least a chance of salvation, such as Kurtz, and the "innocents" who have known no other nature but the darkness of savage life or the barbarity of the Harlequin's Mother Russia). There is a new Darwinian Trinity, too: "We return to face our superiors"—the father figures of the austere officer élite, which is as far as Conrad will permit himself to extend a genuine "public opinion"—and then the closer bond and influence of "our kindred, our friends", a secular picture of God the Father and God the Son, "those whom we obey, and those whom we love" as Marlow says; and, most pervasive of all, is the new Holy Ghost, an unseen biological spirit whose influence those traditionally nearest to God, "the most free, lonely, irresponsible and bereft of ties", feel most powerfully. They "have to meet the spirit that dwells within the land", in its particular Darwinian nature of climate and environment, "under its sky, in its air, in its valleys, and on its rises, in its fields, in its waters and its trees—a mute friend, judge, and inspirer".

Each man must prove himself equal to the challenge of readapting to the external nature which cradled the progress of his race; there must be no secret sharers to cast shadows into his consciousness, no reversion to primitive darknesses: "say what you like, to get its joys, to breathe its peace, to face its truth, one must return with a clear consciousness". This "spirit that dwells within the land" is the invisible force of Darwinian natural selection, of the effects of use and disuse of adaptive abilities, not a Wordsworthian "creator and receiver both" except in the most limited unromantic sense, nor the spirit of nature of loosely imagined popular romanticism. As Marlow remarks of his beliefs about this implacable spirit, "All this may seem to you sheer sentimentalism", but the biological reality is merely obscured beneath the self-comforting ideas of nature so attractive in the past; "and indeed" Marlow adds decisively, "very few of us have the will or the capacity to look consciously under the surface of familiar emotions", to turn the small light of reason downwards into the unexplored, vast, unconscious darkness (as Conrad and Freud were prepared to do), venturing with their faulty Darwinian torchlight into primaeval continents every bit as dangerous and disturbing and unexpected as Marlow's journey to the heart of darkness of Darwinian Africa.

Different external natures revive different stratified levels in the evolutionary history of mind, and, for the morally weakened, for Jim or for Leggatt, the climb upwards from such a descent into the mind's geology may well be beyond their strength. For, as Marlow knows, "Each blade of grass has its spot on earth whence it draws its life, its strength; and so is man rooted to the land from which he draws his faith together with his life." These intellectual and emotional roots are no mere seedling tendrils of shallow patriotism: "I do not mean to imply that I figured to myself the spirit of the land uprising above the white cliffs of Dover." Again, as the lonely know best, the Darwinian spirit, compared with the transient gods of the fireside and the individual life and superficial political ideals of country and frontier, is a "disembodied, external, and unchangeable spirit" whose influence is felt in "its severity, its saving power", and which gives "the grace of its secular right to our fidelity, to our obedience". But there is no atonement for biological sins, no redemption. The implacable and inscrutable spirit goes about its work of natural selection without the individual's direct knowledge: "few of us understand, but we all feel it though, and I say *all* without exception, because those who do not feel do not count." Those without the slightest glimmer of conscious response have already sunk without trace into the unconscious past of mere instinct; like the rest of the officers of the *Patna*, they have become a part of that implacable force of inscrutable intention—the nature which existed before consciousness evolved, and from which, even now, only a very few societies of man have struggled free.

The "spirit of the land" acts for "the good of the community" as Darwin describes such a spirit in his documentation of the social instincts of the hive bee, for instance, in *The Origin of Species*, but, as Darwin also insists, such a spirit is a-moral in any conventional sense, and "maternal love or maternal hatred . . . is all the same to the inexorable principle of natural selection."[5] The Queen-bee benefits her species as a whole by destroying the "young queens her daughters",[6] and, likewise, Conrad's idea of the spirit of the land: "as becomes the ruler of great enterprises, is careless of innumerable lives. Woe to the stragglers! We exist only in so far as we hang together." Like Tennyson's Lamarckian spirit of *In Memoriam* "so careless of the single life"[7] Darwin and Conrad's "inexorable principle" or "implacable force" is careless of Jim's single life; but "he was aware of it with an intensity that made him touching, just as a man's more intense life makes his death more touching than the death of a tree". Jim is aware of the spirit of the land and the spirit of his race, where he is "not good enough", not fit to live any more in such a nature; at least, as Marlow says, "I know he felt, he felt confusedly but powerfully, the demand of some such truth or some such illusion — I don't care how you call it, there is so little difference, and the difference means so little."

The inexorable principle and the demand rule in time and space and within and between each organism in nature, reducing absolute and eternal truths from their one divine sameness "all over the world" to multitudinous local restrictions within the changing varieties of man and his differently evolved communities. Darwin ended the long debate about the number of different species of man and their relative positions upon the great chain of being which led up *via* the angels to god; but he also ended the essential distinction between the varieties and species themselves. So, while nominally placing all the various races of mankind together, he yet removed both the external and the internal imagined boundaries of species and of varieties, straggled them out across a time that extended before and beyond the mind's capacity to imagine and enclose it; he ranged them across geographical space which had lost its comfortable eighteenth-century solidity, maps and compasses and meticulous voyages being but trivial reassurances in a world so precarious, an earth surface of advancing and retreating ice, of rocks no longer rock-like but rising and subsiding, of seas and continents which capriciously changed places. In such a world it really matters little whether the instinctively held standards of conduct of a particular variety of men are classified as truth or illusion. Natural selection, "the ruler of great enterprises", acts ruthlessly upon variations of social instinct whatever the individual man may imagine he believes rationally or mystically; Jim is no longer fit to survive socially in the land of his particular variety of race and moral code, but his reaction is deep and biological — disgust. With the unconscious expression of the same inner brute that produced his jump or his sudden violence before "the idea of going home", Marlow tells us, Jim (in exactly the reverse of his reaction to an appeal to his social instinct to overcome his fear, to resist the degenerate call to jump and be true to the spirit of his land) "would grow desperately stiff and immovable with lowered chin and pouted lips, and with those candid blue eyes of his glowing darkly under a frown, as if before something unbearable, as if before something revolting".

No wonder that Jim's destiny matters to those who are still biologically able to return home to the land of their societies' origins, those amongst the "favoured races" who are preserved "in the struggle for life". Marlow is emphatic: "The thing is that in virtue of his feelings he mattered. He would never go home now. Not he. Never." Jim's feelings, his unconscious regression to a previous level in the evolution of his society's social instincts are significant just because the spirit of the land is a-moral; even in the first edition of *The Origin of Species* Darwin wrote: "The external conditions of life, as climate and food, etc., seem to have induced some slight modifications. Habit in producing constitutional difference and use in strengthening, and disuse in weakening and diminishing organs, seem to have been more potent in their effects."[8] And "It will be universally admitted that instincts are as important as corporeal structure for the welfare of each species";[9] as "modifications of corporeal structure arise from, and are increased by, use or habit, and are diminished or lost by disuse, so I do not doubt it has been with instincts".[10] And so, whether by the inexorable principle of natural selection working upon "the effects of habit" or "what may be called accidental variations of instincts",[11] the social instincts evolve; they evolve along the same irregular branching paths into the Darwinian future as they have left criss-crossed out across the great abandoned reaches of the Darwinian past. The journey into the Darwinian future, however, is slow.

It is one of the few repetitive (and, as Huxley was shrewd enough to realise, unnecessary) dogmas in *The Origin of Species* that evolution "progresses" in small and gradual steps—"nature makes no jumps"—and the "canon of '*Natura non facit saltum*' applies with almost equal force to instincts as to bodily organs".[12] Darwin adopted this naturalist's dictum partly as a defence against the intervention of sudden miraculous creation in his self-regulating secular nature, partly as an extension into biological detail of Lyell's general geological principle of uniform change. But, when there is no possibility of the hand of a beneficent God at work perfecting his creation, Darwin inconsistently ignores his own dogma; when biological change appears to be moving backwards in time Darwin is content to allow it to do so with Satanic abandon in leaps and bounds across the generations. Discussing the occasional presence of the supra-condyloid foramen (a hole for the nerve and the artery in the lower end of the humerus) in man, Darwin writes, for instance, "if the . . . development of this structure . . . is, as seems probable, due to reversion, it is a return to a very ancient state of things, because in the higher Quadrumana it is absent".[13] For those unconsciously involved in the social progress of their race, for Captain Allistoun and Captain Archbold and the dogged chief mate of *The Secret Sharer*, the ascent into the future is made slowly, in terms of the evolution of the social instinct, "by the slow and gradual accumulation of numerous, slight, yet profitable, variations".[14] They obey Darwin's dogma, the "canon of '*Natura non facit saltum*'", which "applies with almost equal force to instincts as to bodily organs". But, for those unconsciously regressing into the past, the comforting rule that "nature makes no jumps" does not apply; Jim's "unnatural" act, his breach of social trust, "a disgrace to human natur'" as Captain O'Brien says—what is it but a jump?

To Marlow it appears "strange, this fatality that would cast the complexion of a flight upon all his acts, of impulsive unreflecting desertion—of a jump into the unknown". But for Conrad the direction of Jim's jumps against nature is precise. Whilst Kurtz journeyed into the far past of the species, toward the space and time of the origin of man in the heart of darkness of Africa, Jim journeys into the specifically European past, toward a space and time that Darwin imagined as intermediate between man's savage origins and his highest civilised society, toward the twilight of the Malay Archipelago. As Darwin writes in *The Origin of Species*, "The Malay Archipelago is of about the size of Europe from the North Cape to the Mediterranean, and from Britain to Russia" and "I fully agree . . . that the present condition of the Malay Archipelago with its numerous large islands separated by wide and shallow seas, probably represents the former state of Europe, when most of our formations were accumulating."[15]

Within this geographical space which is yet distant in time, Jim travels toward a destination which Conrad is careful to give further intellectual definition, a sharp focus of idea with the most authoritative instruments which contemporary science could provide. As Darwin writes, the "Malay Archipelago is one of the richest regions of the whole world in organic beings"[16] and it is obvious that Conrad, in his own way, agrees; but within this rich region the seethe of life and the varieties of man which Conrad compresses into Patusan are themselves of a special kind. The favoured races naturally selected to become dominant branches upon Darwin's tree of life establish themselves over the great continents; but, just as Conrad tells us that

Jim "had straggled in a way" and "woe to the stragglers!", so Darwin remarks that "we here and there see a thin straggling branch springing from a fork low down in a tree" and "so we occasionally see an animal . . . which has apparently been saved from fatal competition by having inhabited a protected station".[17] Jim, "a straggler yearning inconsolably for his humble place in the ranks" makes his way toward just such a station.

The main "stream of civilisation", we remember, "branches" away to the north of Patusan, "leaving its plains and valleys, its old trees and its old mankind, neglected and isolated". Patusan is "an insignificant and crumbling islet between the two branches of a mighty, devouring stream". And, as Darwin observes: "On a small island, the race for life will have been less severe, and there will have been less modification and less extermination."[18] Jim retreats into an island (although we will discover that Conrad is still more scientifically detailed in his precise placing of Patusan in evolutionary time) and his halting migration is also true to Darwinian predictions. He descends upon Patusan from the north to dominate its "old mankind". More precisely, Jim comes as a counterfeit inheritor of another man's characteristics and achievements; Jim only appears to come "from the right place". The man whose privileged position in the struggle for existence he inherits "was a Scot—even to the length of being called Alexander McNeil—and Jim came from a long way south of the Tweed" Conrad tells us, but "at the distance of six or seven thousand miles Great Britain, though never diminished, looks foreshortened enough even to its own children to rob such details of their importance".

Yet such details are indeed important, and we know that Conrad imagines Jim to have inherited the acquired characteristics of a special intellectual habitat, a "plague spot" hidden within Darwin's generally designated area of origin of those "more dominant forms" which have been "generated in the larger areas and more efficient workshops of the north".[19] From these (most Victorian) workshops of the north of the world have migrated strong forms (like McNeil) "from the north to the south", Darwin writes, and

I suspect that this preponderant migration from north to south is due to the greater extent of land in the north, and to the northern forms having existed in their own homes in greater numbers, and having consequently been advanced through natural selection and competition to a higher stage of perfection or dominating power, than the southern forms.[20]

And, once settled, "many of these wanderers, though still plainly related by inheritance to their brethren of the northern or southern hemispheres, now exist in their new homes as well-marked varieties or as distinct species".[21] Jim in Patusan "looked with an owner's eye at the peace of the evening, at the river, at the houses, at the everlasting life of the forests, at the life of the old mankind, at the secrets of the land, at the pride of his own heart", but, as Marlow remarks in a particularly Darwinian aside, Jim's real relations to the old nature are deeper and more sinister: "it was they that possessed him and made him their own to the innermost thought, to the slightest stir of blood, to his last breath". This is the way in which Jim "was approaching greatness as genuine as any man ever achieved"; "greatness" is now a combination of so many determining biological conditions that its old meaning is simply dispersed into the new nature.

Conrad considers Jim's arrival in Patusan, "the land he was destined to fill with the fame of his virtues, from the blue peaks inland to the white ribbon of surf on the coast". Jim journeys away from the open struggle of the sea for ever: "he lost sight of the sea with its labouring waves for ever rising, sinking, and vanishing to rise again", like the constantly changing relations of the races and varieties of individuals and societies within the species man, according to the late Darwinian idea of the changing places of the favoured and degenerating races in the struggle for life, or, as Conrad says, "the very image of struggling mankind". And as well as the easy encompassing of geographical space and the lateral interrelations of conflicting, adapting, habit-forming men and societies in the immediate habitat, in "the immovable forests rooted deep in the soil", Jim as always, travels in biological and geological time. Living fossils of the past line the muddy banks of the river, and Jim "tried by looking ahead to decide whether the muddy object he saw lying on the water's edge was a log of wood or an alligator . . . Always alligator . . . Then in a long empty reach he was very grateful to a troop of monkeys who came right down on the bank and made an insulting hullabaloo on his passage." Jim enters his new environment with a movement whose significance in terms of his hidden instincts, his position in Darwinian time, and in Conrad's vertically imagined scale of his descent, is, by now, obvious enough: he "became instantaneously aware . . . of his boatmen leaping out together upon a low point of land and taking to their heels. Instinctively he leaped out after them."

And what is our first direct impression of Patusan, this "crumbling

114

islet", the "isolated station"? It is a land of twilight, of half-light, not the full light of reason and Marlow's "clear consciousness" of the open sea or the searching light of the "spirit of the land" of "home", and nor is it the heart of darkness, but "the ghost of dead sunlight". Marlow, immediately after the passage describing Jim's entry, is moved to describe his Western impression of the Patusan moon "like an ascending spirit out of a grave; its sheen descended, cold and pale" and the "light of the moon . . . has all the dispassionateness of a disembodied soul, and something of its inconceivable mystery".

At last, the "inconceivable" within Jim has found a nature to which it is adapted, and his misty, mystical, romantic consciousness can safely cloud itself with dreams, because such a light, Marlow continues, "is to our sunshine, which—say what you like—is all we have to live by" as the light of clear-sighted reason as well as the ultimate biological energy of all organisms: "what the echo is to the sound: misleading and confusing whether the note be mocking or sad. It robs all forms of matter—which, after all, is our domain—of their substance, and gives a sinister reality to shadows alone. And the shadows were very real around us . . ."

The energy of this whole passage, Conrad's insistence upon the shadowy nature of this isolated retreat hidden in the dim prehistory of the race, not only tells us that he is deliberately setting the scene, painting in the particular background light that pervades Patusan, but also leads us to the probable intellectual source of that light. In an especially powerful and evocative series of images in the argument of *The Origin of Species*, discussing those individuals who have retreated away from the open sunlight of their homes towards isolated, shadowy, "protected stations", where they have degenerated to form new species, Darwin writes that rather than suppose them especially created to fit their environment:

> on my view we must suppose that . . . animals, having ordinary powers of vision, slowly migrated by successive generations from the outer world into the deeper and deeper recesses of the Kentucky caves, as did European animals into the caves of Europe. We have some evidence of this gradation of habit; for, as Schiödte remarks, "animals not far remote from ordinary forms, prepare the transition from light to darkness. Next follow those that are constructed for twilight; and, last of all, those destined for total darkness." By the time that an animal had reached, after numberless generations, the deepest recesses, disuse will on this view have more or less perfectly obliterated its eyes . . .[22]

Darwin makes it clear that he imagines such blindness not to be the result of natural selection: "As it is difficult to imagine that eyes, though useless, could be in any way injurious to animals living in darkness, I attribute their loss wholly to disuse."[23] Such an idea gathers all the suggestive power of the commonplace images of the light of reason, clearsighted perception, the acute senses developed by Western man in the scientific exploration of nature; Darwin himself uses just such imagery to describe vestigial structures: "In some of the crabs the foot-stalk for the eye remains, though the eye is gone; the stand for the telescope is there, though the telescope with its glasses has been lost."[24]

H. G. Wells's time traveller, into the future, discovers that a whole class within the race has retreated to "the deepest recesses" and become adapted to twilight; but Wells's Morlocks are clearly the favoured variety in terms of social evolution:[25] efficient tool-makers, a dominant strain, the masters of their sleek and un-Victorian machines (the time traveller's time-machine is a mere modified new invention, the bicycle) and masters of their divergent variety in the open sunlight, the aristocratic, Decadent, Aesthetic, degenerate Eloi, who are nevertheless highly nutritious. But this biological future, true to H. G. Wells's intellectual character, is a conceptual reversal of Darwin's specific image in terms of Darwin's general theory; the very literally ground-under lower classes will one day very literally feed upon the upper classes; Darwin's "deepest recesses"[26] inhabited by his "wrecks of life",[27] "anomalous forms" in man though they may now appear to be, will one day emerge dominant in the twilight, made ruthless, strong and knowledgeable by the "effects of use", of excessive toil; their eyes, unlike the degenerate majority of cave-living species, not vestigial at all, but, like those of Darwin's cave rat, "of immense size".[28]

Conrad's time travellers, voyaging into the past (although with as strong a moral warning about potential futures) are more orthodox; Conrad only transmutes the minor details of contemporary science, with the grotesque alchemy of his humour, into more permanent life, never concepts. James Wait threatens to pull advanced society down from the open light of hard nature, by the weight of the evolutionary past, into "the deepest recesses"; Jim travels through time to the twilight; Leggatt's "anomalous form" in the recess of the ship is briefly illuminated by the society above—Marlow's society of "the different atmosphere that seemed to vibrate with a toil of life, with the energy of an impeccable world"—defined, as Leggatt is carried toward the darkness, by the chief mate's repetition of the crew's collective indignation that they would "harbour such a thing" and their instinctive reaction: "would you like to look for him in our coal-hole?"[29]

And so in a lost nature in *Lord Jim* inhabited by Darwin's organisms that are "constructed for twilight", Conrad himself constructs an early series of the diverse stages in moral evolution amongst "the old mankind". Darwin writes: "I am only surprised that more wrecks of ancient life have not been preserved, owing to the less severe competition to which the inhabitants of these dark abodes will probably have been exposed."[30] Patusan, almost all its dark abodes full of wrecks of ancient life, might have satisfied him. Certainly the nature in which Marlow contemplates Jim harbours those "animals not far remote from ordinary forms" which "prepare the transition from light to darkness" and "those that are constructed for twilight", a nature where "even on the river the moonbeams slept as on a pool" in a "moment of immobility that accentuated the utter isolation of this lost corner of the earth". And in this twilight nature the "houses crowding along the wide shining sweep without ripple or glitter, stepping into the water in a line of jostling, vague, grey, silvery forms mingled with black masses of shadows, were like a spectral herd of shapeless creatures pressing forward to drink in a spectral and lifeless stream."

6

Stein

So we now understand the "why and the wherefore" of Jim's inability to return home, his wanderings, and the nature of his final retreat; but what of the man who sends Jim to Patusan, generally imagined together with the French lieutenant as one of Conrad's "wise men"? Certainly the light in which Stein is introduced to us would place him far from advanced evolutionary Enlightenment and deep into the new Dark Ages of evolutionary prehistory, into the light of "the deeper and deeper recesses" of Darwin's caves, or, as Marlow describes the shadows in Stein's room, "into shapeless gloom like a cavern".

Indeed, Stein's immediate surroundings are first characterised in almost precisely the same way as are Jim's in the nature of Patusan. Marlow, "after traversing an imposing but empty diningroom very dimly lit" in the silent, spectral, lofty dark abode of Stein's where he is preceded, most suitably, by a native of the once prehistoric dark abode of speechless Java man, "an elderly grim Javanese servant" who "vanished in a mysterious way as though he had been a ghost only momentarily embodied", describes Stein and his self-created habitat in images of subterranean darkness, of isolation and deathly quiet, of a house or a cave in which to hide a secret sharer.

Round the walls of the "shapeless gloom" run "dark boxes of uniform shape and colour . . . in a sombre belt . . . catacombs of beetles . . . and the word *Coleoptera* . . . glittered mysteriously upon a vast dimness". Stein enters the twilight whenever he passes

out of the bright circle of the lamp into the ring of fainter light—into shapeless dusk at last. It had an odd effect—as if these few steps had carried him out of this concrete and perplexed world. His tall form, as though robbed of its substance, hovered noiselessly over invisible things with stooping and indefinite movements; his voice, heard in that remoteness where he could be glimpsed mysteriously busy with immaterial cares, was no longer incisive, seemed to roll voluminous and grave—mellowed by distance.

And indeed Stein has been distanced in another dimension, like the distance to be measured out between the sunlit present of the practical empiricism of the Englishman in his home countryside (or upon the open sea which he had made his own habitat, and where his was so obviously the favoured race in the struggle for dominance) and the deepening gloom of the past leading to the living fossils to be found within Darwin's "deep limestone caverns".[1] Like the distance between that nature to which Marlow is adapted (where he "revelled in the vastness of the opened horizon . . . This sky and this sea were open to me . . . there was a sign, a call in them—something to which I responded with every fibre of my being" and that nature of twilight and spectral forms, silent, vague, shadowy, robbed of their substance. Like the time travellers of H. G. Wells or the faint voices of those unfortunates in the fifth dimension (but without the jocular self-congratulation of the once professional scientist which neutralises the potential emotional poisons of Wells's stories, without that "scientific scandal-mongering" Conrad denounces in *Lord Jim*), Stein half disappears into the past whenever he leaves the "one corner of the vast room" which "was strongly lighted by a shaded reading lamp", or whenever he leaves, for instance, that "narrow circle of the psychic life which is illumined by the little lamp of consciousness"[2] which, as Max Nordau wrote in *Degeneration*, was all the rationalists believed determined "the thoughts and actions of men" and from whom all "that wide region of organic needs and hereditary impulses, all that E. von Hartmann calls the 'Unconscious' lay hidden."[3]

In Stein's rooms, as in Marlow's first description of Patusan, that "spectral herd of shapeless creatures pressing forward to drink in a spectral and lifeless stream", Nordau's image of the brain of the mystic is enlarged, projected through the tortuous and complex but nevertheless consistent and precise thought of a mind beside which Nordau's own intellect appears a little Ramapithecine, and given genuine intensity and fictional life. The judgment of Nordau's "mystic", lost amongst the "faint, scarcely recognisable, liminal presentations . . . grows drifting and nebulous . . . consciousness, aware of the spectrally transparent shapes, seeks in vain to grasp them" and "a man fancies that he perceives inexplicable relations between distinct phenomena and ambiguous formless shadows."[4]

This is precisely how Stein makes his most famous pronouncement, couched in the language of the twilight rather than that of Nordau's "true depth of strong select minds" which is "wholly luminous. It scares shadows out of hidden corners, and fills abysses with radiant light."[5] Away from the "little lamp of consciousness" upon Stein's writing desk, there is only the "mystic's pseudo-depth"[6] to be found in his house; a remoteness, a "shapeless dusk" as Marlow says, where his voice, "no longer incisive", reaches Marlow from an "obscurity" which Nordau describes as the essential murky characteristic of the thought of the mystical dreamer which "causes things to appear deep by the same means as darkness . . . by reason of its rendering their outlines imperceptible".[7]

The "shadow prowling amongst the graves of butterflies" declares from the dusk:

"A man that is born falls into a dream like a man who falls into the sea. If he tries to climb out into the air as inexperienced people endeavour to do, he drowns—*nicht wahr?* . . . The way is to the destructive element submit yourself, and with the exertions of your hands and feet in the water make the deep, deep sea keep you up!" . . . His voice leaped up extraordinarily strong, as though away there in the dusk he had been inspired by some whisper of knowledge.

Stein in the shadows is indeed inspired, in a "state of mind in which the subject imagines that he perceives or divines unknown and inexplicable relations amongst phenomena"[8] as Nordau has it, and "With a hasty swish-swish of his slippers he loomed up in the ring of faint light" like the fishy form of the secret sharer looming up from the dark depths of the past, and "suddenly appeared in the bright circle of the lamp . . . his deep-set eyes seemed to pierce through me, but his twitching lips uttered no word, and the austere exaltation of a certitude seen in the dusk vanished from his face". Once in the light, Nordau's "emergent thought-phantoms can acquire no influence over the thought-procedure because attention either lightens up their faces, or banishes them back to their underworld of the Unconscious."[9] Or, as Marlow says of Stein, the "light had destroyed the assurance which had inspired him in the distant shadows".

As all those know who can return home with a "clear consciousness", such as Captain Allistoun, Captain Archbold, the chief mate in *The Secret Sharer*, Stein's pronouncement from the shadows is false. Not all men fall into a dream as a man falls into the sea when they are born (although, apart from the rare Darwinian variation, all primitive men do); some men in civilised societies are born with an inherited capacity for the exercise of enlightened reason and the courageous ability, selected and nurtured by their ancestors' long struggle, to look objectively upon nature. Conrad's quiet heroes are not afraid of the empty cosmos or of their own restricted biological nature and they know "how to be". They instinctively answer Stein's agonised question, without considering Stein's "one remedy! . . . one way"— without suicide, without the protective escape into the dream, the illusion, the destructive element, the deep, deep sea. Within Conrad's vertically imagined world of the open sky, the open sea and the depths, they command the symbolic ships of society, guide their vessels safely through the worst that nature blindly can do either from within or from without, the brute or the storm, and they carry out their life's work upon the open surface of the sea, and sail home, as Marlow says, to "touch their reward with clean hands".

Marlow listens to Stein, and tells us that the

> whisper of his conviction seemed to open before me a vast and uncertain expanse, as of a crepuscular horizon on a plain at dawn—or was it, perchance, at the coming of the night? One had not the courage to decide; but it was a charming and deceptive light; throwing the impalpable poesy of its dimness over pitfalls—over graves.

The landscape is again much the same as Nordau's large vision of degeneration in Europe and the "light of the Dusk of the Nations" where "Over the earth the shadows creep with deepening gloom, wrapping all objects in a mysterious dimness, in which all certainty is destroyed and any guess seems plausible. Forms lose their outlines, and are dissolved in floating mist."[10] It is certainly the same light which Marlow describes in Patusan, one of the most isolated of those places in the archipelago which Stein had "seen in the original dusk"—not darkness—"of their being"; Stein's thought, his house, the nature in which he used to live—they are all almost adapted to each other.

As Marlow walks through Stein's rooms, through "empty dark rooms . . . the flicker of two flames could be seen for a moment stealing silently across the depths of a crystalline void" and it is here that Marlow has his "vision" of Jim's essential nature. Just as the

Marlow of *Heart of Darkness*, contemplating the Harlequin (who is as effortlessly adapted to the nature of past darkness as is Jim to past twilight) tells us: "His very existence was improbable, inexplicable, and altogether bewildering";[11] so Marlow found that "at that moment it was difficult to believe in Jim's existence", the surface trappings of "externals", his mere geographical journey from a "country parsonage"; but his "imperishable reality", the somebody or something deeper, "came to me" Marlow exclaims,

> with a convincing, with an irresistible force! I saw it vividly, as though in our progress through the lofty silent rooms amongst . . . the sudden revelations of human figures stealing with flickering flames within un- fathomable and pellucid depths, we had approached nearer to absolute Truth, which, like Beauty itself, floats elusive, obscure, half submerged, in the silent still waters of mystery.

A mystical vision certainly, irrational formless shapes in a dream undisciplined by harsh reason, but Conrad means more than this; in Darwin's deep cave-like recesses, the isolated stations inhabited by outcast Europeans, who for one reason or another cannot return to the open country of their home, the lost thought-processes of the past, by a series of Darwinian gradations, begin to reappear. The confusion of subjective desires with objective nature is a habit of mind which Darwin, Lubbock, Tylor and Frazer all declared to be a primitive characteristic, and such a desire includes the longing for unchanging, immortal absolutes such as Truth and Beauty, which the new objective science purported to place firmly in the process of evolution with ignoble but ancient pedigrees, whether of simple invention or witchcraft, myth and tribal ritual, or of sexual selection; which is why, in Conrad's vertical metaphor, such absolutes should float half submerged in the deep, deep sea of Stein's dreams. And it is a suitable place for Marlow to see Jim's brutish imperishable reality. Stein, like Jim, cannot go home; and Stein, like Jim, appears to Marlow as a man following a linear course: "I saw only the reality of his destiny, which he had known how to follow with unfaltering footsteps, that life . . . rich in generous enthusiasms . . . in all the exalted elements of romance." Whether or not Jim is romantic, Marlow has no doubt that the dreamer Stein is: "no one could be more romantic than himself." It is fitting in both the fictional and the Darwinian sense that the betrayed woman Jewel who had once relied upon her surrounding nature to keep her Jim—the "land, the people, the forests were her accomplices, guarding him with vigilant accord, with an air of seclusion, of mystery, of invincible possession"—should seek Stein's artifical, Darwinian and cave-like "anomalous"[12] mirroring of such a nature. There is then no doubt of the meaning of Stein's rooms which "you enter . . . as you would a scrubbed cave underground". The "white figure" of Jim's Jewel is transformed in a kind of psychic thermodynamical death, "shaped in snow; the pendant crystals of a great chandelier clicked above her like glittering icicles . . . I was chilled as if these vast apartments had been the cold abode of despair."

Stein cannot go home; he lives in his cave-like recess far from the society of his kind, ostensibly because, as Marlow tells us, "when a youth of twenty two" he had "taken an active part in the revolutionary movement of 1848. Heavily compromised, he managed to make his escape, and at first found refuge with a poor republican watchmaker in Trieste. From there he made his way to Tripoli with a stock of cheap watches to hawk about." Now these two clusters of ideas are most interestingly interrelated in Conrad's work. Stein the revolutionary is one with Stein the seller of cheap watches and Stein the collector of butterflies; different steps along the same path guided by the same dream; an illusion, which, "charming and deceptive", as Marlow describes it, throws its "dimness", the "impalpable poesy" of its cave-like twilight "over pitfalls—over graves". Stein's dream is a false idea of time and nature, a projection of the superficial time of watches upon the immeasurable past of man's evolved inner nature; and his sacrifices and enthusiasms are merely the reverse image of a Brierly's dream; Stein deludes himself that one small change in the present structure of society, a revolution, one adjustment to a merely faulty mechanical balance, is all that is needed to produce the static Absolute Beauty and Truth and Harmony. Brierly deludes himself, as he consults his gold chronometer, that this man-made time and social absolute really exist in nature; both men disregard the vast threatening legacy of Darwinian time past, and the slow, painfully unglamorous struggle necessary to preserve some small hope of a tolerable future in such a nature.

But Stein the dreamer of revolutionary utopias still possesses one strong biological protection which both Brierly and Jim have lost: the "physical courage that could have been called reckless had it not been like a natural function of the body . . . completely unconscious of itself". It is this instinctive characteristic which enables Stein to survive his awakening from the dream. He tells Marlow: "it is not good for you to find you cannot make your dream come true, for the reason that you not strong enough are, or not clever enough"; and, although Stein's advice to lesser men is to remain within their dream, he at least knows that it is "the destructive element".

And where is Stein's dream now—what acquired characteristics, habits of thought, have survived the ardent youth and (that nightmare year for Conrad), 1848, the year of revolutions?[13] Stein the revolutionary, the hawker of instruments to measure the pitifully small, reassuringly ordered and absolute units of superficial, social time, has become a famous collector and describer of "bushels of dead insects", which in Darwinian time and nature is an activity, a path across the plain, as misguided by siren illusions as preaching revolution or selling watches. The loving, "charming and deceptive" light which Stein brings to his blackened slips of paper is a pardonable indulgence; the intense pleasure of classification, the half-fanatical catalogue, is a path trodden in the euphoric dream that such naming and ordering reflect an equally real permanence, order and balance in a Scale of Nature, a self-projected world of small measurements in a time-scale of watches and a nature of Newtonian or Natural Theological equilibrium where only man is throwing the Providential beam out of true and where, by analogy, only one small revolutionary adjustment is needed to make man conform and all nature perfect.

In the same way Conrad describes Marlow, half-amused but half-envious (just as he is more seriously confused by Jim, after all) and contemplating Stein's present pursuit: "the intense, almost passionate, absorption with which he looked at a butterfly, as though on the bronze sheen of those frail wings . . . he could see other things, an image of something as perishable and defying destruction as these delicate and lifeless tissues displaying a splendour unmarred by death." Here is Stein's dream, his "charming and deceptive" illusion that an evolving, time-enmired society of men could ever produce an unchanging institution, a government by perfection as "unmarred" by the diverse, unconscious, messy demands of organic life as the inorganic, deceptively "living" harmonious order measured out by the hand of a watch. Such a false hope is primitive because it is so obviously not a result of the rational contemplation of time and nature. A modern expression of ideas of God-in-Nature, a mystical refusal to be objective, to dream of absolute truths and the higher rules of Justice, whilst surrounding nature is a savage chaos of atrocities, is to dream much as the Harlequin from primitive Russia dreams of Kurtz and his political light at the heart of darkness, whilst Kurtz himself continues to eat his subjects.

Stein's dream of perfection in nature now fastens upon butterflies rather than men; many-coloured Harlequin hopes in his butterflies which, he has convinced himself, are themselves outside the time and nature, the random change and constant transformation of the new biology, and are, instead, secure in the balanced stability of a Newtonian universe and a law-giving God of Nature: "'Marvellous!' he repeated, looking up at me" Marlow remembers,

> 'look! The Beauty—but that is nothing—look at the accuracy, the harmony. And so fragile! And so strong! And so exact! This is Nature— the balance of colossal forces. Every star is so—and every blade of grass stands *so*—and the mighty Kosmos in perfect equilibrium produces— this. This wonder; this masterpiece of Nature—the great artist.'

This is hardly the speech of a contemporary scientist, as Marlow himself observes: "Never heard an entomologist go on like this"; such a romantic celebration of nature belongs to an earlier time, to 1848, to mystical belief in the absolute Truth and Beauty which Marlow imagines in Stein's cavernous rooms, or even to Natural Theology and God the master-artist, creator of unchanging perfection in the wings of each of his immutable species of butterfly. It is no accident that Stein should eventually catch the most beautiful and the rarest of all his butterflies—"This species fly high with a strong flight"— in the midst of a civil war in which Stein has sided with the rebellious party of the younger son in a primitive contest for political power, a tribal mimicry of the year 1848 in Europe, and that he should find it surrounded by the bodies of men he has shot ("One was curled up like a dog"); or that he should first see his butterfly, the species of his dreams, indirectly, in its shadow upon a dead man's face, and "At last I saw him sitting on a small heap of dirt ten feet away". Amongst the carnage, and in a country of barbaric social anarchy, in pursuit of his dream, as Stein tells Marlow:

> "On that day I had nothing to desire; I had greatly annoyed my principal enemy; I was young, strong; I had friendship; I had the love" (he said "lof") "of woman, a child I had, to make my heart very full . . . Friend, wife, child," he said, slowly . . . He sighed and turned again to the glass case. The frail and beautiful wings quivered faintly, as if his breath had for an instant called back to life that gorgeous object of his dreams.

Conrad writes of Stein with a deep energy of conviction and excitement, an energy with sources that are closely personal as well as sustained and meticulously directed by an intellectual passion. Stein's character is indeed legion, and he is strong, multiple, "rounded" enough to serve as a temporary trap for several of Conrad's accessible demons, bearing them (after all) within his dream and so into the "destructive element" of the deep, deep sea. Held in the cavernous twilight of his rooms, Stein encapsulates and enshrouds the idealistic dreams of both the revolutionary Apollo and the optimistically conservative Thaddeus, defines their place in the dim evolutionary past of Europe, and places them, in the geography of Conrad's emotions, in a far distant country, in Germany; and the irritant suggestive power of their ideas is controlled and enclosed with outward details of the life of Alfred Russel Wallace and his assistant, drawn from *The Malay Archipelago*.

Like Conrad's father, in his revolutionary past, the romantic dream, and in his "loss", the indirect betrayal of his wife the "princess" and their child, a loss later vastly enlarged almost to emotional annihilation in Patusan, Stein also carries the taint of other small but not trivial images: the Apollo-like air of eternal youth, the "long flaxen locks", the lofty rooms, the lofty hopes, the romantic mysticism in which Apollo Korzeniowski died. And his words in the "vast dimness" encircle and hold the beliefs of the conservative Thaddeus Bobrowski too; small but highly emotive images of Conrad's experience with this different dream play in the shadows. Stein's certain knowledge in the shadows of "how to be", which falters in the light, is exactly the same: "'And yet it is true . . . In the destructive element immerse . . . To follow the dream . . . *usque ad finem*'" — or, as Thaddeus exhorts Conrad: "I have gone through a lot, I have suffered over my own fate and the fate of my family and my Nation, and perhaps just because of these sufferings and disappointments I have developed in myself this calm outlook on the problem of life, whose motto, I venture to say, was, is, and will be 'usque ad finem'."[14] Bearing this knowledge, in the moment of looming up in the light, Marlow is startled to see that Stein's "extended hand aimed at my breast like a pistol; his deep-set eyes seemed to pierce through me". The High Victorian (or conservative Polish landowner's) elevation of Duty, "Honour" en masse, into a creed, the celebration of such an empty civic deity — where does it lead the dreamer? In sharp contrast to its celebration in George Eliot, for instance (where its

vacuous euphoric ideal beckons her heroines from their so very wilful
egoism to the same emotion in altruistic disguise, keeping the whole
limited and comfortingly familiar) Brierly's exemplary social conduct
beckons him in the dream towards Duty to the Last too; awakened
from the siren dream there is no egotistically sublime social sainthood;
only suicide, desertion. Likewise, the belief in duty and social order
as an abstract entity (which Thaddeus believed could be preserved
even within the barbaric past of Russian rule)[15] leads upon its
"betrayal" (or upon awakening) for the young Conrad, to desertion;
and perhaps, in his own life, to attempted suicide in the face of
gambling losses in Marseilles; to a shot in the breast with a pistol
which pierced, like Stein's hand and his eye proclaiming a false
belief, "durch and durch near the heart" as Thaddeus Bobrowski
wrote in a letter to Buszczyński.[16] In Conrad's world of Darwinian
time and the evolution of instinctive moral behaviour, he who
must proclaim his intellectual belief in Duty—simple instinctive
social reactions—is already lost. Conrad's quietly indomitable
captains, like Allistoun, do not need to render their instinctive social
sense into Latin exhortations and idealistic dreams or to congratulate themselves upon their superior righteousness in the service of
Duty.

Around these close and painful irritant ideas Conrad oyster-pearls
the protection of the physical appearance of an Englishman whom he
undoubtedly admired (and who went "home" to touch his reward
with clean hands), Alfred Russel Wallace. Yet Stein is in itself a
strange name for a man of Conrad's highly sensitive political knowledge to pick for a German "revolutionary" living in exile unless it
carries an intentional and sinister echo of the German nationalist,
Baron von Stein, who was responsible for the final abolition of
serfdom in Prussia, the creation of peasant landowners, the removal
of barriers to free trade, the promotion of municipal government; in
short, he began to push his country perilously far along the road to
that "democracy" which Conrad described to Spiridion Kliszewski
as the dream of "every disreputable ragamuffin in Europe" who now
"feels that the day of universal brotherhood, despoliation and disorder
is coming apace, and nurses daydreams of well-plenished pockets
amongst the ruins of all that is respectable, venerable and holy".[17]
And worse (although it is both nicely true to Conrad's predictions
of the results and to his convictions as to the real nature of such
"charming and deceptive" dreams) the Baron Heinrich Friedrich

Carl von Stein was an equally zealous maker of myths and dreams about a German Destiny; and he committed three other lesser but still grave Conradian crimes (one, admittedly, posthumous): he wrote a *Political Testament*, he chose to go and live in exile in Russia, and a lavish three-volume biography by J. R. Seeley was published in England in 1878.[18]

7

Heart of twilight

Upon the dubious directions from Stein's cavernous twilight rooms Jim journeys further East towards that nature which Stein himself saw "in the original dusk of its being". The man who captains Jim's last voyage at sea is, appropriately, a "little half-caste", a member of that class, "Borderland dwellers"[1] between races, marked out as particularly likely to be degenerate by contemporary biology. Conrad allows himself temporary relief from the intellectual strain of forcing an idea into the closest possible mimicry the language can be made to perform, a task which for Conrad was about as technically (and psychologically) formidable as it was possible to be. But Conrad, unlike Proust, for instance, enjoying himself with the malapropisms of the hotel manager at Balbec, or all the linguistic catherine wheels of wit spinning down the history of imagination in English literature from Joyce to Shakespeare, poises his character, not between social strata, but between evolutionary strata.

Besides the sinister undertow of actual truth in the half-caste's unconscious "mistakes"—he will carry Jim to the mouth of the river but would "never ascend" into Patusan (from that external nature, indeed, one can only descend into Patusan) where the Rajah, not even dog-like, is a "laughable hyaena" and his country is like a "cage of beasts made ravenous by long impenitence", men whose primitive instincts are unchecked by Darwin's "remorse"[2]—besides the suggestion of the true nature that awaits Jim and which for Marlow "had given more reality to the miserable dangers of his path than Stein's careful statements", it is biologically fitting that a half-caste, proud of his mastery of the language of an advanced society, should take the degenerate Jim to degenerate Patusan and should himself, in reality, speak a degenerate English which "seemed to be derived from a dictionary compiled by a lunatic"[3]—an atavistic lunatic. Darwin concludes a detailed discussion upon the origins of language in *The Descent of Man* (a discussion which Conrad himself elaborates upon in *Nostromo*) by remarking that: "A great stride in the development of the intellect will have followed, as soon as the half-art and half-instinct of language came into use; for the continued use of language will have reacted on the brain and produced an inherited effect; and this again will have reacted on the improvement of language."[4] Jim journeys back across the lost time of that "great stride in the development of the intellect".

On his way, he passes, we later learn, another biologically interesting European, another half-caste, degenerate, "a third-class deputy assistant resident" on the coast; "a big, fat, greasy, blinking fellow of mixed descent, with turned-out, shiny lips", who, just like the captain of the *Patna*, "perspired, puffed, moaning feebly . . . scratching himself with such horrible composure". Just as the degenerate captain of the *Patna* had reminded Marlow of "a trained baby elephant walking on hind legs" — an unnatural, against-nature grotesque, a bizarre degenerate in the full scientific orthodoxy of the time, "extravagantly gorgeous too — got up in a soiled sleeping suit, bright green and deep orange vertical stripes" — so Jim eventually makes his way to the protection of the captain of the *Patna*'s natural counterpart (at that particular stage of the captain's degeneration, which accelerates at a perhaps faster than orthodox veolocity). Jim will eventually find his own level in the society of the ruler Doramin, who "with his imposing bulk and haughty little eyes darting sagacious, inquisitive glances . . . reminded one irresistibly of a cunning old elephant".

But at first Jim descends, or rather jumps, to a level which, in its own different degeneracy, is lower than his own. Jim is now biologically weak beside those ancestors of his own kind, those real adventurer-seamen whose romanticised exploits had served to lend shadowy substance to his egoistic dreams; men who in "the seventeenth century" had sailed to the East "pushing out into the unknown in obedience to an inward voice, to an impulse beating in the blood": a biological impulse, a primitive "inward voice" perhaps, but not a disguised degeneration, not an escape from social standards of civilised conduct beyond the power of their will to observe, and not an impulse which would prevent their return to their northern home. Their desire, their motive, was certainly bizarre, but not a secret illusion; it was a biological need, but also a simple shared social hunger for something to make their food palatable—spices, "because the passion for pepper seemed to burn like a flame of love in the breast of Dutch and English adventurers about the time of James the First". The "bizarre obstinacy of that desire made them defy death in a thousand shapes . . . It seems impossible to believe that mere greed could hold men to such a steadfastness of purpose, to such a blind persistence in endeavour and sacrifice." It is not mere greed, but the instinctive "impulse beating in the blood", a hardened unconscious need to push out "into the unknown", a desire for exploration and for wealth which Conrad, and Darwin, imagined as a particularly English characteristic—as Darwin writes, the "remarkable success of the English as colonists . . . has been ascribed to their 'daring and persistent energy' . . . but who can say how the English gained their energy?".[5] Conrad specifically links this daring energy, this "passion . . . like a flame of love" with another characteristic which we already know that he and Darwin considered to be a biological possession of the English; the habit of objective observation, the prosaic empiricism of the English explorer, so unlike the mystical romantic pilgrimage of the Russian Harlequin: "They were wonderful; and it must be owned they were ready for the wonderful. They recorded it complacently in their sufferings, in the aspect of the seas, in the customs of strange nations, in the glory of splendid rulers." And later, lest we are tempted to imagine Marlow's Jim as a "less tried" successor to such men (in any sense other than his "less tried" and so weakened descent) Conrad introduces the last and in some ways most interesting and complex of the major figures in his chorus, Gentleman Brown, a surviving vestige from such desperate and "heroic" times rather than a degenerate who has descended far below them.

But Jim's ancestral line is not the only one in Patusan which has looped grotesquely backward in time since the seventeenth century. Those seamen-adventurers had been "impressed by the magnificence and wisdom of the Sultan"; but now there is only "an imbecile youth with two thumbs on his left hand", who takes his seat amongst his councillors, a seat of government above a "rotten bamboo floor" through which can be seen "twelve or fifteen feet below the heaps of refuse and garbage of all kinds lying under the house". The Rajah Allang's ideas of trade are likewise no longer likely to ensure the evolutionary progress of the society he rules— "his idea of trading was indistinguishable from the commonest forms of robbery" and his "cruelty and rapacity had no other bounds than his cowardice".

It is to this level of social anarchy, "at the mercy of the first casual ragamuffin with a chopper" that Jim first descends, in a "tumble-down shed" amongst the "effluvia of filth and rotten matter". While concentrating upon an equally decayed version of a Brierly's gold chronometer, a reminder of his own superficial social time, "a nickel clock", he instinctively decides to escape. "He dropped the thing—he says—'like a hot potato', and walked out hastily, without the slightest idea of what he would, or indeed, could do." He jumps the stockade, attempts to jump the creek, and falls instead into the primaeval mud itself: "He reached and grabbed desperately with his hands, and only succeeded in gathering a horrible cold shiny heap of slime against his breast—up to his very chin. It seemed to him he was burying himself alive, and then he struck out madly, scattering the mud with his fists. It fell on his head, on his face, over his eyes, into his mouth."

Jim's disgust is as instinctive (and, the cause being both consciously and unconsciously immediate, a great deal more obvious) as is his revulsion before the thought of returning home. " 'I remember how sick I felt wriggling in that slime', he tells Marlow, 'I mean really sick—as if I had bitten something rotten' ". And Conrad writes with a pre-Freudian, Lamarckian conviction, of the terrible exertion of will needed to struggle upwards from one stratum of the social evolutionary past to another: "He made efforts, tremendous sobbing, gasping efforts, efforts that seemed to burst his eyeballs in their sockets and make him blind . . . culminating into one mighty supreme effort in the darkness to crack the earth asunder, to throw it off his limbs—and he felt himself creeping feebly up the bank." Jim struggles upward to join a more advanced society; from one tribe of primaeval men to another, better organised for the future dominance Darwin predicts when "two tribes of primaeval man, living in the same country" come into

> competition, if (other circumstances being equal) the one tribe included a great number of courageous, sympathetic and faithful members, who were always ready to warn each other of danger, to aid and defend each other, this tribe would succeed better and conquer the other. Let it be borne in mind how all-important in the never-ceasing wars of savages, fidelity and courage must be. The advantage which disciplined soldiers have over undisciplined hordes follows chiefly from the confidence which each man feels in his comrades.[6]

Or, as Conrad writes of the "organised power of the Celebes men": "men of that race are intelligent, enterprising, revengeful, but with a more frank courage than the other Malays, and restless under oppression".

And Jim, with this race, will soon enjoy the "moral effect of his victory in war" when "his word decided everything". It is a victory, too, over a Kurtz-like figure who, as Marlow tells us, is a degenerate "wandering stranger, an Arab half-breed", with a Kurtzian mystical vision, "who, I believe, on purely religious grounds, had incited the tribes in the interior (the bush-folk, as Jim himself called them) to rise"; and having "devastated the open country" he leaves the Kurtz-like result of his dream behind him where "whole villages deserted, rotted on their blackened posts", in a reversion to a nature-before-man, "with a curious effect of natural decay as if they had been a form of vegetation stricken by blight at its very root".

Jim bands the Celebes-men together into a powerful social unit, an organised tribe as Darwin and Huxley imagined individual and competing societies. Marlow remembers Jim asserting that " 'They were all afraid . . . each man afraid for himself' ", but after their organised attack and victory, after their struggle to free themselves from "imbecile jealousies" and "senseless mistrusts", the Celebes men, more faithful and courageous than their neighbours and so the possessors of a more advanced moral sense, become "the favoured race in the struggle for life" in Patusan.

But Jim does not achieve such Darwinian success, the elevation of a whole society from one stage to another in the evolution of morals, entirely by himself. Evolution by natural selection requires chance variations within the race or the species and, just as Razumov, the man of reason, is such a potentially beneficial but actually premature variation in the barbaric Russia of *Under Western Eyes*, so, more fortunate in his time and place in nature, is "Dain Waris, the distinguished youth". In an interesting aside which details those qualities which Conrad thought to be the most desirable goals of moral evolution, Marlow tells us that

> Of Dain Waris, his own people said with pride that he knew how to fight like a white man. This was true; he had that sort of courage—the courage in the open, I may say—but he had also a European mind. You meet them sometimes like that, and are surprised to discover unexpectedly a familiar turn of thought, as unobscured vision, a tenacity of purpose, a touch of altruism.

Jim has already lost that "courage in the open" and Stein that "unobscured vision". Dain Waris is no dreamer, but a man of practical reason, of "silent disposition" with "a firm glance, an ironic smile", and a naturally civilised "courteous deliberation of manner" which is no Alvan Harvey-like veneer over the Darwinian degenerative decay within, but "seemed to hint at great reserves of intelligence and power".

Marlow's remarks further foreshadow the conception of *Under Western Eyes*, and Razumov's role as a biological glass through which the advanced Western races may peer down into the dark past of a Dostoyevskian Russia which is otherwise incomprehensible. "Such beings open to the Western eye, so often concerned with mere surfaces," as Marlow says of Dain Waris, "the hidden possibilities of races and lands over which hangs the mystery of unrecorded ages." And Dain has risen, upon his own ascent into his own potential racial future, to an evolutionary level which corresponds to the time and place in nature which Jim has reached upon his own descent into his own racial past. Dain, Marlow observes, "not only trusted Jim, he understood him, I firmly believe". True friendship involves a Darwinian marriage of minds attuned to the same evolutionary time, if it is not to be a façade of "mere surfaces", and, as Marlow tells us: "I seemed to behold the very origin of friendship." But the bonds of friendship are now more than a figure of speech; precise biological bonds of conscious and unconscious response to the inner Darwinian nurture and the outer nature, which includes the unseen influence of other minds, they are more than a little sinister: "If Jim took the lead, the other had captivated his leader. In fact, Jim the leader was a captive in every sense. The land, the people, the friendship, the love, were like the jealous guardians of his body. Every day added a link to the fetters of that strange freedom."

And what of the coming of Gentleman Brown to Patusan, the rumoured "son of a baronet", who is perhaps an exiled, biological vestige of characteristics once dominant in the English race and now tolerated no longer within the home nature and society? Perhaps Gentleman Brown really belongs amongst those other "knights all"[7] in Conrad, those inspired robber-barons who sailed from the Thames estuary upon their piratical aristocratic adventuring and whose conquests Conrad so ambiguously celebrates at the beginning of *Heart of Darkness*.

Dain Waris, biologically whole amongst the people and nature of his own race, would be more than a match for such an adversary, in a simple Darwinian battle depending upon warrior-loyalty and fighting skills. But Jim, Tuan Jim, the counterfeit aristocrat bearing the plague spot of his degeneration, is no longer upon the evolutionary heights of "unobscured vision" and "firm glance" possessed by those quiet and austere captains of his unreachable homeland; captains who have driven the Gentleman Browns in their society far into the very backwaters of forgotten biological niches like Patusan. Jim himself escapes Eastward even from second engineers of the *Patna*, from Donkins, let alone men of Gentleman Brown's altogether different biological kind.

In Europe, so Nordau prides himself, there is no longer a place for the "new" Nietzchian man who is, in "scientific" reality, no more than a primitive reversion. "All our labour," he writes, "is performed by men who esteem each other, mutually aid each other, and know how to curb their selfishness for the general good. There is no place among us for the lusting beast of prey . . ."[8] Gentleman Brown is partly such a man; partly he is the counterpart to Jim in Stein's mystically over-simple, wearily Christian pronouncement upon the poles of human nature—which is only true, and then superficially, for dreamers of false dreams like himself. Stein imagines that man "wants to be a saint, and he wants to be a devil—and every time he shuts his eyes he sees himself as a very fine fellow—so fine as he can never be . . . In a dream . . ."

In the evocative details of his character, Gentleman Brown reveals himself to be very much more interesting than his mirage of a literary ancestry suggests; and Conrad's own fascination reveals its intensity in his insistent prose, which, to a later and uncomprehending age of readers, whose intellectual inheritance has long discovered such fears to be scientifically groundless (and substituted others for them) itself appears overblown, rhetorical Conradese.

Gentleman Brown, like those "seventeenth century Dutch and English adventurers" who, in their turn, like the Romans in ancient and savage Britain, were "men enough to face the darkness";[9] and who set out to conquer "into the unknown in obedience to an inward voice, to an impulse beating in the blood", is driven by inherited, biological and unconscious forces acting within him as Darwin described; like his older Roman and English counterparts, he is no colonist, but akin to the Romans Marlow imagines invading prehistoric England, who possessed only "brute force" and "grabbed what they could get for the sake of what was to be got. It was just robbery with violence, aggravated murder on a great scale . . ."[10]

England, the homeland of democracy and liberty in Conrad's Polish eyes, has become so because of the evolved characteristics of its nature and people; and Conrad's Polish intelligence enjoys the complex Darwinian conclusion. The surviving robber-barons such as Gentleman Brown are still plagued by an implacable force of their inherited nature, an "unreasoning, cold-sweat, nerve-shaking, blood-to-water turning sort of horror at the bare possibility of being locked up". Flamboyantly piratical upon weaker races in the harsh open nature of the high seas, disdainfully avaricious, earnest in the idealism of a biological, racial idea, these men, ready to risk their lives for pepper in Patusan, or to return in "the *Golden Hind* . . . with her round flanks full of treasure, to be visited by the Queen's Highness",[11] possessed of a deep biological fear of confinement in small niches in nature, let alone of imprisonment, as a simple biological result, become the founders of a "free" society.

At one stage in the later biological development of the mental characteristics of the English (and we must remember that the imagined time-scale was short and imagined biological change still rapid in the 1890s) the race had briefly reverted, in Conrad's eyes, to the role of men like Gentleman Brown, in whom certain once essential but now outlawed unconscious characteristics were fiercely dominant. And, as Marlow listens to Gentleman Brown's extraordinary death-bed defiance (which is too consistently related to a complex cluster of ideas to be Dickensian horror merely distorted by Conrad's tougher sense of the grotesque) he realises that:

> There was in the broken, violent speech of that man, unveiling before me his thoughts with the very hand of Death upon his throat, an undisguised ruthlessness of purpose, a strange vengeful attitude towards his own past, and a blind belief in the righteousness of his will against all mankind, something of that feeling which could induce the leader of a horde of wandering cut-throats to call himself proudly the Scourge of God.

From the barons of Magna Carta to the primal horde of impossible Puritan dreamers, purifying, bringing the one true light to the land in the English Revolution, is hardly a progressive step in Conrad's idea of social evolution. One of the guiding principles of the man-of-reason, Razumov, we remember, is "Evolution not Revolution"[12] (a principle which, despite his artistic part-genesis in Wallace, has little meaning for Stein). The barons were at least plain-spoken, openly predatory, and egotistical only in Darwin's sense of being replete with all the animal appetites and the fighting loyalty of the savage in his tribe. The revolutionary Puritans have the dream of personal salvation and the enticing illusion of a righteousness whose possession licenses Kurtz-like gratifications of the instinctive lust for blood, destruction and power, and at the same time promises immortality as a reward for such gratification.

Gentleman Brown, like Conrad's Cromwell, the "Scourge of God" and "leader of a horde of wandering cut-throats", is possessed by a "natural senseless ferocity"; an unconscious, inherited, mental characteristic which is very different from Jim's equally deep, instinctive desire to avoid danger and to preserve his idea of self. Half hidden in the unconscious motivating darkness beneath Brown's shrewd political negotiations in Patusan, Marlow perceives that "what he had really described" and, most importantly, "almost in spite of himself", was to gratify his inborn racial characteristic instinct, "to play havoc with that jungle town which had defied him, to see it strewn over with corpses and enveloped in flames". He shares this desire with Cromwell, the dreamer with an egotistical mission, the King-killer, revolutionary—and Scourge of God. Relating how Brown murders Dain Waris and decimates his men, Marlow insists: "Notice that even in this awful outbreak there is a superiority as of a man who carries right—the abstract thing—within the envelope of his common desires. It was not a vulgar and treacherous massacre; it was a lesson, a retribution." For Marlow (and Conrad) it was "a demonstration of some obscure and awful attribute of our nature which, I am afraid, is not so very far under the surface as we like to think".

Marlow remarks of Brown telling his triumphantly cold-blooded story that there are "sights one never forgets", specifically about the moment when the primitive Brown, "bowed and hairy, glared at me sideways like some man-beast of folklore". Gentleman Brown's hairy body emphasises his survival from an earlier age. It at least places a part of Brown biologically close to that sinister revolutionary in *Nostromo* who, in the new Marxist dream this time, is in reality bent upon the gratification of his "various lusts", his primitive and destructive desires; reappearing, the latest inheritor of the ancestral branch which would somewhere include Cromwell and the Stein of

1848, he, too, dreams so single-mindedly of Utopian futures that he foregoes all chance to contribute to the struggle of evolutionary social progress in the present. But he belongs, unlike Gentleman Brown, to Nordau's degenerate "band who dare to speak of liberty and progress. They wish to be the future . . . We have, however, seen in all individual cases that it is not the future but the most forgotten, far-away past."[13] This very minor, but for Conrad most prophetically sinister of all the characters in *Nostromo*, the "pale photographer",[14] is engaged in an appropriate occupation: a maker of images which appear to stop time altogether, to offer the illusion of a static permanence, fixed against evolving societies and evolving nature; one unpleasant click and all will be frozen into unchanging perfection according to the latest revolutionary mechanism. The photographer is "small, frail, bloodthirsty"[15] like the dying Brown; and he, too, is "shock-headed, wildly hairy, like a hunchbacked monkey".[16]

But Brown is not corrupted by ideas, lays no emptily enticing claims upon the future, and belongs firmly in an English aristocratic-adventurer biological mould, a danger of another primitive, but perhaps less primitive, type. The "courageous . . . and faithful members" of Darwin's tribes "who were always ready . . . to aid and defend each other" are not expected to extend such tribal or racial loyalty to their neighbours, but to conquer and survive in mutual aid and united external ruthlessness. Brown, with no impossible ideals of the colonists, no self-flattering dream of benign and loyal white man's burdening for another race, is more consistent and whole than is Jim; and he is loyal, as he justly avows to his "men in the same boat". There is no taint about him of his own summary of Jim as "a hollow sham", no emptiness of the self-projected dream. And Brown could never be described as the youngest human being now in existence as Marlow says of Jim, or be the target of Cornelius's odd and reiterated abuse that Jim is "no more than a little child". Jim, in biological time, is now older than Brown; or, imagined in the metaphor of the ages of man, where the savage is but a child when compared either with civilised man or with the old and decayed races that have passed their maturity and withered away amongst their ancestral pyramids, temples and amphitheatres, Jim is now younger than Gentleman Brown. He is caught as a child of his race at the stage before it had fully developed towards adulthood, before it had finally separated from the unimaginably old line of its prehistoric forefathers, and begun to struggle towards civilised consciousness.

Marlow tells us that Jim "dominated . . . the old mankind" and "was like a figure set upon a pedestal, to represent in his persistent youth the power, and perhaps the virtues, of races that never grow old, that have emerged from the gloom".

Jim's child-like dream of godly power and romantic heroism, in a nature where his unconscious holds him enmeshed in a past time of lost river and jungle, amongst a lost child-like people whose myth and legend weaves itself around him, is no match against the younger (in evolutionary time) or older (in terms of the race growing to manhood) English objectivity; he cannot hope to compete against Brown's straightforward readiness to seize upon all possible ways and means when it comes to winning wealth in the struggle for life. But Brown also possesses a much more important, although inter-related, inherited characteristic.

In the time of his "greatest glory", with an "armed barque", and men in his crew who have at least deserted from ships which venture into the harshest of Conradian natures, "runaway whalers", Gentleman Brown "ran off . . . with the wife of a missionary". He is accustomed to victory in crudely literal processes of Darwinian natural selection with his victims: "some lonely white trader" he has robbed and then chivalrously invited to "fight a duel with shotguns on the beach". He is victorious, too, in the equally literal process of sexual selection. The prize is a "very young girl from Clapham way, who had married the mild, flat-footed fellow in a moment of enthusiasm"; the defeated is the missionary victim, degenerate, dreaming impossibly and egotistically that he will "Bag Gentleman Brown for Glory", as a "leery-eyed loafer" puts it. But Brown's conduct is exemplary in one sense in Conrad's world: his passionate fidelity is far from egotistical abandonment, betrayal, of his chosen mate; Brown's curious history in love is no digression, but highlights the terrible failure of Jim and, by implication, Stein. It is the first hint at an immense emotional power to come (too powerful, as yet, for Conrad to control artistically, and so dissipated in a desperately awkward authorial insistence that almost forces the reader to pass by upon the other side and to forget); it heralds that disproportionate investment of unworked personal rather than creative energy which unbalances the novel, but which also leads us to its source.

In the care of the missionary dreamer, the flat-footed visionary, his young neglected wife becomes fatally ill (much as did Conrad's own mother with a more powerful dreamer, also in exile) and even Brown, who has no self-conjured solace for his egoism in the future or in illusory Providence elsewhere, would perhaps have saved her with his undivided fidelity. His beloved, however, was "ill at the time he carried her off, and died on board his ship. It is said—as the most wonderful part of the tale—that over her body he gave way to an outburst of sombre and violent grief"—from which he and his exploits never quite recover. Marlow listens to Brown's boasting vehemence, his defiance before his last adversary, death, and he weighs Brown's "scorn for mankind at large", his instinctive ferocious desire for dominance, for "never-ceasing wars",[17] as Darwin described it, for destruction, against his memory of "the chuckling talk relating to the time . . . when, during a year or more, Gentleman Brown's ship was to be seen for many days on end, hovering off an islet befringed with green upon azure"; the islet where lived the girl from Clapham whom Brown so tenaciously and loyally wooed, and an islet of a nature whose "green upon azure" are the colours of the emerald. The emerald, Marlow tells us, "seems to appeal more to the Eastern imagination than any other precious stone". And the emerald is also rumoured, upon the coast, to be the plunder which Jim discovered for himself in Patusan, "an emerald of enormous size, and altogether priceless"; a rumour which, as Marlow implies, has the "deep hidden truthfulness of works of art". And so it does—the hidden truthfulness of an opportunity, an Eastern bride altogether priceless, but still veiled from Jim's eyes, which are peering only into the shadowy exaltations of his dream.

"Jim called her", Marlow tells us, "by a word that means precious, in the sense of a precious gem—Jewel." But, unlike Brown (and unlike Conrad) Jim remembers vaguely "having been deserted in the fullness of possession", not "by someone", a mistress or a mother, but "by something": his own idea of himself in his secret dreams, a courageous hero, honoured throughout his homeland, like the romantic seamen adventurers in popular literature. This is the "something", a hollow sham, not the real living promise of a less egotistical achievement and happiness, which for Jim is "more precious than life"; whilst the woman, the someone he calls by a word which means precious, will later be brutally betrayed and abandoned. Jewel would have had no cause to be so deeply and intuitively distrustful of the promises of Gentleman Brown.

Brown is a bloodthirsty cut-throat, a piratical English savage, but he is also a courageous leader loyal to his small tribe of warriors, and he is tenaciously faithful in love to his potential mate; these are no mean qualities in Darwin's stages of moral evolution within the race; they are both essential to direct dominance in the natural selection of races themselves and also powerful factors in the process of sexual selection: the one force in nature strong enough (in Conrad as in Hardy) temporarily to banish the empty vastness of the rest of the new biology and physics, its remorseless struggle and necessary suffering.

Brown, who disdains glory and honour and public opinion, who is not afraid of death or the onslaught of nature, marauding into the "protected station"[18] of Patusan, defeats Jim in a more complex duel of Darwinian natural selection, in which he demonstrates his biological, a-moral superiority, objectively perceiving Jim's weaknesses, undercutting Jim's pretensions and dreams and his illusion that he can be priest and king in a race not his own, by playing upon the real biological bond between them, their common racial inheritance. Jim is now unconsciously dominated by instincts which belong to a time in the social evolution of the English race far more ancient than the period from which Gentleman Brown is a vestigial survivor; he is defeated at every turn by Brown's "vein of subtle reference to their common blood . . . a sickening suggestion of common guilt, of secret knowledge that was like a bond of their minds and of their hearts". A more sophisticated Lamarckian spell cast upon Jim's unconscious than the simple animal yells to which he responds in jumping from the *Patna*, it is a daunting display of biological superiority on Brown's part, which belongs to the intricate nexus of biological ideas which lies behind the conclusion of *Lord Jim*. Jim's psychological defeat is nonetheless as uncontrollable, as instinctive an escape as his earlier desertion of that similar cargo of people upon the *Patna* who trusted him. And so, like the river flowing from the heart of darkness, "Henceforth events move fast without a check, flowing from the very hearts of men like a stream from a dark source"; because Jim's inherited biological destiny, his "fate, revolted, was forcing his hand".

"Man is the rival of other men; he delights in competition, and this leads to ambition which passes too easily into selfishness,"[19] Darwin writes in *The Descent of Man*; but there is a biological check upon this "selfishness", because when

> two men are put into competition . . . both possessed of every mental quality in equal perfection, save that one has higher energy, perseverance, and courage, the latter will generally become more eminent in every

pursuit, and will gain the ascendancy. He may be said to possess genius—for genius has been declared . . . to be patience; and patience in this sense, means unflinching, undaunted perseverance. But this view of genius is perhaps deficient; for without the higher powers of the imagination and reason, no eminent success can be gained in many subjects.[20]

This passage upon genius seems to have fascinated Conrad; he explores Darwin's crude remarks upon its origin and effects within society with an intricate thoroughness; his quiet captains certainly possess a kind of high Darwinian genius, a most unliterary and unromantic genius, energy, courage, and "unflinching, undaunted perseverance". They also possess "reason", and "imagination", in Darwin's sense, the ability to create an accurate, objective mental picture of some possible event or idea by projecting or re-forming past experience. MacWhirr in *Typhoon* is perhaps Conrad's idea of a Darwinian "genius" who is flawed by the lack of this "imagination"; Jim suffers the results of its overdevelopment and the corresponding decline of reason; Nostromo and Gould develop their own complex commentary upon Darwin's simple social mechanism.

Jim himself, when, in Darwin's words, he is "put into competition" with Gentleman Brown, a rival possessed of "higher energy, perseverance, and courage" is caught by the Darwinian mesh, naturally selected not for the "ascendancy" but for plucking, trapped by his male dream "ambition" which, Darwin admits, "passes too easily into selfishness". Conrad makes his own comment upon Darwin's optimism about the utilitarian social value of this check. Although, in Darwinian orthodoxy, Brown is the more "moral" of the two in his loyalty to his tribe and to his mate, his fighting courage and his "observation, reason, invention, or imagination", such a conception of the evolution of morals is in itself no cause for optimism, involving suffering, chaos and death at every step of the conqueror. And it is also, of course, nothing to do with Justice, but a consequence of "chance variations" upon which natural selection works or, as Marlow remarks of Jim's "fate": "There is a law, no doubt, and likewise a law regulates your luck in the throwing of dice."[21] It is not "Justice the servant of men", but inhuman time and nature, "accident, hazard, Fortune—the ally of patient Time—that holds an even and scrupulous balance". Tamb'Itam, denied his rightful protection by a Lord who is indeed, biologically, "not good enough", states the blind result of this law of chance variations, which are naturally selected in the struggle for life, more simply: "He would not fight! He would not fight!"

And here we are close to one deep but complex source of the genesis of the Patusan chapter of *Lord Jim*. Bearing this scene in mind, we must also remember that Cornelius is the agent of the German-born (and once revolutionary idealist) Stein; that he has been the unwilling husband of Jewel's mother (hardly a wise or even benign match on Stein's part), in an arrangement that Marlow leaves in darkness. Upon Marlow's first mentioning Patusan as a suitable "burial ground" for Jim, Stein, like the French lieutenant, almost embarks upon a story, or a confession, but draws back: "'And the woman is dead now,' he added incomprehensibly." Marlow remarks: "Of course I don't know that story; I can only guess that once before Patusan had been used as a grave for some sin, transgression or misfortune. It is impossible to suspect Stein." Marlow's gratuitous disclaimer is precisely of the kind to convey its opposite; the unnecessary and unexpected assertion that Stein is innocent when he had not been considered guilty is enough to associate him one way or another with the betrayal of "the woman" in Patusan. And, after all, Stein is about to be instrumental in the betrayal of her daughter, and, once again, is about to "use" Patusan to dispose of "some sin", sending, with the aid of the trusted talisman, a dangerous and deceptive new agent to Doramin—who, without his son, with a land in chaos, with "hell loose" as Jim imagines it, might well have reservations about Stein's romantic wisdom.

The German revolutionary Stein, courageous and half-awakened from his dream but of semi-philosophical, abstract and empty utterance, unwittingly unleashed chaos upon the country. His agent Cornelius is very much more primitive and local in his effect, though equally devastating, and so adapted to the ground, the primaeval mud into which his hut is rotting, that he is almost a part of it; he is as close in nature as *Homo sapiens* can be to that ground without actually evolving into a Morlock, or a worm; he is unbridled, raw emotion, tossed by the forces of the unconscious, a natural counterpart to Stein's lofty ideals, and his impossible generalisations upon the human condition. Cornelius, abject, the "Nazarene", who is forever "seen moving off deviously, his face over his shoulder, with either a mistrustful snarl or a woe-begone, piteous, mute aspect", is the natural counterpart of the mystical pilgrim son of the Archpriest, the Russian Harlequin with his siren song of disconnected nonsenses void of reason. And, likewise, the treacherous Cornelius, creeping near the ground, skulks through nature at the same level as that other Russian, the Dostoyevskian Underground man, which might explain his venomous victimisation by Conrad, and the fact that "no assumed expression could conceal this innate irremediable abjectness of his nature, any more than an arrangement of clothing can conceal some monstrous deformity of the body".

Jim attacks Sherif Ali on behalf of his adopted tribe, but is powerless when confronted by Brown; and, despite Marlow's warnings, he is inactive before the threat of the "shadowy Cornelius", who has usurped that place in Jim's consciousness once so amply filled by the bulk of the captain of the *Patna* who, just as Cornelius now, had once "seemed to be the hateful embodiment of all the annoyances and difficulties he had found in his path". To descend from the secret heights of his dream to concern himself with such a mud-creature, such an unrestrained unconsciousness, would be to contaminate the glorious egotistical exaltation of the dream; and Cornelius uncontrolled, like Jim's own unconscious left uncontrolled by his half-absent objective reason, eventually proves how deadly he can be.

Cornelius, the hysterical half-caste degenerate, the fit bearer of one code of Christian conduct — "blessed are the meek, for they shall inherit the earth" — inherits the earth with a grotesque proximity. He is given to throwing "handfuls of mud", that Patusan "primaeval . . . fecund earth" at his nominal wife and her daughter Jewel and, as Marlow helpfully adds, "there was plenty of mud around the house". He will cross a midday courtyard "bathed in intense light" by "creeping across . . . with an inexpressible effect of stealthiness, of dark and secret slinking. He reminded one of everything that is unsavoury." Cur-like, he is "often seen circling slowly amongst the sheds, as if following a scent".

Conrad expends much creative energy upon the unfortunate and unconvincing Cornelius, whose conduct, Marlow insists, "was marked by . . . abjectness . . . That was his characteristic; he was fundamentally and outwardly abject" and is seen "neither in the background nor in the foreground of the story; he is simply seen skulking on its outskirts, enigmatical and unclean". Cornelius is burdened with derogatory animal similes which almost push him bodily into the undergrowth; detestation is yahooed upon him by his creator; the fury he arouses is much greater than his character can support. The ferocious authorial emphasis generates its own phosphorescent enlightenment in the blackest stretches of Jim's journey to extinction: the historical Cornelius, the first centurion to become a Christian, would have been the first man with "the least drop of something rare and accursed" in his nature, of whom the Marlow of *Heart of Darkness* could not reminisce with racial admiration, as he does about those Romans who "first came here, nineteen hundred years ago", who were, unlike the abject "Nazarene", "men enough to face the darkness".[22]

As Marlow looks upon the landscape of Patusan one evening, a landscape which seems closer than ever to the shadows and visions of plains in crepuscular light in Stein's cavernous rooms; as the moon "threw its level rays afar as if from a cavern" and, in the "darkened moonlight", reason is dislocated, so that the "interlaced blossoms" upon Jewel's mother's grave "took on shapes foreign to one's memory and colours indefinable to the eye", he feels as "if the earth had been one grave", and his conscious faculties, dangerously confused, anarchically lead him near to that final and annihilating vision Conrad reserves for Decoud.

With a "sense of utter solitude" so complete that image, civilised memory, language, begin to fragment and leave a void for the unconscious to enter, Marlow feels that: "all I had lately seen, all I had heard, and the very human speech itself, seemed to have passed away out of existence . . . as though I had been the last of mankind". Marlow thinks this illusion to be but a vision "of remote unattainable truth, seen dimly" which, for Conrad, and for contemporary physicists, it was. A cold thermodynamical death awaits the earth, when, as Marlow feels, "all sound and all movements in the world" will indeed seem to "come to an end" in "a great peace" and the earth will indeed be "one grave". And his other "illusion" was likewise a truth for Conrad and for contemporary biologists: Patusan "was, indeed, one of the last, forgotten, unknown places of the earth"; Marlow feels that when he has "left it for ever" it will live only in his own memory until he, too, passes "into oblivion"; and so, after the murder of the one biological hope, Dain Waris, Patusan and its people may indeed regress to extinction in tribal wars and ungoverned degeneration. With these thoughts, in this time and place, and with this threatened reason, sanity and social order, in the barbarous twilight, it is fitting that Cornelius, skulking along the ground, should finally "capture" Marlow for the first time. "He bolted out, vermin-like, from the long grass growing in a depression of the ground . . . his house was rotting somewhere nearby . . ."

Conrad is also careful to document Jewel's immediate heredity for us; Jim takes his place in time and nature as the unconscious successor of two previous generations of white men with whom he shares his most damning Darwinian characteristic. Jewel's own father had been a white, "a high official"; and her mother, too, had been betrayed by an idealistic dreamer, just as Jewel tells Marlow of Jim's own promise: "'He swore to me he would never leave me . . . He swore to me!'" They all desert their trust, for, as Jim tells Marlow, such an oath of loyal conduct, like the conduct expected of officers at sea with crew and passengers to protect, is indeed a trust: "'You take a different view of your actions when you come to understand'" proclaims Jim (once of the *Patna* and now the untested guardian of another tradition), "'every day that your existence is necessary— you see, absolutely necessary—to another person . . . Well, it is a trust, too . . . I believe I am equal to it . . .'" But then, as Jewel continues: "'Other men have sworn the same thing . . . My father did'". And, still further back in the Lamarckian time of her inherited womanly experience, back in a third ancestral generation of romantic dreamers of impossible dreams and swearers of empty promises, there is the shadowy figure of the idealistic betrayer of her grandmother.

"Woman seems to differ from man in mental disposition" Darwin observes,

> chiefly in her greater tenderness and less selfishness . . . It is generally admitted that with woman the powers of intuition, of rapid perception, and perhaps of imitation, are more strongly marked than in man; but some, at least, of these faculties are characteristic of the lower races, and therefore of a past and lower state of civilisation.[23]

Jewel is certainly a woman bearing all these faculties which, commonplace though they are without their Darwinian explanation, are yet specifically emphasised by Conrad. Jewel's "tenderness hovered over" Jim "like a flutter of wings"; her "rapid perception" and her "powers of intuition" (Marlow is oddly insistent about the broken, quick turn of her speech and thought), together with her inherited acquired distrust of the fidelity of the outwardly impeccable but inwardly degenerate white man, enable her accurately to sense the "plague spot" within Jim. Conrad is careful, also, to describe her power of "imitation", both in its outward, visible action and in its deeper biological meaning. She had "learned a good bit of English from Jim, and she spoke it most amusingly, with his own clipping, boyish intonation" and, more profoundly, she "lived so completely in his contemplation that she had acquired something of his outward aspect, something that recalled him in her movements, in the way she stretched her arm, turned her head, directed her glances".

True to Darwin's faulty but authoritative logic, her mind belongs to the past because it is a woman's mind. And, like Gentleman Brown, Jewel is stronger, more courageous than Jim, protected against the ease of mind of those individuals within advanced Western society which leads to their ever faster degeneration. Her "less selfishness" is no dream of ambitious egotistical achievement disguised as love, no conscious talk of semi-mystical "trusts", like Jim's, to which as hero he will be equal; her love is not decoyed into the self by ideas, but is innate, part unconscious, emanating from her in Lamarckian influence, so that her "vigilant affection had an intensity that made it almost perceptible to the senses; it seemed actually to exist in the ambient matter of space, to envelop him like a peculiar fragrance, to dwell in the sunshine like a tremulous, subdued, and impassioned note". This is a deliberate expression of primitive, wordless love; unconscious, biological forces act at a level unknown to reason or to language and so, like much of Conrad's apparently most "obscure" and needlessly evasive prose, the inscrutable and inexpressible is approached with the greatest possible care, and its supposed place in nature, time and space indicated without surrender to the falsely comforting and absolute precision of the accepted but false formulae of past literary tradition.

Marlow insists that his memory is working its description not from "romantic" but from "sober impressions". His images are apt enough, drawn, firstly, from the sense of smell which, of all the senses, Darwin considered to be the most primitive (and almost vestigial in civilised man) and, secondly, from music, equally wordless and almost equally old in preconscious development. Those "sensations and ideas" which are "excited in us" by music (acting like Jewel's love), Darwin believed to originate as an emotive accompaniment to the process of sexual selection, and "appear from their vagueness, yet depth, like mental reversions to the emotions and thoughts of a long-past age".[24] In Jim, the most primitive and involuntary, unconscious expression of the emotions, which is not subject to the control of reason or deliberate wish—his "stubborn blushing"—is odd enough to be noted repeatedly as an unusual characteristic; but of Jewel Marlow simply observes admiringly that "her movements were free, assured, and she blushed a dusky red".

So whatever the possible Freudian explanations of Conrad's general artistic failure to create convincing women in his novels and his apparent awkwardness when attempting to describe the thought and emotion of men and women in love[25] there are certainly pre-Freudian intellectual reasons within his ideas of mind and nature which would make such awkwardness inevitable.

Women live in time past, creatures from a biological lost world, as far as men are concerned; they are inscrutable to his advanced objective reason but exert their powerful Darwinian attraction upon his lowest conscious faculties and his unconscious instincts. They are set apart upon a different evolutionary level in nature; traditional language will no longer serve to depict the interrelations of the sexes. And, indeed, for novelists with temperaments so different that one of the few characteristics they have in common is their awareness of contemporary biology and psychology, for Hardy, Conrad, Proust and D. H. Lawrence, who are all preoccupied, in their best work, with possible attitudes to adopt and with possible meanings to find for man's emotional and intellectual life amidst the new ideas about scientific time, space, sex, chance and nature, it is perhaps their attitude to sex and love which appears to be most alien or most oddly emphasised in comparison with the works of their precursors. There love and sex are considered and described with all the complexities and exhaustive intricacy which such a multitudinously various power demands, but always in relation to the structure of society, or to moral codes, and within the comfortingly close focus of the time spans of a lifetime or two, and the tiny space of social interactions or, (even more self-reflectingly localised) in the struggles of a timeless and space-less God and Devil (who had, wish-fulfillingly, escaped from nature altogether, and were yet firmly enough moulded in man's own image to guarantee his own later escape even as they flattered him with obsessive desires for his most significant soul).

Conrad's younger women, even in his greatest works, may be justly if roughly divided, first, into lofty idealist dreamers, who are not dangerous, unless they happen to be Russian, and, in any case, are to be humoured, because such is their natural, if retarded, place in a past evolutionary time. To try to communicate with the past which woman inhabits, from the potentially progressive present of man, is to try to bridge the unbridgeable gulf of time, which Jim, for instance, senses at the last between himself and Western man: a hopeless psychological task in Conrad's world. And, second, there are those more obvious servants of Schopenhauer's "will" of the species or Darwin's "instincts" who simply obey the implacable force driving their half-animal, feline or splendidly statuesque selves to compete in the contest of the sexual selection of the next generation.

Conrad's women idealist dreamers, revolutionaries and upholders of faiths or of pure beliefs in their chosen mates, are as primitive as his other, apparently less noble, female savages; their impossibly fine feelings and lofty aspirations, subjective illusions, belong to Spencer's and Darwin's conception of undeveloped imagination, not the disciplined, scientific process of thought conquering the self in an imaginative exercise of man's most recently evolved capacity to be objective about nature, but the simple surrender to savage superstition which fills nature with egotistical dreams and nightmares.[26] It is fitting from a scientific as well as a literary point of view that Kurtz and his Intended should be so well matched, so placed in time that the civilised Marlow senses just how abnormally close they are: the degenerate European man and the woman whose European environment has given her only a veneer of civilised mannerisms and language. Both live outside civilised time, the time of those "young" nations who have "emerged from the gloom", so that Marlow feels that the Intended of Mr. Kurtz "was one of those creatures that are not the playthings of Time . . . I saw her and him in the same instant of time . . . Do you understand? I saw them together—I heard them together . . . I asked myself what I was doing there, with a sensation of panic in my heart . . ."[27]

The Marlow of *Lord Jim* is himself exposed to the full force of Jewel's primitive, unconscious will and need, and to her "rapid perception", her instinctive "intuition" that Jim is indeed "not good enough", and will desert her; and Marlow is put to the test. His sudden vertiginous time travelling begins as he allows himself to look unguardedly into the very depths of the past down the vertical fall of Conrad's imagined descent into the time lost of the unconscious; a journey which almost disintegrates Marlow's own reason.

Confronted by Jewel's primitive intuition and her knowledge of sudden and savage betrayal, which is deep and voiceless enough to have been inherited in the acquired characteristics of the repeated emotional experience of her immediate female line of descent, Marlow looks into the "big sombre orbits of her eyes, where there seemed to be a faint stir, such as you may fancy you can detect when you plunge your gaze to the bottom of an immensely deep well. What is it that moves there? . . . Is it a blind monster or only a lost gleam from the universe?" We are in the time past of Darwin's blind monsters adapted to the cavernous twilight; to the lost gleams and misleading light of Stein's rooms, or to the spectral moonlight which haunts Marlow in Patusan and comes "as if from a cavern . . . this mournful eclipse-like light . . ." It is a "Freudian" image, perhaps, but certainly it is also pre-Freudian and created from the same Lamarckian-Darwinian intellectual sources as Freud himself used to create his own imagined nature and mind. The mind of man and woman contain within the conscious and unconscious, in descending strata of memory and instinct, the entire evolutionary past, but their two evolutionary pasts have long ago diverged: sexual selection, since the time and the nature when sex itself evolved, because of its advantages in producing a greater diversity of variations upon which natural selection works, has acted continuously to further differentiate the sexes.

"My mother had wept bitterly before she died" Jewel explains to Marlow, who, already forced to look into his own unconscious, and to half-visualise the dark shadows of Jim's primitive weakness in his unsteady attempt to reassure her, remembers that "an inconceivable calmness seemed to have risen from the ground around us, imperceptibly, like the still rise of a flood in the night, obliterating the familiar landmarks of emotions."

Marlow feels the inconceivable-by-reason, the dumb past before language, the calmness of instinctive life before moral struggle, the pre-social unconscious welling up within himself. Like the "rising . . . silent flood" in Alvan Hervey's mind after the shock of betrayal,[28] it forces its way into the open consciousness "obliterating the familiar landmarks of emotions". Marlow, for the first time in the novel, is alone without his conscious defences; and, like Brierly, whose conscious idea of himself was overwhelmed by the rising flood of Jim's evidence and Jim's contagious unconscious which refused to return "twenty feet underground and stay there", he is shocked by his own unconscious conviction, always expressed in the wordless terms of sudden darkness and desolation upon the landscape. There "came upon me", Marlow remembers, "as though I had felt myself losing my footing in the midst of waters, a sudden dread, the dread of the unknown depths". Jewel's deserted mother, tormented by the mud creature Cornelius, died forsaken in her hut, and "the passive, irremediable horror of the scene" which Marlow imagines, resurrects the emotional centre of *Lord Jim*, forces Marlow out of the dark, threatening, wordless, but, at least, encircling and claustrophobically protective biological past, and—for one far more terrible instant of revelation in Conrad's world—he is projected across the circular boundary of the local, biological insignificance of organic time and nature and mind into the empty inorganic cosmos of physics. "The scene had the power to drive me out of my conception of existence, out of that shelter each of us makes for himself to creep under in moments of danger, as a tortoise withdraws within its shell. For a moment I had a view of a world that seemed to wear a vast and dismal aspect of disorder . . . I seemed to have lost all my words in the chaos of dark thoughts I had contemplated for a second or two beyond the pale."

And is there, perhaps, as we might expect, a quiet Conradian man of unobtrusive self-possession despite his full knowledge of nature? Perhaps he is the "privileged man", whose Western eyes appear to see with an unobscured vision and the symbolic light of a reason which has enabled him and his kind to survive the harshest and most open of natures: "His rooms were in the highest flat of a lofty building, and his glance could travel afar beyond the clear panes of glass, as though he were looking out of the lantern of a lighthouse."

This man has survived the tests of his unconscious moral health and the whispers of the dark racial past from the nature within and without; and he has returned to touch his reward with clean hands, to live quietly knowledgeable of "how to be" in the home of his own kind (and in the immediate environment of rooms very different from Stein's "scrubbed cave underground"). Even his city surroundings reflect the struggle of his race with the nature of the high seas, a nature which has in turn produced the tough objectivity of Conrad's quiet captains in "England, where men and sea interpenetrate",[29] as the narrator of *Youth* remarks. The "slopes of the roofs glistened" outside the window of the "privileged man" and their "dark broken ridges succeeded each other without end like sombre, uncrested waves . . ."

151

Such a man's diagnosis of Jim's destiny will not be in terms of man-made moral codes conjured from the self-comforting dream figures within the old religions, or from romanticism, or from political idealism and its siren utopias; amongst the sombre waves, the "spires of churches, numerous, scattered haphazard, uprose like beacons on a maze of shoals without a channel . . . the booming of a big clock . . . rolled past in voluminous, austere bursts of sound, with a shrill vibrating cry at the core". He is able to face this implacable time which, like the surrounding roofs, Conrad has here projected out into a nature very different from the homely reassurance of the small measurements of civilised stabilities, of the society or the time of Brierly's chronometer. The booming of the big clock is transformed into another order of nature and a scale of time which is indeed voluminous and austere, inhuman, becoming a sound implacable, inscrutable and menacing in the vastating forces of its anarchic indifference; like "that prolonged deep vibration of the air, like the roll of an immense and remote drum beating",[30] those messenger sounds "as of innumerable drums beating far off", the "shrieks"[31] to be heard in the storm winds round the *Narcissus* and the *Nan-Shan*, or the "very loud cry, as of infinite desolation"[32] of the natives forced to face time, god-deprived, at the heart of darkness—the cry of humanity, crushed "at the core" inside the circles of outer nature. The "privileged man" is well aware that for him there are now "No more horizons as boundless as hope, no more twilights within the forests as solemn as temples, in the hot quest of the Ever-undiscovered Country over the hill . . ."

The wisdom which this Conradian seer possesses is certainly not composed of anything remotely resembling the Absolute Truth which floats so mystically in those "silent still waters of mystery" in Stein's shadowy rooms. It is the truth of contemporary science, a-moral, Darwinian truth. As Marlow writes in his letter to the privileged man, the only one to understand Jim's story, "I remember well you would not admit he had mastered his fate . . . You said . . . that 'giving your life up to them' (*them* meaning all of mankind with skins brown, yellow, or black in colour) 'was like selling your soul to a brute'." But this man's knowledge extends further than such a reversal of Kipling's early idealistic celebration of the toilful responsibility and moral necessity of the white man assuming his burden; with full Darwinian logic it includes the idea that such a burden is itself an evolved racial characteristic; and, in Conrad's Polish eyes, it is a characteristic with obviously profitable advantages for the English colonists in the struggle for life, or wealth. "You contended", continues Marlow,

> that "that kind of thing" was only endurable and enduring when based on a firm conviction in the truth of ideas racially our own, in whose name are established the order, the morality of an ethical progress. "We want its strength at our backs", you had said. "We want a belief in its necessity and its justice, to make a worthy and conscious sacrifice of our lives".

Or, as Wallace himself passed judgment in his last shadowy shaping of Lord Jim: "we are right when we are dealing with men of our own race, and of similar ideas and equal capacities with ourselves."[33] To be strong enough to survive the darkness, the belief must be racial, inherited, well rooted in the acquired characteristics of unconscious ancestral memory; but also a conscious conviction safeguarded by reason (without, however, the implication that there will ever be any external sanction for such beliefs, any suggestion of the old hierarchy of moral values applied to different racial ideas). The only Darwinian and Conradian crime is to regress along the past evolution of such belief, to lose it altogether: "Without it the sacrifice is only forgetfulness, the way of offering is no better than the way to perdition."

Marlow, himself half "captivated" by Jim as he is by Dain Waris, cannot be allowed to admit the truth of such a starkly relativistic, value-less judgment. He acknowledges that "You ought to know . . . you who have rushed into one or two places single-handed and come out cleverly, without singeing your wings". Marlow protests with a romantically overblown assertion, which yet, as is often Conrad's way, carries a literal (and usually sinister) worm of biological truth within: "The point . . . is that of all mankind Jim had no dealings but with himself, and the question is whether at the last he had not confessed to a faith mightier than the law of order and progress." In the easy, religious legacy, the popular romantic and exalted cliché—images of "all mankind" and the heroic solitary confessing to uplifting, unstated faith, mightier than inconvenient law, Marlow places an already-wilted wreath of splendid self-hood around Jim's death. But the biological truth wriggling within the language of such fine sentiment states, simply, that Jim indeed harbours the evolutionary history of all mankind (and even the worm) within himself; and if his "faith", his reversion back into that history, is indeed mightier than the "laws of order and progress", then the future for all mankind is desolate.

Jim's final "fate" or his "destiny" is a destination in past time, a journey's end to *Lord Jim* which reflects back upon the novel and out beyond its fictional frame, with an intensity in its harsh light of enquiry and unease, a doubt as to the reader's own emotional reaction, an "ambiguity", only in its own complex waiting and refusal to "enlighten" within the old tradition of literary values. Conventional literary-moral judgment upon Jim's suicide, giving its verdict according to a static mental balance which, in the interest of an intellectual neatness of calibration and that emotional satisfaction in a paucity of dimensions which was once rather more subtly provided in Christian concepts of Eternity, can never begin to understand the nature of such ambiguity. Like Stein's Absolute Truth and Absolute Beauty, such Absolute Moral Standards, in whatever form, are tacitly timeless and universal; but Jim's biological "destiny" was unavoidable, racial, local, and, above all, it took place in four dimensions in a nature whose power changes across geographical space, which also traverses different time; Jim's suicide, the extinction of an individual rendered unfit to survive in the "struggle for life" by the disadvantages of his accumulated inheritance, unconsciously relapsing into a niche which traps him in time lost, has nothing to do with absolutes. Such judgment of Jim, whether finally heroically "saved" or heroically "damned" (or mysteriously, ambiguously, mystically obscure between the two) ignores both his own time travelling and also *Lord Jim*'s place in intellectual time. The real "ambiguity", as Conrad was writing, seemed to lie massively before him in time-future, nightmared into being by his knowledge of the intellectual present. Jim's fate is indeed a cautionary "tale" for the rest of his countrymen who may even yet suffer with the contagion of hidden "plague spots" in their society, spread by the vigorous psychological carrier whose mechanism Novalis describes in the aphorism which Conrad takes as an epigram for *Lord Jim*: "It is certain any conviction gains infinitely the moment another soul will believe in it."

There is sinister meaning, too, at the biological heart of darkness, within Marlow's final remarks. Jim goes to his false opportunity and way from the "living woman" and that real trust, Marlow tells s, "in his exalted egoism", exactly as Kurtz (who is equally and inescapably held in a more distant past time in nature), crawls towards his mystical dream of immortal life in "his own exalted and incredible degradation".[34] And Jim, who now, through Western eyes, is as inscrutable as the nature at the heart of darkness whose "implacable force" breeds "over an inscrutable intention",[35] has himself become implacable, in his instinctive indifference to the needs, not just of Darwin's "strangers"[36] (about whom savages are not expected to be altruistic) but of his own "precious" mate; and he is "gone", Marlow tells us, "inscrutable at heart".

Notes

CHAPTER I

Biology and the politics of progress; physics and the politics of permanence

1. F.R. Leavis, *The Great Tradition*, London, 1948, p.180.
2. James Clerk Maxwell, "Molecules: A Lecture" (1873), reprinted in *Scientific Papers of James Clerk Maxwell*, ed. W.D. Niven, 2 vols., Cambridge, 1890, vol.II, pp.376–7.
3. Bernard C. Meyer, *Joseph Conrad: A Psychoanalytic Biography*, Princeton, 1967, p.32.
4. J.H. Retinger, *Conrad and his Contemporaries*, London, 1941, p.116.
5. Ibid., p.116.
6. For an excellent introduction to nineteenth-century Polish politics, see *Conrad's Polish Background: Letters to and from Polish Friends*, ed. Zdzisław Najder, London, 1964, pp.2–14.
7. Ibid., p.11.
8. *Joseph Conrad's Letters to R.B. Cunninghame Graham*, ed. C.T. Watts, Cambridge, 1969, p.50; letter dated Dec. 6th, 1897. *Joseph Conrad: Life and Letters*, ed. G. Jean-Aubry, 2 vols., London, 1927, vol.I, p.213.
9. *Letters*, ed. Edward Garnett, London, 1928, p.188; letter dated Dec. 22nd, 1902.
10. Ibid., p.265; letter dated Feb. 23rd, 1914.
11. Ibid., p.260; letter dated May 27th, 1912. G. Jean-Aubry, op. cit., vol.II, p.140.
12. C.T. Watts, op. cit., p.70; letter dated Jan. 31st, 1898 (there are slight textual variants in the less authoritative G. Jean-Aubry, op. cit., vol.I, p.225).
13. See Zdzisław Najder, op. cit., p.223, n.3.
14. See Eloise Knapp Hay, *The Political Novels of Joseph Conrad: a Critical Study*, Chicago, 1963, p.192, n.79.
15. *Letters of Joseph Conrad to Marguerite Poradowska, 1890–1920*, trans. from the French and ed. John A. Gee and Paul J. Sturm, London, 1940, p.42.
16. Ibid., p.36; letter dated Sept. 15th, 1891.
17. C.T. Watts, op. cit., pp.70–7; letter dated Jan. 31st, 1898. G. Jean-Aubry, op. cit., vol.I, pp.225–6.
18. J.H. Retinger, op. cit., p.105.
19. Ibid., p.104.
20. Ibid., p.105.
21. G. Jean-Aubry, op. cit., vol.II, p.65.
22. Ibid., vol.II, p.65.
23. C.T. Watts, op. cit., p.71; letter dated Jan. 31st, 1898. G. Jean-Aubry, op. cit., vol.I, p.225.
24. G. Jean-Aubry, op. cit., vol.I, pp.79–85.
25. Joseph Conrad, *Nostromo: a Tale of the Seaboard*, London, 1904, part I, chap.1.
26. C.T. Watts, op. cit., pp.10–11.
27. Ibid., p.56; letter dated Dec. 20th, 1897. G. Jean-Aubry, op. cit., vol.I, p.216.
28. Of his evasion of the honour: "What a foolish idea seems to prevail in Germany on the connection between Socialism and Evolution through Natural Selection". (Letter from Charles Darwin to Dr. Scherzer, quoted in *The Life and Letters of Charles Darwin, Including an Autobiographical Chapter*, ed. Francis Darwin, 3 vols., London, 1887; vol.III, p.237.) See also Sir Arthur Keith, *Darwin Revalued*, London, 1955, p.234, quoting Darwin's letter to Karl Marx: "Possibly I have been too strongly influenced by the thought of the concern it might cause some members of my family, if in any way I lent my support to direct attacks on religion."
29. C.T. Watts, op. cit., p.56; letter dated Dec. 20th, 1897. G. Jean-Aubry, op. cit., vol.I, p.216.
30. Quoted in Rupert Hart-Davis, *Hugh Walpole: a Biography*, London, 1952, p.168. Cf. Wells's uneasy sparring with Conrad's

massive intellectual presence in H.G. Wells, *Experiment in Autobiography*, 2 vols., London, 1934, vol.II, pp.615–19. And cf. also a characteristic Conradian drollery, dedicating *The Secret Agent*, of all books, to Wells.

31. C.T. Watts, op. cit., p.65; letter dated Jan. 14th, 1898. G. Jean-Aubry, op. cit., vol.I, p.222.

32. Ibid.

33. See also William Thomson's (Lord Kelvin) later papers: "The Age of the Sun's Heat", *Macmillan's Magazine*, 1862, vol.II, pp.388–93; his attacks upon Lyell and Darwin, "The Doctrine of Uniformity in Geology Briefly Refuted", *Royal Society Editions*, 1865, and especially his remarks to the British Association in 1861: "As for the future we may say with . . . certainty that inhabitants of the earth cannot continue to enjoy the light and heat essential to their life for many million years longer, unless new sources now unknown to us, are prepared in the great storehouse of creation."

34. "Henry James", *North American Review*, Jan. 1905; reprinted in Joseph Conrad, *Notes on Life and Letters*, London, 1921, pp.15–16.

35. C.T. Watts, op. cit., p.53; letter dated Dec. 4th, 1897. G. Jean-Aubry, op. cit., vol.I, p.215.

36. The luminiferous ether, through which Clerk Maxwell's electro-magnetic waves appeared to be transmitted, was perhaps the last omnipresent all-in-one *deus in* and *ex machina* to be widely contemplated both for its metaphysical comfort and its theoretical physical necessity; the Michelson-Morley experiment, designed to provide factual basis for ethereal speculation, projected a powerful light of empiricism into the empyrean atmosphere hoping to measure a displacement of reflection as the earth moved relative to the ether. The nothingness revealed nothing, however, and the negative result was the first bewildering signal of an end to the sensible, visual, literary-theological physics whereby the commonsensical concerns of man and his geometer God, the levers, pulleys, circles, triangles, perfect balances, absolute space and times, musical spheres and profit-and-loss thermodynamical steam engines, had once been obviously applicable, by the practical man, to a contained cosmos.

37. For a good recent account with excellent documentation see Ronald W. Clark, *Einstein: The Life and Times*, London, 1973, pp.105–12. For the details of the debate see "Einstein, Michelson and the 'crucial' Experiment," *ISIS*, vol. 60, part 2, no.202 (Summer 1969), pp.133–97.

38. "The Ascending Effort", *Daily Mail*, July 30th, 1910; reprinted in Joseph Conrad, *Notes on Life and Letters*, p.74.

39. Edward Garnett, op. cit., pp.136–7; letter dated Sept. 29th, 1898. In 1895 Röntgen wrote to Lord Kelvin describing the greenish glow on his tray of crystals and asked for help with his "devil's science, to see through objects"; Kelvin wrote at once to John McIntyre, Conrad's "scientific swell" (Ibid., p.136) and he was thus one of the very first scientists to grasp the medical implications of x-rays and to test Röntgen's results.

40. Ibid., p.31; letter dated May 24th, 1896.

41. See Jocelyn Baines, *Joseph Conrad: A Critical Biography*, London, 1959, pp.215–223; pp.238–40.

42. Zdzisław Najder, op. cit., pp.153–4; letter dated Oct. 28th/Nov. 9th, 1891.

43. See Bernard C. Meyer, op. cit., pp.36–39.

44. Zdzisław Najder, op. cit., p.153; letter dated Oct. 28th/Nov. 9th, 1891.

45. Ibid., p.154.

46. C.T. Watts, op. cit., p.65; letter dated Jan. 14th, 1898. G. Jean-Aubry, op. cit., vol.I, pp.222–3.

47. Edward Garnett, op. cit., p.153; letter dated Sept. 16th, 1899.

48. Joseph Conrad, *Nostromo*, part I, chap.1.

49. Edward Garnett, op. cit., p.152; letter dated Sept. 16th, 1899.

50. E.M. Forster, *Abinger Harvest*, London, 1936, p.135: "Is there not . . . a central obscurity, something noble, heroic, beautiful, inspiring half a dozen great books; but obscure, obscure? . . . These essays do suggest that he is misty in the middle as well as at the edges, that the

secret casket of his genius contains a vapour rather than a jewel . . ."

51. "Confidence", *Daily Mail*, June 30th, 1919; reprinted in Joseph Conrad, *Notes on Life and Letters*, p.208.

52. "Well Done", *Daily Chronicle*, Aug. 22nd–24th, 1918; reprinted in Joseph Conrad, *Notes on Life and Letters*, p.182.

53. "Memorandum On the Scheme for Fitting Out a Sailing Ship" (1926), reprinted in Joseph Conrad, *Last Essays*, p.79.

54. Joseph Conrad, "Lord Jim; a Tale", *Blackwood's Magazine*, Oct. 1899–Nov. 1900; *Lord Jim; a Tale*, Edinburgh, London, New York and Toronto, 1900, chap.24.

55. R.B. Cunninghame Graham, *Thirteen Stories*, London, 1900.

56. C.T. Watts, op. cit., p.101; letter dated Aug. 26th, 1898. G. Jean-Aubry, op. cit., vol.I, p.245.

57. Ibid., p.87; letter dated June 11th, 1898. Ibid., vol.I, p.239.

58. Bertrand Russell, "Mind and Matter," *Portraits from Memory*, London, 1956, p.135.

59. Paul Kirschner, *Conrad: The Psychologist as Artist*, Edinburgh, 1968, footnote p.247: "Borys Conrad has confirmed for me that Dostoyevsky was one of the authors his father read most assiduously." And Galsworthy remembered that Conrad once admitted Dostoyevsky to be "deep as the sea". (*Castles in Spain and Other Screeds*, London, 1927, p.90.)

60. H.R. Lenormand, "Note on a Sojourn of Conrad in Corsica", *La Nouvelle Revue Française*, Paris, *Nouvelle Série*, 135 (Dec. 1st, 1924); reprinted in *The Art of Joseph Conrad: a Critical Symposium*, ed. R.W. Stallmann, Michigan, 1960, p.7.

61. Ibid., p.5.

62. William Rothenstein, *Since Fifty, 1922–1938* (*Men and Memories, Recollections* vol.III), London, 1939, p.159; letter dated May 20th, 1910.

63. H.R. Lenormand, op. cit., p.7.

64. Ibid., p.7.

65. G. Jean-Aubry, op. cit., vol.I, p.301; letter dated Nov. 11th, 1901.

66. For a simple descriptive comparison see Alan M. Hollingsworth, "Freud, Conrad, and The Future of an Illusion", *Literature and Psychology*, 5 (Nov. 1955), pp.78–83.

67. Sigmund Freud, *The Future of an Illusion*, trans. W.D. Robson-Scott, London, 1928, p.27.

68. Ibid., p.27.

69. Joseph Conrad, "Books", *Speaker*, July 15th, 1905; *Living Age*, Aug. 19th, 1905; *Notes on Life and Letters*, London, Toronto and New York, 1926.

70. A.O. Lovejoy, *The Great Chain of Being*, London, 1942, p.17.

71. Alfred North Whitehead, *Science and the Modern World*, Cambridge, 1933, p.93.

CHAPTER 2

Joseph Conrad's cosmology: time, space, sex, chance and nature in Lord Jim

1. Karl Pearson, *The Chances of Death and Other Studies in Evolution*, 2 vols., London, 1897, vol.II, p.256. Karl Pearson was Professor of Applied Mathematics at University College, London, and, with Francis Galton, has a claim to be considered one of the founding fathers of medical statistics; more parochially, he was a friend of the Garnetts: see David Garnett, *The Golden Echo*, London, 1953, p.112.

2. Charles Darwin, *The Origin of Species*, London, 1859, chap.V (Variorum edition, Philadelphia, 1959, p.275 ff.); *The Descent of Man*, London, 1871, p.12 and ff., *inter alia*.

3. Charles Darwin, *The Variations in Animals and Plants under Domestication*, London, 1868. For an incisive critique of Darwin's theory of pangenesis, see C.D. Darlington, *Genetics and Man*, Oxford, 1959; for documented detail, Hans Stubbe, *History of Genetics from Prehistoric Times to the Rediscovery of Mendel's Laws*, trans. T.R. Waters (from

the revised second edition, 1965), London, 1972, p.165 ff.; and G. L. Geison, "Darwin and Heredity: The Evolution of his Hypothesis of Pangenesis", *J.Hist.Med.*, 24 (1969), pp.375–411.

4. Ernst Haeckel's pithy naming of the missing link shackling man to monkey was potently popularised by a suitably unsophisticated and despondently globular couple drawn by Hanfstaangl and entitled *Ancestors of Man* (*Pithecanthropus Alalus*) which appeared in England even in primers such as Edward Clodd's *The Story of "Primitive" Man*, London, 1895.

5. Joseph Conrad, *Heart of Darkness*, 1899, chap.2.

6. Ibid., chap.2.

7. James Sully, *Sensation and Intuition*, p.3.

8. Ibid., p.3.

9. Théodule Ribot, *The Psychology of the Emotions*, London, 1897, p.2.

10. Ibid., p.11.

11. Ibid., p.161.

12. Ibid., p.162.

13. Ibid., p.2.

14. Joseph Conrad, *Heart of Darkness*, chap.2.

15. Henry Maudsley, *Body and Will*, London, 1883, p.252.

16. Charles Darwin, *The Descent of Man*, p.52.

17. Cf. Ernst Haeckel, *The History of Creation*, vol.II, p.293: "Those processes of development which led to the origin of the most Ape-like Men out of the most Man-like Apes must be looked for in the two adaptational changes which, above all others, are distinctive of Man, namely, *upright walk* and *articulate speech.*"

18. Ibid., p.52.

19. Ibid., p.52.

20. Charles Darwin, *The Expression of the Emotions*, London, 1872, p.364.

21. Ibid., pp.310–11.

22. Ibid., p.364.

23. Ibid., p.364.

24. Ibid., p.310.

25. Ibid., p.333.

26. Ibid., p.347.

27. Charles Darwin, *The Descent of Man*, p.97.

28. Ibid., p.98.

29. Ibid., p.110.

30. Ibid., p.110.

31. Ibid., p.110.

32. Ibid., p.110.

33. Ibid., p.110.

34. Ibid., p.121.

35. Ibid., p.12 and ff.; and Charles Darwin, *The Origin of Species*, chap.V (Variorum edition, p.275 ff.).

36. Henry Maudsley, op. cit., p.183.

37. Charles Darwin, *The Origin of Species*, chap.V: "Laws of Variation" (Variorum edition, p.275 ff.).

38. Charles Darwin, *The Descent of Man*, p.125.

39. Ibid., p.618.

40. Ibid., p.618.

41. Ibid., p.619.

42. Ibid., p.619.

43. Henry Maudsley, op. cit., p.319.

44. Ibid., p.319.

45. Or, more succinctly, "Ontogeny recapitulates phylogeny" as Von Baer so famously (and inaccurately) remarked in a lecture "On the most general laws of Nature in all development", 1834, quoted in H. F. Osborn, *From the Greeks to Darwin*, London, 1874. And see Charles Darwin, *The Origin of Species*, Variorum edition, p.686.

46. Henry Maudsley, op. cit., p.321.

47. Charles Darwin, *The Descent of Man*, p.155.

48. Henry Maudsley, op. cit., p.319.

49. Ibid., pp.252–3.

50. Théodule Ribot, op. cit., p.175.

51. Ibid., p.175.

52. Ibid., p.165.

53. Ibid., p.175.

54. Ibid., p.216.

55. Ernest Jones, *Sigmund Freud: Life and Work*, 3 vols, London, 1953–7, vol.II, p.219; vol.III, p.308, and especially pp.332–7.

56. Ibid., vol.III, p.293 ff.

57. Charles Darwin, *The Descent of Man*, p.132.

58. See note, p.61, for Haeckel's extreme, clear and imaginative ideas of life with the speechless hordes of *Pithecanthropus Alalus*. For a variety of individual preferences, see

Lewis H. Morgan, *Ancient Society*, London, 1877; T.F. McLennan, *Studies in Ancient History*, London, 1886.

59. See Cyril Bibby, *T.H. Huxley: Scientist, Humanist, Educator*, London, 1959, pp.46, 59; T.H. Huxley, "The Evolution of Theology: an Anthropological Study", 1886, reprinted in *Collected Essays*, vol.IV, p.287 ff.

60. Huxley himself, for instance, was an original member of the London School Board implementing the Education Act of 1870; a member of the Clarendon Commission; a Governor of Owen's College and of Eton; the maestro midwife at the breech birth of science (and English literature) teaching at Oxford; a founder and champion of Imperial College; of adult popular education; of mind over magpie in museums; and a matador to John Bull's educated ignorance.

61. Max Nordau, *Degeneration*, London, 1895, p.7.

62. Ibid., p.554.

63. Ibid., p.554.

64. Ernst Haeckel, *History of Creation: or the Development of the Earth and its Inhabitants by the Action of Natural Causes*, trans. Ray Lankester, 2 vols., London, 1876; *The Riddle of the Universe*, trans. Ray Lankester, London, 1900.

65. B.A. Morel, *Traité des Dégénérescences physiques, intellectuelles et morales*, Paris, 1857.

66. Cesare Lombroso, *L'uomo delinquente in rapporte all' antropologia*, Turin, 1884, trans. *Criminal Anthropology*, London, 1897.

67. Max Nordau, op. cit., p.vii.

68. Ibid., p.560.

69. E.M. Forster, *Abinger Harvest*, London, 1936, p.135.

70. Max Nordau, op. cit., p.6.

71. Ibid., p.27.

72. Ibid., p.537.

73. Ibid., pp.556–7.

74. Ernest Jones, op. cit., vol.I, p.205.

75. See C.T. Watts, *Notes and Queries*, June 1974, pp.226–7.

76. Max Nordau, op. cit., p.145.

77. Joseph Conrad, *Notes on Life and Letters*, p.47.

78. Max Nordau, op. cit., p.22.

79. Ibid., p.45.

80. Ibid., p.45.

81. Ibid., p.57.

82. Ibid., p.57.

83. Ibid., p.18.

84. Ibid., p.18.

85. Ibid., p.18.

86. Ibid., p.31.

87. Ibid., p.31.

88. Ibid., p.67.

89. Ibid., p.78.

90. Ibid., p.78.

91. Ibid., p.22.

92. Ibid., p.560.

93. Ibid., pp.58–9.

94. Ibid., p.59.

95. Henry Maudsley, op. cit., p.191.

96. Ibid., p.191.

97. Charles Darwin, *The Descent of Man*, p.138.

98. Ibid., p.137.

99. Ibid., p.137.

100. Ibid., p.134.

101. Ibid., p.137.

102. Joseph Conrad, *Heart of Darkness*, chap.2.

103. Charles Darwin, *The Descent of Man*, p.180.

104. Ibid., p.155.

105. Ibid., p.157.

106. Ibid., p.157.

107. Ibid., p.157.

108. Charles Darwin, *The Descent of Man*, p.157, quoting T.H. Huxley, *Man's Place in Nature*, London, 1863, p.105.

109. Charles Darwin, *The Descent of Man*, pp.157–8.

110. Henry Maudsley, op. cit., p.321.

111. Charles Darwin, *The Descent of Man*, p.162.

112. Ibid., p.162.

113. Ibid., p.159.

114. Ibid., pp.160–1.

115. Joseph Conrad, *Heart of Darkness*, chap.2.

116. Joseph Conrad, "The Return", *Tales of Unrest*, London, 1898.

117. Ibid., pp.181–2.

118. Charles Darwin, *The Descent of Man*, p.160.

119. Ibid., p.161.

120. Ibid., p.161.

121. Ibid., p.161.

122. Ibid., p.137.

123. Max Nordau, op. cit., p.556.
124. Charles Darwin, *The Descent of Man*, p.158.
125. Ibid., p.158.
126. Max Nordau, op. cit., pp.45–7 and ff.
127. Ibid., p.34.
128. Ibid., p.56.
129. Charles Darwin, *The Descent of Man*, p.609.
130. Ibid., p.567.
131. Max Nordau, op. cit., p.56.
132. Charles Darwin, *The Descent of Man*, p.567.
133. Max Nordau, op. cit., p.56.

CHAPTER 3

A biological familiar

1. Joseph Conrad, *Heart of Darkness*, chap.2.
2. Charles Darwin, *The Descent of Man*, pp.35–6.
3. James Burnet, Lord Monboddo (1714–1799), *Of the Origin and Progress of Language*, 6 vols., Edinburgh, 1773–92.
4. Max Nordau, op. cit., p.72.
5. Joseph Conrad, *Heart of Darkness*, chap.2.
6. Ibid., chap.2.
7. Ibid., chap.1.
8. Joseph Conrad, "The Nigger of the Narcissus", 1897, chap.5.
9. Joseph Conrad, "Youth", 1898, chap.1.
10. Joseph Conrad, *Heart of Darkness*, chap.2.
11. Ibid., chap.2.
12. George Eliot, *Middlemarch*, London, 1871–2, chap.XV: "Lydgate's spots of commonness lay in the complexion of his prejudices."
13. Joseph Conrad, *Heart of Darkness*, chap.3.
14. John A. Gee, op. cit., p.36; Sept. 15th, 1891.
15. Charles Darwin, *The Descent of Man*, p.112.
16. Théodule Ribot, op. cit., p.162.
17. Charles Darwin, *The Descent of Man*, p.10.
18. Ibid., p.17.
19. Ibid., p.41.
20. Ibid., p.130.
21. Joseph Conrad, *Heart of Darkness*, chap.1.
22. Ibid., chap.1.
23. Charles Darwin, *The Descent of Man*, pp.35–6.
24. Joseph Conrad, *Heart of Darkness*, chap.3.
25. Ibid., chap.1.

CHAPTER 4

The degenerate chorus

1. Théodule Ribot, op. cit., p.245.
2. Ibid., p.245.
3. Charles Darwin, *The Descent of Man*, p.45, *inter alia*.
4. Ibid., p.70.
5. Joseph Conrad, *Heart of Darkness*, chap.3.
6. Charles Darwin, *The Descent of Man*, p.36.
7. Joseph Conrad, *Heart of Darkness*, chap.1.
8. Ibid., chap.3.
9. Charles Darwin, *The Descent of Man*, p.142.
10. Ibid., pp.110–12.
11. Charles Darwin, *The Descent of Man*, p.12 and ff., *inter alia*; see also the first edition, vol.I, p.90: "in the earlier editions of my 'Origin of Species' I perhaps attributed too much to the action of natural selection on the survival of the fittest." Charles Darwin, *The Origin of Species*, chap.V (Variorum edition, p.275 ff.).
12. Charles Darwin, *The Descent of Man*, p.112.

13. Ibid., p.114.
14. Charles Darwin, *On the Origin of Species by means of Natural Selection or the Preservation of Favoured Races in the Struggle for Life.*
15. Herbert Spencer, "The Development Hypothesis", *Leader*, March 20th, 1852, reprinted in *Collected Essays*, 3 vols., London, 1891, vol.I, pp.1–7.
16. T.H. Huxley, "Administrative Nihilism", 1871, reprinted in *Collected Essays*, 9 vols., London, 1893–4, vol.I, pp.251–89; "The Struggle for Existence in Human Society", 1891, vol.IX, pp.195–236; "Evolution and Ethics", 1893, vol.IX, pp.46–116.
17. J.G. Frazer, *The Golden Bough: a Study in Magic and Religion*, 2 vols., London, 1890, vol.I, p.146. Edward B. Tylor, *Primitive Culture: Researches into the Development of Mythology, Philosophy, Religion, Art and Custom*, 2 vols., London, 1871, vol.I, p.387. Edward B. Tylor, *Researches into the Early History of Mankind and the Development of Civilisation*, London, 1870, pp.7–8, *inter alia*. John Lubbock, *The Origin of Civilisation and the Primitive Condition of Man, Mental and Social Condition of Savages*, third edition, London, 1875, pp.206–7 (first edition 1870).
18. Charles Darwin, *The Descent of Man*, p.130.
19. Ibid., p.130.
20. See Francis Galton, *Inquiries into Human Faculty and its Development*, London, 1883. Sigmund Freud, *The Interpretation of Dreams*, trans. A. Brill, London, 1913, and *Wit and its Relation to the Unconscious*, trans. A. Brill, London, 1916.
21. Joseph Conrad, "The Idiots", *Tales of Unrest*, London, 1898, p.64.
22. F.R. Leavis, *The Great Tradition*, London, 1948, p.180.
23. John A. Gee, op. cit., p.36.
24. Charles Darwin, *The Descent of Man*, p.114.
25. John A. Gee, op. cit., p.36.
26. Joseph Conrad, *Heart of Darkness*, chap.1.
27. Joseph Conrad, "An Outpost of Progress", *Tales of Unrest*, chap.1.
28. Joseph Conrad, "The Idiots", *Tales of Unrest*, p.63.
29. Joseph Conrad, *Heart of Darkness*, chap.1.
30. Ibid., chap.1.
31. Max Nordau, op. cit., p.31.
32. Henry Maudsley, op. cit., pp.326–7.
33. Ibid., p.327.
34. Charles Darwin, *The Descent of Man*, p.133.
35. Ibid., p.135.

CHAPTER 5

Wallace lines and shadow lines

1. Charles Darwin, *The Descent of Man*, p.110.
2. Ibid., p.110.
3. Ibid., p.18.
4. Ibid., p.601.
5. Charles Darwin, *The Origin of Species*, chap.VI (Variorum edition, pp.374–5).
6. Ibid., chap.VI (Variorum edition, p.374).
7. Alfred Lord Tennyson, *In Memoriam A.H.H.*, 1850, canto LV.
8. Charles Darwin, *The Origin of Species*, chap.V (Varorium edition, pp.317–318).
9. Ibid., chap.VII (Variorum edition, p.382).
10. Ibid., chap.VII (Variorum edition, p.382).
11. Ibid., chap.VII (Variorum edition, p.382).
12. Ibid., chap.VII (Variorum edition, p.383).
13. Charles Darwin, *The Descent of Man*, p.21.
14. Charles Darwin, *The Origin of Species*, chap.VII (Variorum edition, p.382).
15. Ibid., chap.IX (Variorum edition, p.503).
16. Ibid., chap.IX (Variorum edition, p.504).
17. Ibid., chap.IV (Variorum edition, p.274).

18. Ibid., chap.IV (Variorum edition, p.199).
19. Ibid., chap.XI (Variorum edition, p.606).
20. Ibid., chap.XI (Variorum edition, p.605).
21. Ibid.
22. Charles Darwin, *The Origin of Species*, chap.V (Variorum edition, pp.284–5).
23. Ibid., chap.V (Variorum edition, p.283).
24. Ibid., chap.V (Variorum edition, p.283).

25. H.G. Wells, *The Time Machine*, London, 1895, chap.V (first published *New Review*, 1894–5).
26. Charles Darwin, *The Origin of Species*, chap.V (Variorum edition, p.285).
27. Ibid., chap.V (Variorum edition, p.286).
28. Ibid., chap.V (Variorum edition, p.283).
29. Joseph Conrad, *The Secret Sharer*, chap.2.
30. Charles Darwin, *The Origin of Species*, chap.V (Variorum edition, p.286).

CHAPTER 6

Stein

1. Charles Darwin, *The Origin of Species*, chap.V (Variorum edition, p.284).
2. Max Nordau, op. cit., p.72.
3. Ibid., p.72.
4. Ibid., p.57.
5. Ibid., p.59.
6. Ibid., p.59.
7. Ibid., p.59.
8. Ibid., p.45.
9. Ibid., p.56.
10. Ibid., p.6.
11. Joseph Conrad, *Heart of Darkness*, chap.3.
12. See Charles Darwin, *The Origin of Species*, chap.V (Variorum edition, p.286): "Far from feeling any surprise that some of the cave-animals should be very anomalous . . . I am only surprised that more wrecks of ancient life have not been preserved, owing to the less severe competition to which the inhabitants of these

dark abodes will probably have been exposed."
13. 1848 was indeed a year when it seemed that "every disreputable ragamuffin in Europe" might feel that the day of "universal brotherhood, despoliation and disorder" was at hand (Conrad to Spiridion Kliszcewski, Dec. 19th, 1885, in G. Jean-Aubry, op. cit., vol.I, p.84). There were revolutionary uprisings or serious riots in Venice, Parma, Milan, Paris, Vienna and Warsaw, where the Prussians suppressed a Polish insurrection in April.
14. Zdzislaw Najder, op. cit., p.154.
15. Ibid., p.5.
16. Ibid., p.177; and see pp.20, 183–202.
17. G. Jean-Aubry, op. cit., vol.I, p.84 (Dec. 19th, 1885).
18. J.R. Seeley, *Life and Times of Stein, or Germany and Prussia in the Napoleonic Age*, 3 vols., Cambridge, 1878.

CHAPTER 7

Heart of twilight

1. Max Nordau, op. cit., p.18.
2. Charles Darwin, *The Descent of Man*, p.114, *inter alia*; *The Expression of the Emotions*, p.333, *inter alia*.
3. Cf. Charles Darwin, *The Descent of Man*, p.35.

4. Charles Darwin, *The Descent of Man*, p.610.
5. Ibid., p.142.
6. Ibid., p.130.
7. Joseph Conrad, *Heart of Darkness*, chap.1.
8. Max Nordau, op. cit., p.557.

9. Joseph Conrad, *Heart of Darkness*, chap. 1.
10. Ibid., chap. 1.
11. Ibid., chap. 1.
12. Joseph Conrad, *Under Western Eyes*, London, 1911, chap. 2.
13. Max Nordau, op. cit., p.554.
14. Joseph Conrad, *Nostromo*, part III, chap. 13.
15. Ibid., chap. 13.
16. Ibid., chap. 13; and of Almayer's monkey, *vide infra*.
17. Charles Darwin, *The Descent of Man*, p. 130.
18. Charles Darwin, *The Origin of Species*, chap. IV (Variorum edition, p.274).
19. Charles Darwin, *The Descent of Man*, p.563.
20. Ibid., pp.564–5.
21. See Karl Pearson, "The Scientific Aspect of Monte Carlo Roulette", *Fortnightly Review*, Feb. 1894, reprinted in *The Chances of Death*, p.42 ff.
22. Joseph Conrad, *Heart of Darkness*, chap. 1.
23. Charles Darwin, *The Descent of Man*, pp.563–4.
24. Charles Darwin, *The Descent of Man*, p.572. (See also Edward Westermarck's summary and critique of Darwin's and Wallace's theories of scent and song in sexual selection, *The History of Human Marriage*, London, 1891, pp.246–52.)
25. See Thomas Moser, *Joseph Conrad: Achievement and Decline*, London, 1966, "The Uncongenial Subject: Love's Tangled Garden", p.62 ff.; Bernard C. Meyer, op. cit., passim.
26. For forceful connections of imagination, superstition, religion and savage life, see especially Herbert Spencer, *Principles of Psychology*, London, 1855, p.349 ff., p.583 ff; see also the second edition, London, 1870, where the evolutionary emphasis is very much stronger. See also John Lubbock, *Pre-Historic Times*, London, 1865, p.571 ff.; *The Origin of Civilisation*, London, 1870, p.246. Edward B. Tylor, *Researches into the Early History of Mankind*, London, 1870, p.6 ff. Charles Darwin, *The Descent of Man*, pp.563–6.
27. Joseph Conrad, *Heart of Darkness*, chap.3.
28. Joseph Conrad, "The Return", p.181.
29. Joseph Conrad, "Youth: A Narrative", p.3.
30. Joseph Conrad, *Typhoon*, chap.2.
31. Joseph Conrad, "The Nigger of the Narcissus", chap.3.
32. Joseph Conrad, *Heart of Darkness*, chap.2.
33. Alfred Russel Wallace, *The Malay Archipelago*, vol.I, p.398.
34. Joseph Conrad, *Heart of Darkness*, chap.3.
35. Ibid., chap.2.
36. Charles Darwin, *The Descent of Man*, p.110.

Select Bibliography

I

The works of Joseph Conrad

Almayer's Folly; a Story of an Eastern River, London and New York, 1895.

An Outcast of the Islands, London and New York, 1896.

"The Idiots", *Savoy*, Oct. 1896; *Tales of Unrest*, London and New York, 1898.

"The Lagoon", *Cornhill Magazine*, Jan. 1897; *Tales of Unrest*, London and New York, 1898.

"An Outpost of Progress", *Cosmopolis*, June–July 1897; *Tales of Unrest*, London and New York, 1898.

"The Nigger of the *Narcissus*; a Tale of the Forecastle", *New Review*, Aug.–Dec., 1897; reprinted as *Children of the Sea, A Tale of the Forecastle*, New York, 1897, and as *The Nigger of the 'Narcissus'; a Tale of the Sea*, London, 1898.

"Karain; A Memory", *Blackwood's Magazine*, Nov. 1897; *Living Age*, Dec. 18–25, 1897; *Tales of Unrest*, London and New York, 1898.

"Alphonse Daudet", *Outlook*, April 9, 1898; *Notes on Life and Letters*, London, Toronto and New York, 1921.

"An Observer in Malay", *Academy*, April 23, 1898; *Notes on Life and Letters*, London, Toronto and New York, 1921.

"Tales of the Sea", *Outlook*, June 4, 1898; *Notes on Life and Letters*, London, Toronto and New York, 1921.

"The Return", *Tales of Unrest*, London and New York, 1898.

"Youth", *Blackwood's Magazine*, Sept. 1898, *Outlook*, Oct. 1, 1898; *Youth, a Narrative; and Two Other Stories*, Edinburgh and London, 1902.

"Heart of Darkness", *Blackwood's Magazine*, Feb.–April 1899, *Living Age*, June 16–Aug. 4, 1900; *Youth, a Narrative; and Two Other Stories*, Edinburgh and London, 1902.

"Lord Jim; a Tale", *Blackwood's Magazine*, Oct. 1899–Nov. 1900; *Lord Jim; a Tale*, Edinburgh, London, New York and Toronto, 1900.

The Inheritors; an Extravagant Story (with F.M. Hueffer), New York and London, 1901.

"The End of the Tether", *Blackwood's Magazine*, July–Dec. 1902; *Youth, a Narrative; and Two Other Stories*, Edinburgh and London, 1902.

"Amy Foster", *Illustrated London News*, Dec. 14, 21, 28, 1901; *Typhoon; and Other Stories*, London, 1903, New York, 1923.

"Typhoon", *Pall Mall Magazine*, Jan.–March 1902, *Critic* (New York), Feb.–May 1902; *Typhoon*, London and New York, 1902.

"Tomorrow", *Pall Mall Magazine*, Aug. 1902; *Typhoon; and Other Stories*, London, 1903, New York, 1923.

"Falk; a Reminiscence", *Typhoon; and Other Stories*, London, 1903, New York, 1923.

Romance, a Novel (with F.M. Hueffer), London, 1903, New York, 1904.

"Nostromo; a Tale of the Seaboard", *T.P.'s Weekly*, Jan. 29–Oct. 7, 1904; *Nostromo; a Tale of the Seaboard*, London and New York, 1904.

"Overdue and Missing", *Daily Mail*, March 8 and Nov. 16, 1904; *The Mirror of the Sea; Memories and Impressions*, London and New York, 1906.

"Anatole France—I. *Crainquebille*", *Speaker*, July 16, 1904; *Notes on Life and Letters*, London, Toronto and New York, 1921.

"The Faithful River", *World Today*, Dec. 1904; *The Mirror of the Sea; Memories and Impressions*, London and New York, 1906.

"The Grip of the Land", *Daily Mail*, Dec. 2, 1904; *The Mirror of the Sea; Memories and Impressions*, London and New York, 1906.

"Landfalls and Departures", *Pall Mall*

Magazine, Jan. 1905, *Reader Magazine*, Feb. 1905; *The Mirror of the Sea; Memories and Impressions*, London and New York, 1906.

"Henry James", *North American Review*, Jan. 1905; *Notes on Life and Letters*, London, Toronto and New York, 1921.

"Emblems of Hope", *Pall Mall Magazine*, Feb. 1905, *Reader Magazine*, March 1905; *The Mirror of the Sea; Memories and Impressions*, London and New York, 1906.

"The Character of the Foe", *Pall Mall Magazine*, March 1905, *Reader Magazine*, April 1905; *The Mirror of the Sea; Memories and Impressions*, London and New York, 1906.

"The Fine Art", *Pall Mall Magazine*, April 1905; *The Mirror of the Sea; Memories and Impressions*, London and New York, 1906.

"Rulers of East and West", *Pall Mall Magazine*, May–June 1905, *Reader Magazine*, Aug. 1907; *The Mirror of the Sea; Memories and Impressions*, London and New York, 1906.

"Cobwebs and Gossamer", *Harper's Weekly*, June 10, 1905; *The Mirror of the Sea; Memories and Impressions*, London and New York, 1906.

"The Weight of the Burden", *Harper's Weekly*, June 17, 1905; *The Mirror of the Sea; Memories and Impressions*, London and New York, 1906.

"Autocracy and War", *Fortnightly Review*, July 1905, *North American Review*, July 1905; *Notes on Life and Letters*, London, Toronto and New York, 1921.

"Books", *Speaker*, July 15, 1905, *Living Age*, Aug. 19, 1905; *Notes on Life and Letters*, London, Toronto and New York, 1921.

"In Captivity", *Blackwood's Magazine*, Sept. 1905; *The Mirror of the Sea; Memories and Impressions*, London and New York, 1906.

"The Heroic Age", *Standard*, Oct. 21, 1905; *The Mirror of the Sea; Memories and Impressions*, London and New York, 1906.

"John Galsworthy", *Outlook*, March 31, 1906; *Last Essays*, London, Toronto and New York, 1926.

"An Anarchist", *Harper's Magazine*, Aug. 1906; *A Set of Six*, London, 1908.

"The Secret Agent; a Simple Tale", *Ridgeway's; a Militant Weekly for God and Country*, Oct. 6, 1906–Jan. 12, 1907; *The Secret Agent; a Simple Tale*, London and New York, 1907.

"The Informer", *Harper's Magazine*, Dec. 1906; *A Set of Six*, London, 1908.

"The Brute", *Daily Chronicle*, Dec. 5, 1906, *McClure's Magazine*, Nov. 1907; *A Set of Six*, London, 1908.

"The Tremolino", *The Mirror of the Sea; Memories and Impressions*, London and New York, 1906.

"The Censor of Plays", *Daily Mail*, Oct. 12, 1907; *Notes on Life and Letters*, London, Toronto and New York, 1921.

"The Duel", *Pall Mall Magazine*, Jan.–May 1908, *Forum*, July–Oct. 1908; *A Set of Six*, London, 1908.

"The Black Mate", *London Magazine*, April 1908; *Tales of Hearsay*, London and New York, 1925.

"Il Conde", *Cassell's Magazine*, Aug. 1908, *Hampton's Magazine*, Feb. 1909; *A Set of Six*, London, 1908.

"Anatole France—II L'Ile des Pingouins", *English Review*, Dec. 1908; *Notes on Life and Letters*, London, Toronto and New York, 1921.

"A Personal Record", *English Review*, Dec. 1908–June 1909; as *Some Reminiscences*, New York, 1908; *A Personal Record*, London and New York, 1912.

"The Nature of a Crime" (with F.M. Hueffer), *English Review*, April–May 1909; *The Nature of a Crime*, London and New York, 1924.

"The Life Beyond", *Daily Mail*, July 16, 1910; *Notes on Life and Letters*, London, Toronto and New York, 1921.

"A Happy Wanderer", *Daily Mail*, July 23, 1910; *Notes on Life and Letters*, London, Toronto and New York, 1921.

"The Ascending Effort", *Daily Mail*, July 30, 1910; *Notes on Life and Letters*, London, Toronto and New York, 1921.

"The Secret Sharer", *Harper's Magazine*, Aug.–Sept. 1910; *'Twixt Land and Sea; Tales*, London and New York, 1912.

"Under Western Eyes; a Novel", *English Review*, Dec. 1910–Oct. 1911, *North American Review*, Dec. 1910–Oct. 1911; *Under Western Eyes; a Novel*, London and New York, 1911.

"A Smile of Fortune", *London Magazine*, Feb.

1911; *'Twixt Land and Sea; Tales*, London and New York, 1912.

"Prince Roman", *Oxford and Cambridge Review*, Oct. 1911, *Metropolitan Magazine* (New York), Jan. 1912; *Tales of Hearsay*, London and New York, 1925.

"The Partner", *Harper's Magazine*, Nov. 1911; *Within the Tides; Tales*, London and Toronto, 1915; New York, 1916.

"Chance; a Tale in Two Parts", *New York Herald*, Jan. 21–June 30, 1912; *Chance; a Tale in Two Parts*, London and New York, 1913.

"Certain Aspects of the Admirable Inquiry into the Loss of the *Titanic*", *English Review*, July 1912; *Notes on Life and Letters*, London, Toronto and New York, 1921.

"Freya of the Seven Isles", *Metropolitan Magazine* (New York), April 1912, *London Magazine*, July 1912; *'Twixt Land and Sea; Tales*, London and New York, 1912.

"Some Reflections on the Loss of the *Titanic*", *English Review*, May 1912; *Notes on Life and Letters*, London, Toronto and New York, 1921.

"The Future of Constantinople", *The Times*, Nov. 7, 1912; *Last Essays*, London, Toronto and New York, 1926.

"A Friendly Place", *Daily Mail*, Dec. 10, 1912; *Notes on Life and Letters*, London, Toronto and New York, 1921.

"The Inn of Two Witches", *Pall Mall Magazine*, March 1913, *Metropolitan Magazine* (New York), May 1913; *Within the Tides; Tales*, London and Toronto, 1915; New York, 1916.

"The Planter of Malata", *Metropolitan Magazine* (New York), June–July 1914; *Within the Tides; Tales*, London and Toronto, 1915; New York, 1916.

"Protection of Ocean Liners", *Illustrated London News*, June 6, 1914; *Notes on Life and Letters*, London, Toronto and New York, 1926.

"Because of the Dollars", *Metropolitan Magazine* (New York), Sept. 1914; *Within the Tides; Tales*, London and Toronto, 1915; New York, 1916.

"Guy de Maupassant", Introduction to *Yvette and Other Stories*, Guy de Maupassant, trans. Ada Galsworthy, London, 1914; *Last Essays*, London, Toronto and New York, 1926.

"Victory; an Island Tale", *Munsey's Magazine* (New York), Feb. 1915, *Star*, Aug. 24–Nov. 9, 1915; *Victory; an Island Tale*, New York and London, 1915.

"Poland Revisited", *Daily News*, March 29, 31, April 6, 9, 1915, *The Book of the Homeless*, New York, 1916; *Notes on Life and Letters*, London, Toronto and New York, 1921.

"The Shadow-Line; a Confession", *English Review*, Sept. 1916–March 1917, *Metropolitan Magazine* (New York), Oct. 1916; *The Shadow-Line; a Confession*, London, Toronto and New York, 1917.

"The Warrior's Soul", *Land and Water*, March 29, 1917, *Tales of Hearsay*, London and New York, 1925.

"Flight", *Fledgeling*, June 1917; *Notes on Life and Letters*, London, Toronto and New York, 1921.

"The Tale", *Strand Magazine*, Oct. 1917; *Tales of Hearsay*, London and New York, 1925.

"Turgenev", Introduction to *Turgenev; a Study*, Edward Garnett, London, 1917; *Notes on Life and Letters*, London, Toronto and New York, 1921.

"Tradition", *Daily Mail*, March 8, 1918; *Notes on Life and Letters*, London, Toronto and New York, 1921.

"First News", *Reveille*, Aug. 1918; *Notes on Life and Letters*, London, Toronto and New York, 1921.

"Well Done!" *Daily Chronicle*, Aug. 22, 1918, *Living Age*, Oct. 1918; *Notes on Life and Letters*, London, Toronto and New York, 1921.

"The Arrow of Gold; a Story Between Two Notes", *Lloyd's Magazine*, Dec. 1918–Feb. 1920; *The Arrow of Gold; a Story Between Two Notes*, New York and London, 1919.

"The Rescue; a Romance of the Shallows", *Land and Water*, Jan. 30–July 31, 1919, *Romance* (New York), Nov. 1919–May 1920; *The Rescue; a Romance of the Shallows*, New York, London and Toronto, 1920.

"The Crime of Partition", *Fortnightly Review*, May 1, 1919, *Collier's Weekly* (New York), June 14, 1919; *Notes on Life and Letters*, London, Toronto and New York, 1921.

"Confidence", *Daily Mail*, June 30, 1919; *Notes on Life and Letters*, London, Toronto and New York, 1921.

Select Bibliography

"Stephen Crane; a Note without Dates", *London Mercury*, Dec. 1919, *Bookman* (New York), Feb. 1920; *Notes on Life and Letters*, London, Toronto and New York, 1921.

"The Dover Patrol", *The Times*, July 27, 1921; *Last Essays*, London, Toronto and New York, 1926.

"The Loss of the Dalgonar", *London Mercury*, Dec. 1921; *Last Essays*, London, Toronto and New York, 1926.

"A Note on the Polish Problem", *Notes on Life and Letters*, London, Toronto and New York, 1921.

"Cookery", *Delineator*, Aug. 1922; Preface to *A Handbook of Cookery for a Small House*, Jessie Conrad, London, 1923.

"Outside Literature", *Manchester Guardian Literary Supplement for 1922*, Dec. 4, 1922, *Bookman* (New York), Feb. 1923; *Last Essays*, London, Toronto and New York, 1926.

"Ocean Travel", *Evening News*, May 15, 1923; *Last Essays*, London, Toronto and New York, 1926.

"The Rover", *Pictorial Review*, Sept.–Dec. 1923; *The Rover*, New York and London, 1923.

"The *Torrens*; a Personal Tribute", *Blue Peter*, Oct. 1923, *Collier's Weekly*, Oct. 27, 1923; *Last Essays*, London, Toronto and New York, 1926.

"Christmas Day at Sea", *Daily Mail*, Dec. 24, 1923, *Delineator*, Dec. 1923; *Last Essays*, London, Toronto and New York, 1926.

"Stephen Crane; a Preface to Thomas Beer's *Stephen Crane*", *Stephen Crane; a Study in American Letters*, New York, 1923; *Last Essays*, London, Toronto and New York, 1926.

"Travel", *Into the East; Notes on Burma and Malaya*, Richard Curle, London, 1923; *Last Essays*, London, Toronto and New York, 1926.

"Geography and Some Explorers", *Countries of the World*, Feb. 1924, *National Geographic Magazine*, March 1924; *Last Essays*, London, Toronto and New York, 1926.

"Legends", *Daily Mail*, Aug. 15, 1924; *Last Essays*, London, Toronto and New York, 1926.

Preface to *The Shorter Tales of Joseph Conrad*, London, 1924; *Last Essays*, London, Toronto and New York, 1926.

"Suspense; a Napoleonic Novel", *Saturday Review of Literature*, June 27–Aug. 12, 1925; *Suspense; a Napoleonic Novel*, New York, London and Toronto, 1925.

"A Glance at Two Books", *T.P.'s and Cassell's Weekly*, Aug. 1, 1925, *Forum*, Aug. 1925, *Living Age*, Sept. 5, 1925; *Last Essays*, London, Toronto and New York, 1926.

"The Unlighted Coast", *The Times*, Aug. 18, 1925; *Last Essays*, London, Toronto and New York, 1926.

"The Congo Diary", *Blue Peter*, Oct. 1925, *Yale Review*, Jan. 1926; *Last Essays*, London, Toronto and New York, 1926.

"His War Book", Preface to *The Red Badge of Courage*, Stephen Crane, London, 1925; *Last Essays*, London, Toronto and New York, 1926.

"Memorandum on the Scheme for fitting out a Sailing Ship", *Last Essays*, London, Toronto and New York, 1926.

Three Plays; Laughing Anne; One Day More; and The Secret Agent, London, 1934.

Conrad's letters

Jean-Aubry, G., *Joseph Conrad: Life and Letters*, 2 vols., London and New York, 1927.

Garnett, E., *Letters from Conrad, 1895–1924*, London and Indianapolis, 1928.

Curle, R., *Conrad to a Friend: 150 Selected Letters from Joseph Conrad to Richard Curle*, London and New York, 1928.

Jean-Aubry, G., *Lettres Françaises par Joseph Conrad*, Paris, 1930.

Gee, J.A. and P.J. Strum, *Letters of Joseph Conrad to Marguerite Poradowska, 1890–1920*, London and New York, 1940.

Blackburn, W., *Joseph Conrad: Letters to William Blackwood and David S. Meldrum*, London and Durham, NC, 1958.

Select Bibliography

Najder, Z., *Conrad's Polish Background: Letters to and from Polish Friends*, London and New York, 1964.

Watts, C.T., *Joseph Conrad's Letters to R.B. Cunninghame Graham*, Cambridge and New York, 1969.

II

Contemporary scientific thought

Bain, Alexander, *The Senses and the Intellect*, London, 1855.

—, *The Emotions and the Will*, London, 1859, 3rd ed., London, 1875.

—, *On the Study of Character, Including an Estimate of Phrenology*, London, 1861.

Basalla, George, William Coleman and Robert H. Kargon, eds., *Victorian Science; a Self-Portrait from the Presidential Addresses of the British Association for the Advancement of Science*, New York, 1970.

Bates, Henry Walter, *The Naturalist on the River Amazons: a Record of Adventures, Habits of Animals, Sketches of Brazilian and Indian Life, and Aspects of Nature under the Equator, during Eleven Years of Travel*, London, 1864.

Bateson, William, *Mendel's Principles of Heredity: a Defence*, Cambridge, 1902.

—, *Problems of Genetics*, New Haven and London, 1913.

Bergson, Henri, *Creative Evolution*, trans. A. Mitchell, London, 1911.

Brown, Robert, *Our Earth and its Story: a Popular Treatise on Physical Geography*, 3 vols., London, 1887.

Buckley, Arabella B., *A Short History of Natural Science*, London, 1876, 4th ed., London, 1888.

Burnet, James (Lord Monboddo), *Of the Origin and Progress of Language*, 6 vols., Edinburgh, 1773–92.

Butler, Samuel, *Evolution Old and New; or, the Theories of Buffon, Dr. Erasmus Darwin, and Lamarck, as Compared with that of Charles Darwin*, London, 1879.

—, *Unconscious Memory: a Comparison Between the Theory of Dr. Ewald Hering and the "Philosophy of the unconscious" of Dr. Edward von Hartmann*, London, 1880.

Campbell, George Douglas, Duke of Argyll, *Primeval Man: An Examination of some Recent Speculations*, London, 1869.

Chambers, Robert, *Vestiges of the Natural History of Creation*, London, 1844.

Clifford, W.K., *Body and Mind. A lecture, reprinted from the "Fortnightly Review"*, London, 1875.

Clodd, Edward, *The Story of Creation: a Plain Account of Evolution*, London, 1888.

—, *The Story of "Primitive" Man*, London, 1895.

Darwin, Charles, *Darwin on Man: a Psychological Study of Scientific Creativity by Howard E. Gruber together with Darwin's Early and Unpublished Notebooks transcribed and annotated by Paul H. Barrett*, London, 1974.

—, *Journal of Researches into the Natural History and Geology of the Countries Visited during the Voyage of H.M.S. Beagle Round the World*, London, 1839.

—, *Charles Darwin and A.R. Wallace. Evolution by Natural Selection* (with a foreword by Sir Gavin de Beer), Cambridge, 1958.

—, *On the Origin of Species by means of Natural Selection, or the Preservation of Favoured Races in the Struggle for Life*, London, 1859.

—, *The Origin of Species by Charles Darwin: a Variorum Text*, ed. Morse Peckham, Philadelphia, 1959.

—, *The Descent of Man and Selection in Relation to Sex*, 2 vols., London, 1871. 2nd ed., London, 1885.

—, *The Expression of the Emotions in Man and Animals*, London, 1872.

—, *The Life and Letters of Charles Darwin, Including an Autobiographical Chapter*, ed. Francis Darwin, 3 vols., London, 1887.

—, *More Letters of Charles Darwin: a Record of his Work in a Series of hitherto Unpublished Letters*, ed. Francis Darwin and A.C. Seward, 2 vols., London, 1903.

—, *The Autobiography of Charles Darwin, 1809–1882. With original omissions restored*, ed. Nora Barlow, London, 1958.

Darwin, Erasmus, *Zoonomia; or Laws of Organic Life*, 2 vols., London, 1794.

—, *Phytologia; or the Philosophy of Agriculture and Gardening*, London, 1800.

—, *The Temple of Nature, or the Origin of Society. A Poem with philosophical notes*, London, 1803.

Du Chaillu, Paul, *My Encounters with the Gorilla*, London, 1861.

Ellis, Henry Havelock, *The Criminal*, London, 1890.

Frazer, J.G., *The Golden Bough: a Study in Comparative Religion*, 2 vols., London, 1890.

Freud, Sigmund, *The Interpretation of Dreams*, trans. A. Brill, London, 1913.

—, *Psychopathology of Everyday Life*, trans. A. Brill, London, 1914.

—, *Wit and Its Relation to the Unconscious*, trans. A. Brill, London, 1916.

—, *Totem and Taboo: Resemblances Between the Psychic Lives of Savages and Neurotics*, trans. A. Brill, London, 1919.

—, *Beyond the Pleasure Principle*, trans. C.J.M. Hubback, London, 1922.

—, *The Future of an Illusion*, trans. W.D. Robson-Scott, London, 1928.

Galton, Francis, *Hereditary Genius; an Inquiry into its Laws and Consequences*, London, 1869.

—, *Inquiries into Human Faculty and its Development*, London, 1883.

—, *Natural Inheritance*, London, 1889.

Geikie, Sir Archibald, *Founders of Geology*, London and New York, 1897.

Gosse, Philip Henry, *Omphalos: an Attempt to Untie the Geological Knot*, London, 1857.

Haeckel, Ernst, *The Evolution of Man: a Popular Exposition of the Principle Points of Human Ontogeny and Phylogeny*, 2 vols., London, 1879.

—, *The Riddle of the Universe at the Close of the Nineteenth Century*, trans. Joseph McCabe, London, 1900.

Hobhouse, Leonard Trelawny, *Mind in Evolution*, London and New York, 1901.

Humboldt, Alexander von, *Personal Narrative of Travels to the Equinoctial Regions of the New Continent during the Years 1799 to 1804*, trans. H.H. Williams, 7 vols., London, 1814–29.

—, *Personal Narrative of Travels to the Equinoctial Regions of America during the years 1799–1804*, trans. and ed. Thomasina Ross, 3 vols., London, 1852–3.

Hutton, James, *Theory of the Earth, or an Investigation of the Laws observable in the Composition, Dissolution, and Restoration of Land upon the Globe*, 2 vols., Edinburgh, 1795.

Huxley, Thomas Henry, *Collected Essays*, 9 vols., London, 1893–4.

—, *The Life and Letters of Thomas Henry Huxley*, ed. Leonard Huxley, 2 vols., London, 1900.

James, William, *The Principles of Psychology*, 2 vols., London and New York, 1890.

—, *The Varieties of Religious Experience*, Gifford Lectures, 1901–2, London, 1902.

Keller, Ferdinand, *The Lake Dwellings of Switzerland and Other Parts of Europe*, trans. John Edward Lee, London, 1866.

Kidd, Benjamin, *Social Evolution*, London, 1894.

Kropotkin, Prince Peter, *Natural Selection and Mutual Aid: an Epitome*, London, 1897.

—, *Modern Science and Anarchism*, trans. David A. Modell, Philadelphia, 1903.

Lamarck, Jean Bapiste Pierre Antoine, *Zoological Philosophy, an Exposition with regard to the Natural History of Animals*, trans. Hugh Elliott, London, 1914.

Lankester, E. Ray, *Degeneration; a Chapter in Darwinism*, London, 1880.

—, *Extinct Animals*, London, 1905.

Lawrence, William, *Lectures on Physiology, Zoology and the Natural History of Man*, London, 1819 (suppressed).

Le Clerc, Georges Louis, Comte de Buffon, *Natural History, General and Particular*, trans. William Smellie, 2nd ed., 9 vols., London, 1785.

Lewes, George Henry, *Problems of Life and Mind*, 4 vols., London, 1874–9.

Lombroso, Cesare, *Criminal Anthropology*, trans., London, 1897.

Lubbock, Sir John, *Pre-Historic Times, as Illustrated by Ancient Remains in the Manners and Customs of Modern Savages*, London, 1865.

—, *The Origin of Civilisation and the Primitive Condition of Man. Mental and Social Condition of Savages*, London, 1870, 3rd ed., London, 1875.

—, *Scientific Lectures*, London, 1879.

Lyell, Sir Charles, *Principles of Geology*, 3 vols., London, 1830–3.

—, *Elements of Geology*, London, 1838.

—, *The Geological Evidences of the Antiquity of*

Man with remarks on theories of *The Origin of Species by Variation*, London, 1863.

Mallock, W.H., *Studies of Contemporary Superstition*, London, 1895.

Malthus, Thomas Robert, *An Essay on the Principle of Population as it affects the Future Improvement of Society. With Remarks on the Speculations of Mr. Godwin, M. Condorcet, and other Writers*, London, 1798.

Maudsley, Henry, *Body and Will, Being an Essay concerning Will in its Metaphysical, Physiological and Pathological Aspects*, London, 1883.

Maxwell, James Clerk, *Matter and Motion*, London, 1873.

—, *Scientific Papers of James Clerk Maxwell*, ed. W.D. Niven, 2 vols., Cambridge, 1890.

Merz, J.T., *A History of European Thought in the Nineteenth Century*, 4 vols., Edinburgh, 1896–1914.

Miller, Hugh, *The Old Red Sandstone; or New Walks in an Old Field*, Edinburgh, 1841.

—, *The Testimony of the Rocks; or, Geology in its Bearings on the Two Theologies, Natural and Revealed*, Edinburgh, 1857.

Mivart, St. G., *On the Genesis of Species*, London, 1871.

Morel, B.A., *Traité de Dégénérescences physiques, intellectuelles et morales de L'Espèce Humaine*, Paris, 1857.

Morgan, C. Lloyd, *Emergent Evolution*, the Gifford Lectures, 1922, London, 1923.

Nordau, Max, *Degeneration*, trans. from the 2nd German ed., London, 1895.

Paley, William, *Natural Theology; or, Evidences of the Existence and Attributes of the Deity*, London, 1802.

Pearson, Karl, *The Grammar of Science*, London, 1892.

—, *The Chances of Death and Other Studies in Evolution*, 2 vols., London and New York, 1897.

Playfair, John, *Illustrations of the Huttonian Theory of the Earth*, Edinburgh, 1802.

Reade, Winwood, *The Martyrdom of Man*, Edinburgh, 1872.

Ribot, Théodule, H., *English Psychology*, London, 1873.

—, *The Psychology of the Emotions*, London, 1897.

Romanes, George, *A Candid Examination of Theism*, London, 1878.

—, *Mental Evolution in Man. Origin of Human Faculty*, London, 1888.

—, *Darwin, and After Darwin: an Exposition of the Darwinian Theory and a Discussion of Post-Darwinian Questions*, 3 vols., London, 1892–7.

Schopenhauer, Arthur, *The World as Will and Idea*, trans. R.B. Haldane and J. Kemp, 3 vols., London, 1883.

Spencer, Herbert, *The Principles of Psychology*, London, 1855.

—, *Essays: Scientific, Political, and Speculative*, 3 vols., London, 1858–74.

—, *First Principles*, London, 1863.

—, *The Principles of Biology*, 2 vols., London, 1864–7.

Sully, James, *Sensation and Intuition: Studies in Psychology and Esthetics*, London, 1874.

—, *Pessimism: a History and a Criticism*, London, 1877.

—, *Illusions: a Psychological Study*, London, 1881.

—, *Outlines of Psychology: with Special Reference to the Theory of Education*, London, 1884.

—, *The Human Mind, a Text-book of Psychology*, 2 vols., London, 1892.

Thomson, Sir William, Lord Kelvin, *Popular Lectures and Addresses*, 3 vols., London, 1889–94.

Tylor, Edward B., *Researches into the Early History of Mankind and the Development of Civilization*, London, 1865, 2nd ed., London, 1870.

—, *Primitive Culture: Researches into the Development of Mythology, Philosophy, Religion, Art and Custom*, 2 vols., London, 1871.

Tyndall, John, *The Glaciers of the Alps*, London, 1860.

—, *Fragments of Science for Unscientific People*, London, 1871.

Wallace, Alfred Russel, *The Malay Archipelago: the Land of the Orang-Utan and the Bird of Paradise. A Narrative of Travel, with studies of man and nature*, 2 vols., London, 1869.

—, *On Miracles and Modern Spiritualism*, London, 1875.

—, *Island Life: or, the Phenomena and Causes of Insular Faunas and Floras; Including a Revision and Attempted Solution of the Problem of Geological Climates*, London, 1880.

—, *Darwinism: an Exposition of the Theory of*

Natural Selection with some of its Applications, London, 1889.

—, *The Wonderful Century, its Successes and its Failures*, London, 1898.

—, *Studies Scientific and Social*, 2 vols., London, 1900.

—, *Man's Place in the Universe, a Study of the Results of Scientific Research in Relation to the Unity or Plurality of Worlds*, London, 1903.

—, *My Life: a Record of Events and Opinions*, 2 vols., London, 1905.

Weismann, A., *Essays upon Heredity and Other Kindred Biological Problems*, trans. E.B. Poulton, S. Schönland and A.E. Shipley, 2 vols., Oxford, 1889.

—, *The Evolution Theory*, trans. J.A. and M.R. Thompson, 2 vols., London, 1904.

Westermarck, Edward Alexander, *The History of Human Marriage*, London, 1891.

White, Gilbert, *The Natural History and Antiquities of Selborne*, 2 vols., London, 1789.

III

Secondary sources

Alden, Douglas W., "Proust and Ribot", *Modern Language Notes*, 58 (1943), 501–507.

Arber, Agnes, *The Mind and the Eye: a Study of the Biologist's Standpoint*, Cambridge, 1954.

Bailey, J.O., "Evolutionary Meliorism in the Poetry of Thomas Hardy", *Studies in Philosophy*, 60 (1963), 569–87.

Baines, Jocelyn, *Joseph Conrad, a Critical Biography*, London, 1959.

Barnett, S.A., *A Century of Darwin*, London, 1958.

Barzun, Jacques Martin, *Darwin, Marx, Wagner: Critique of a Heritage*, London, 1942.

Batho, E. and B. Dobrée, *The Victorians and After, 1830–1914*, London, 1938.

Beach, J.W., *The Concept of Nature in Nineteenth-Century English Poetry*, New York, 1936.

Beebe, Maurice, "Criticism of Joseph Conrad: a Selected Checklist", *Modern Fiction Studies*, 10 (1964), 81–106.

Bell, I.F. and D. Baird, *The English Novel 1578–1956: a Checklist of Twentieth Century Criticisms*, Denver, 1958.

Bergonzi, Bernard, *The Early H.G. Wells: a Study of the Scientific Romances*, Manchester, 1961.

Bibby, Cyril, "Huxley and the Reception of the 'Origin'", *Victorian Studies*, 3 (1959–60), 76–86.

—, *T.H. Huxley: Scientist, Humanist and Educator*, London, 1959.

Bibby, Geoffrey, *The Testimony of the Spade*, London, 1957.

Bradbrook, M.C., *Joseph Conrad: Poland's English Genius*, Cambridge, 1941.

Buckley, J.H., *The Triumph of Time. A Study of the Victorian Concepts of Time, History, Progress and Decadence*, Cambridge, Massachusetts, 1966, London, 1967.

Burrow, J.W., *Evolution and Society: a Study in Victorian Social Theory*, Cambridge, 1966.

Bush, Douglas, *Science and English Poetry 1590–1950*, New York, 1950.

Butterfield, Herbert, *The Origins of Modern Science, 1300–1800*, London, 1949.

Cannon, Walter F., "The Bases of Darwin's Achievement: a Revaluation", *Victorian Studies*, 5 (1961–2), 109–34.

Carr, E.H., *The Romantic Exiles: a Nineteenth Century Portrait Gallery*, London, 1933.

Chapman, Raymond, *The Victorian Debate. English Literature and Society, 1832–1901*, London, 1968.

Charlesworth, Barbara, *Dark Passages: the Decadent Consciousness in Victorian Literature*, Madison, 1965.

Church, Margaret, *Time and Reality. Studies in Contemporary Fiction*, Chapel Hill, 1962.

Clark, G. Kitson, *The Making of Victorian England*, London, 1962.

Clark, Ronald W., *Einstein: the Life and Times*, London, 1973.

Clemens, Florence, "Conrad's Favorite Bedside Book", *South American Quarterly*, 38 (1939), 305–15.

Cohen, I. Bernard, *The Birth of a New Physics*, London, 1961.

Collingwood, Robin George, *The Idea of Nature*, Oxford, 1945.

Conrad, Jessie, *Joseph Conrad as I Knew Him*, London, 1926.

—, *Joseph Conrad and his Circle*, London, 1935.

Cox, C.B. and A.E. Dyson, *The Twentieth Century Mind: History, Ideas and Literature in Britain*, 3 vols., Oxford, 1972.

Cox, Roy Alan, "Dominant Ideas in the Works of Guy de Maupassant", *The University of Colorado Studies*, 19, no. 2. (April 1932).

Curle, Richard, *The Last Twelve Years of Joseph Conrad*, London, 1928.

Dampier-Whetham, W.C., *A History of Science and its Relations with Philosophy and Religion*, Cambridge, 1929.

Daniel, Glyn, *The Idea of Prehistory*, London, 1962.

—, *The Origins and Growth of Archaeology*, London, 1967.

Darlington, C.D., *Darwin's Place in History*, Oxford, 1959.

—, *Genetics and Man*, London, 1964.

de Beer, Sir Gavin, *Charles Darwin: Evolution by Natural Selection*, London, 1963.

Dowden, Edward, *Studies in Literature, 1789–1877*, London, 1878. 5th ed., London, 1889.

Dudley, Frederick A., "Matthew Arnold and Science", *Publications of the Modern Language Association of America*, 57 (March 1942), 275–94.

Dudley, Frederick A., N. Furst and others, ed., *Relations of Literature and Science: a Selected Bibliography, 1930–49*, Washington, 1949.

Eiseley, Loren, *Darwin's Century: Evolution and the Men who Discovered It*, New York, 1958, and London, 1959.

Ellegård, Alvar, *Darwin and the General Reader: the Reception of Darwin's Theory of Evolution in the British Periodical Press, 1859–1872*, Göteborg University årrskv., vol. 64, Göteborg, 1958.

Ellenberger, Henri Frederic, *The Discovery of the Unconscious: the History and Evolution of Dynamic Psychiatry*, London, 1970.

Ford, F.M. (Ford Madox Hueffer), *Joseph Conrad: a Personal Remembrance*, London, 1924.

Forster, E.M., *Abinger Harvest*, London, 1936.

Galsworthy, John, *Castles in Spain and Other Screeds*, London, 1927.

Gantz, K.F., "The Beginnings of Darwinian Ethics, 1859–71", *University of Texas Publications* (1939), 180–97.

Garnett, David, *The Golden Echo*, London, 1953.

Geison, G.L., "Darwin and Heredity: the Evolution of his Hypothesis of Pangenesis", *Journal of the History of Medicine*, 24 (1969), 375–411.

George, Wilma, *Biologist Philosopher: a Study of the Life and Writings of Alfred Russel Wallace*, London, 1964.

Gillispie, C.C., *Genesis and Geology: a Study in the Relations of Scientific Thought, Natural Theology, and Social Opinion in Great Britain, 1790–1850*, New York, 1959.

—, *The Edge of Objectivity*, Princeton, 1966.

Glass, B., O. Temkin and L. Strauss, eds., *Forerunners of Darwin, 1745–1859*, Baltimore, 1959.

Goldman, Irving, "Evolution and Anthropology", *Victorian Studies*, 3 (September 1959), 65–75.

Gosse, Edmund, *Father and Son. A Study of Two Temperaments*, London, 1907.

Greene, J.C., *Darwin and the Modern World View*, New York, 1961.

Guérard, Albert J., *Conrad the Novelist*, London, 1958.

Haddon, A.C., *History of Anthropology*, London, 1934.

Harkness, Bruce, ed., *Conrad's Secret Sharer and the Critics*, Belmont, 1964.

Hart-Davis, Rupert, *Hugh Walpole, a Biography*, London, 1952.

Hay, Eloise Knapp, *The Political Novels of Joseph Conrad: a Critical Study*, Chicago, 1963.

Henkin, Leo J., *Darwinism in the English Novel, 1860–1910*, New York, 1940.

Hewitt, Douglas, *Conrad: a Reassessment*, London, 1952.

Himmelfarb, Gertrude, *Darwin and the Darwinian Revolution*, London, 1959.

Hoffman, Frederick J., *Freudianism and the Literary Mind*, Baton Rouge, 1945.

—, "From Surrealism to 'the Apocalypse': a Development in Twentieth Century

Irrationalism", *Journal of English Literary History*, 15 (1948), 147–65.

Hollingsworth, Alan M., "Freud, Conrad, and the Future of an Illusion", *Literature and Psychology*, 5 (Nov. 1955), 78–83.

Holloway, John, "Science and Literature", *Encounter*, 33 (July 1969) 81–5.

Houghton, Walter Edwards, *The Victorian Frame of Mind, 1830–70*, New Haven, 1957.

Hughes, A., *A History of Cytology*, London, 1959.

Hull, David, *Darwin and his Critics*, Oxford, 1973.

Hutchinson, H.G., *The Life of Sir John Lubbock, Lord Avebury*, 2 vols., London, 1914.

Huxley, Julian Sorell, *Evolution in Action*, London, 1953.

Hyness, Samuel, *The Edwardian Turn of Mind*, Princeton, 1968.

Iltis, Hugo, *Life of Mendel*, trans. Eden and Cedar Paul, London, 1932.

Irvine, William, *Apes, Angels and Victorians; a Joint Biography of Darwin and Huxley*, London, 1955.

—, "The Influence of Darwin on Literature", *Proceedings of the American Philosophical Society*, 103, 616–28.

Jean-Aubry, Gérard, *The Sea Dreamer: a Definitive Biography of Joseph Conrad*, London, 1957.

Jeans, Sir James Hopwood, *The Mysterious Universe*, Cambridge, 1930.

Johnson, Bruce, *Conrad's Models of Mind*, Minneapolis, 1971.

Jones, Ernest, *Sigmund Freud: Life and Work*, 3 vols., London, 1953–7.

Keith, Sir Arthur, *Darwin Revalued*, London, 1955.

Kirschner, Paul, *Conrad: the Psychologist as Artist*, Edinburgh, 1968.

Knight, David M., *Natural Science Books in English 1600–1900*, London, 1972.

Knoepflmacher, U.C., *Religious Humanism and the Victorian Novel: George Eliot, Walter Pater, and Samuel Butler*, Princeton, 1965.

Koyré, Alexander André, *From the Closed World to the Infinite Universe*, Baltimore, 1957.

Krzyzsnowski, Ludwig, ed., *Joseph Conrad: Centennial Essays*, New York, 1960.

Lack, David, *Evolutionary Theory and Christian Belief: the Unresolved Conflict*, London, 1957.

Lenormand, H.R., "Note on a Sojourn of Conrad in Corsica", *La Nouvelle Revue Française*, Nouvelle série, 135 (Dec. 1, 1924), Paris.

Lester, J.A., *Journey through Despair 1880–1914. Transformations in British Literary Culture*, Princeton, 1968.

Lillard, Richard Gordon, "Irony in Hardy and Conrad", *Publications of the Modern Language Association of America*, 50 (1935), 316–22.

Liszt, Franz, *Life of Chopin*, trans. M. Walter Cook, London, 1877.

Loewenberg, Bert James, "The Mosaic of Darwinian Thought", *Victorian Studies*, 3 (Sep. 1959) 3–18.

Lohf, Kenneth A. and Eugene G. Sheehy, *Joseph Conrad at Mid-Century: Editions and Studies, 1895–1955*, Minneapolis, 1957.

Lovejoy, A.O., *The Great Chain of Being*, William James Lectures, 1933, London, 1942.

—, *Essays in the History of Ideas*, Baltimore, 1948.

Lowes, J.L., "Two Readings of Earth", *Yale Review*, 15 (1926), 515–39, reprinted in *Essays in Appreciation*, Boston, 1936, 515–539.

Lurie, Edward, "Louis Agassiz and the Idea of Evolution", *Victorian Studies*, 3 (1959–1960), 87.

MacCarthy, Sir James Desmond, *Portraits*, London, 1931.

McIntyre, Allan D., "Conrad on the Functions of the Mind", *Modern Language Quarterly*, (1964), 187–97.

Mandelbaum, Maurice, "The Scientific Background of Evolution Theory in Biology", *Journal of the History of Ideas*, 18 (June 1957), 342–61.

Marshall, P.T., *The Development of Modern Biology*, Oxford, 1969.

Mason, S.F., *A History of the Sciences*, London, 1953.

Meyer, Bernard, C., *Joseph Conrad: a Psychoanalytic Biography*, Princeton, 1967.

Miller, J. Hillis, *The Disappearance of God: Five Nineteenth Century Writers, 1832–1900*, Oxford, 1963.

Millhauser, Milton, "The Literary Impact of 'Vestiges of Creation'", *Modern Language Quarterly*, 17 (1956), 213–26.

Moser, Thomas, *Joseph Conrad: Achievement and Decline*, Cambridge, Massachusetts, 1957 and London, 1966.

Mudrick, Marvin, ed., *Conrad: a Collection of Critical Essays*, Englewood Cliffs, New Jersey, 1966.

Mumford, L., *The Story of Utopias; Ideal Commonwealths and Social Myths*, London, 1923.

Murry, John Middleton, *Pencillings, Little Essays in Literature*, London, 1923.

Newton, William, "Chance as Employed by Hardy and the Naturalists", *Philological Quarterly*, 30 (1951), 154–75

—, "Hardy and the Naturalists: Their Use of Physiology", *Modern Philology*, 49 (1951), 28–41.

Nicolson, Marjorie Hope, *The Microscope and English Imagination*, Northampton, Massachusetts, 1935.

Nordenskiöld, E., *The History of Biology*, trans. L. B. Eyre, London, 1929.

Osborn, H.F., *From the Greeks to Darwin; an Outline of the Development of the Evolutionary Idea*, New York, 1894.

Passmore, John, "Darwin's Impact on British Metaphysics", *Victorian Studies*, 3 (Sept. 1959), 41–54.

—, *The Perfectibility of Man*, London, 1970.

Peckham, Morse, "Darwinism and Darwinisticism", *Victorian Studies*, 3 (Sept. 1959), 19–40.

—, *Beyond the Tragic Vision: the Quest for Identity in the Nineteenth Century*, New York, 1962.

Penniman, T.K., *A Hundred Years of Anthropology*, London, 1935.

Pledge, H.T., *Science since 1500: a Short History of Mathematics, Physics, Chemistry, Biology*, London, 1939.

Potter, George Reuben, "Tennyson and the Biological Theory of Mutability in Species", *Philological Quarterly*, 16 (Oct. 1937), 321–43.

Poynter, F.N.L., ed., *History and Philosophy of Knowledge of the Brain and its Functions*, Oxford, 1958.

Raven, Charles E., *Organic Design: a Study of Scientific Thought from Ray to Paley*, Oxford, 1953.

Retinger, J.H., *Conrad and his Contemporaries*, London, 1941.

Roppen, Georg, *Evolution and Poetic Belief: a Study in some Victorian and Modern Writers*, (Oslo Studies in English, vol. 5), Oxford, 1936.

Rothenstein, William, *Men and Memories, Recollections*, vol.I, *1872–1900*; vol.II, *1900–1922*; vol.III, *Since Fifty, 1922–1938*. 3 vols., London, 1931–9.

Roussel, Royal, *The Metaphysics of Darkness: a Study in the Unity and Development of Conrad's Fiction*, Baltimore, 1971.

Routh, H.V., ed., *Towards the Twentieth Century: Essays in the Spiritual History of the Nineteenth Century*, Cambridge, 1937.

Russell, Bertrand, *Portraits from Memory*, London, 1956.

Rutland, William R., "Tennyson and the Theory of Evolution", *Essays and Studies*, 26 (1940), 7–29.

Saveson, John E., "Spencerian Assumptions in Conrad's Early Fiction", *Conradiana* 1 (1969), 29–40.

—, "Contemporary Psychology in 'The Nigger of the Narcissus'", *Studies in Short Fiction*, 7 (1970), 219–31.

Selincourt, E. de, "The Interplay of Literature and Science during the last three centuries", *Hibbert Journal*, 37 (Jan. 1939), 225–45.

Sherry, Norman, *Conrad's Eastern World*, Cambridge, 1966.

—, *Conrad's Western World*, Cambridge, 1971.

—, ed., *Conrad: The Critical Heritage*, London, 1973.

—, ed., *Joseph Conrad: a Commemoration. Papers from the 1974 International Conference on Conrad*, London, 1976.

Singer, C.J., *A History of Biology*, 3rd rev. ed., London, 1959.

—, *A Short History of Scientific Ideas to 1900*, Oxford, 1959.

Singer, C.J. and E.J. Homyard, eds., *History of Technology*, 5 vols., Oxford, 1954–8.

Smith, Sydney, "The Origin of 'The Origin'", *British Association for the Advancement of Science*, 64 (1960), 391–401.

Stallmann, R.W., ed., *The Art of Joseph Conrad: a Critical Symposium*, Michigan, 1960.

Stevenson, Lionel, *Darwin among the Poets*, London, 1932.

—, "Darwin and the Novel", *Nineteenth Century Fiction*, 15 (1960), 29–38.

Street, Brian V., *The Savage in Literature: Representations of "Primitive" Society in English Fiction 1858–1920*, London, 1975.

Stubbe, Hans, *History of Genetics. From Prehistoric Times to the Rediscovery of Mendel's Laws*, trans. T. R. W. Waters, Cambridge, Massachusetts, 1972.

Sussman, Herbert L., *The Victorians and the Machine: the Literary Response to Technology*, Cambridge, Massachusetts, 1968.

Sutherland, J.C., *At Sea with Joseph Conrad*, London, 1922.

Symondson, Anthony, ed., *Victorian Society: the Victorian Crisis of Faith, 6 Lectures by R. M. Young*, London, 1970.

Thorburn, David, *Conrad's Romanticism*, New Haven, 1974.

Toulmin, Stephen and June Goodfield, *The Fabric of the Heavens*, London, 1961.

—, *The Architecture of Matter*, London, 1962.

—, *The Discovery of Time*, London, 1965.

Toulmin, Stephen E., Ronald W. Hepburn and Alasdair Macintyre, eds., *Metaphysical Beliefs*, London, 1957.

Vorzimmer, Peter J., *Charles Darwin: the Years of Controversy. "The Origin of Species" and its Critics, 1859–82*, Philadelphia, 1970 and London, 1972.

Wagenknecht, Edward, "'Pessimism' in Hardy and Conrad", *College English*, 3 (1942), 546–54.

Watts, C.T., "Nordau and Kurtz: a Footnote to 'Heart of Darkness'", *Notes and Queries*, June 1974.

Wells, H.G., *Experiment in Autobiography; Discoveries and Conclusions of a Very Ordinary Brain (since 1866)*, 2 vols., London, 1934.

White, Andrew, *A History of the Warfare of Science with Theology in Christendom*, 2 vols., New York and London, 1896.

Whitehead, Alfred North, *Science and the Modern World*, Cambridge, 1926.

Whyte, L.L., *The Unconscious before Freud*, London, 1962.

Wiley, P.L., *Conrad's Measure of Man*, Madison, Wisconsin, 1954.

Willey, Basil, *Darwin and Butler: Two Versions of Evolution*, Hibbert Lectures 1959, London, 1960.

Wilson, J.B., "Darwin and the Transcendentalists", *Journal of the History of Ideas*, 26 (1965) 286–90.

Index

INDEX

Compiled by Douglas Matthews

Index